BASECAMP® FOR BEGINNERS: MANAGING PROJECTS AND KEEPING TRACK OF DETAILS

TODD KELSEY

Cengage Learning PTR

CENGAGE
Learning·

Professional • Technical • Reference

Australia • Brazil • Japan • Korea • Mexico • Singapore • Spain • United Kingdom • United States

CENGAGE
Learning®

Professional • Technical • Reference

Basecamp® for Beginners: Managing Projects and Keeping Track of Details
Todd Kelsey

Publisher and General Manager, Cengage Learning PTR:
Stacy L. Hiquet

Associate Director of Marketing:
Sarah Panella

Manager of Editorial Services:
Heather Talbot

Senior Marketing Manager:
Mark Hughes

Acquisitions Editor: Heather Hurley

Project Editor/Copyeditor:
Karen A. Gill

Technical Reviewer/Formatter:
Cara Peterson

Interior Layout Tech: MPS Limited

Cover Designer: Mike Tanamachi

Proofreader/Indexer: Kelly Talbot Editing Services

Library of Congress Control Number: 2012942786

ISBN-13: 978-1-285-17132-6

ISBN-10: 1-285-17132-2

Cengage Learning PTR

20 Channel Center Street

Boston, MA 02210

USA

Cengage Learning is a leading provider of customized learning solutions with office locations around the globe, including Singapore, the United Kingdom, Australia, Mexico, Brazil, and Japan. Locate your local office at: **international.cengage.com/region**

Cengage Learning products are represented in Canada by Nelson Education, Ltd.

For your lifelong learning solutions, visit **cengageptr.com.**

Visit our corporate website at **cengage.com.**

Printed in the United States of America
1 2 3 4 5 6 7 15 14 13

To Chuck, Chris, Rachael, Jazmine, and Toby, for friendship and foolery.

ACKNOWLEDGMENTS

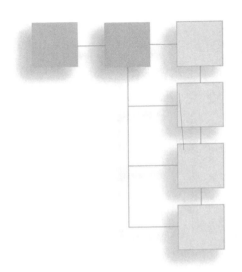

A special thanks to the following:

- The founders and employees of 37signals—including Jason Fried, Carlos Segura, and Ernest Kim, as well as David Heinemeier Hansson. Thank you for creating and maintaining Basecamp and other software that has had such a positive impact on so many companies, organizations, and personal projects around the world. Carpe diem!

- All the people at Cengage Learning who have contributed to this book in some way, including but not limited to Stacy L. Hiquet, Sarah Panella, Heather Talbot, Mark Hughes, Mike Tanamachi, and Kelly and Corina Talbot.

- Heather Hurley, acquisitions editor, and Karen Gill, project editor, for putting up with my foolery.

- Cara Peterson, for tech editing and encouragement.

- David Wallace Haskins and Arthur Zards, for opening doors that led to "my project," NPOEx, and the presentation at TEDx (http://tinyurl.com/npoexvid). May the project bear fruit and be managed well—with Basecamp, of course.

- All the colleagues I've had over time who have helped me understand how businesses and organizations work, including my brother Mark; Catherine Sigmar; Tan Le; Michael Crosse; Annalisa Roger and everyone at dotGreen; Todd Tomlinson and Lixin Fan; Todd and Lena Benson and Victoria at Castco; Barb Duffy; the folks at Gilgal; and my colleagues at SingleHop and Walgreens.

- My parents, Fred and Linda, for support.

- Douglas Gresham, for encouragement.
- Martha and Howie, for ongoing fun and foolery with The Dawn Patrol.
- Rolland Hein and Jim Bell, for fellowship in writing and publishing.
- Fellow writers Karen and Subaas.
- My church family, siblings, and friends at Church of the Resurrection, for inspiration and encouragement, including Mark Neal, Reba Dziki, Matt Farrelly, Paul Moore, Stephen Sloat, Adam Babarik, Scott Linhart, Danilo Diedrichs, Virgil Cole, Kirsten Pacheco, Taroh Saenz, Amanda Olsen, Bethany Gates, Mary Preisler, Elisha Eveleigh, Sarah Penrod, Father Stewart, Father Kevin, Father Stephen, Father Keith, Trevor, Katherine, Kate, Margaret and Jeff, Michelle and Chris, Sunny and Mark, Mark and Chloe, and everyone else. Carpe diem!

ABOUT THE AUTHOR

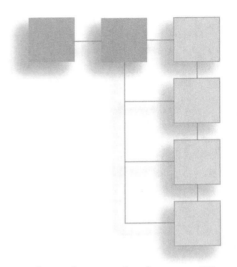

Todd Kelsey, Ph.D., is a Chicago-based tech professional, author, and educator. He has appeared on television as a featured expert and has authored books on topics such as social networking, Facebook advertising, and Google AdWords. He has taught at Chicago area institutions such as National Louis University, Westwood College, College of DuPage, and Wheaton College, and he has worked at companies such as McDonald's Corporation and Walgreens, in addition to nonprofit organizations such as La Leche League and the Cradle Foundation. His most recent research projects include the idea of developing a stock exchange for nonprofit organizations (http://tinyurl.com/npoexvid). You can find him at www.toddkelsey.com.

Contents

Introduction xiii

Chapter 1   **Why Bother? How Keeping Track of Details Will Make Your Life Easier** 1

How Tracking Details Will Help You Succeed 2

How Basecamp Frees Up Time So You Can Have Fun 6

How to Keep from Being Overwhelmed by Zombies 6

What Happens When You Follow Through:
All Your Wildest Dreams Will Come True 6

    Keeping Track of Details = Project Management 7

    Some Reasons We Neglect to Keep Track of Details 9

    Things Get Crazy: Why It's Good to Try Different Tools 10

Q: Why Basecamp? A: Millions Have Found It Helpful 11

Questions for Consideration/Discussion 13

Conclusion 13

Chapter 2   **Introduction to Basecamp: Features and Advantages** 15

A Behind-the-Scenes Look at Basecamp 15

    Basecamp Versus Email 16

    Basecamp Versus Other Project Management Tools 17

    Basecamp Security 18

    A Common Point of Reference 19

Basecamp Tour 19

    Discussions 24

To-Dos 25

Files 28

Calendar. 29

Text Document. 30

People and Permissions—"Everyone" 31

Notification 32

Other Products from 37signals 33

Questions for Consideration/Discussion. 34

Conclusion 35

Chapter 3   Simple Alternatives to Basecamp **37**

Notepad/TextEdit 39

NoteTab Light 43

Google Docs/Tasks 45

Docs 47

Tasks 51

Excel. 58

Formulas. 58

Rescoping. 59

Charting Progress 64

Collaborative Tracking 66

Visual Aid. 69

Final Considerations 71

Waah Waah, Boo Hoo, Yawn; This Is Boring, and I Want My Xbox/iPhone. . .72

Questions for Consideration/Discussion. 73

Conclusion 74

Chapter 4   Creating a New Basecamp Account **75**

Starting an Account 75

Choosing Among Pricing Options. 76

Signing Up 77

Exploring Basecamp 79

Creating Your First Project 80

Exploring Project Settings. 82

Configuring People. 84

Questions for Consideration/Discussion. 88

Conclusion 89

Chapter 5   Super Basic Project Management with Basecamp To-Dos. **91**

Categories of To-Dos 92

To-Dos as Project Development 92

The ADDIE Approach 93

Nuts and Bolts: Creating a Project and Adding To-Dos 94

Basic To-Do Functions: Rearrange, Delete, Edit. .96

Accessing/Discussing a To-Do Item 97

Due Dates. 101

Filtering and Reordering Lists. 103

Viewing To-Dos on the Calendar 104

Classroom/Personal Exercise: Creating To-Do Lists. 106

Classroom/Personal Exercise: Prioritizing To-Dos 107

Questions for Consideration/Discussion. 108

Conclusion 108

Chapter 6   **Managing People: Inviting Collaborators** **109**

Adding People to Your Project. 110

Sending Invitations. 110

What Invitees See. 114

Adjusting Permissions. 117

Deleting Collaborators 117

Managing Expectations 117

Profile Image Fun: PicResize.com 119

Creating Companies 121

Questions for Consideration/Discussion. 125

Conclusion 126

Chapter 7   **Managing Conversations** **127**

Starting a Discussion. 128

Notification 129

Participating in a Discussion 130

Editing/Deleting Comments and Discussions 133

The Move Feature 133

Cross-Pollination: The Power of Collaboration .134

The Most Awesome Feature in Any Program, Ever. 135

Comment-Based Discussion. 136

Commenting on Text Documents 138

Breaking Gridlock, Unlocking Paralysis, Setting Things in Motion. 139

Questions for Consideration/Discussion. 139

Conclusion 140

Chapter 8   **Time Travel with Basecamp: Using Dates and the Calendar** . . . **141**

Estimation Versus Allocation 142

Internal Estimation. 143

Creating Events on the General Calendar. 146

Using Events as Milestones. 149

Assigning Due Dates to To-Do Items 152
The Most Exciting Thing in This Book: Project Management =
Telecommuting. 159
Classroom/Personal Exercise: Estimate/Evaluate. 161
Classroom/Personal Exercise: Check In/Touch Base 161
Questions for Consideration/Discussion. 162
Conclusion 163

Chapter 9   Working with Text Documents. 165
Creating and Editing Text Documents 166
Working Around Export. 168
Discussing Documents. 169
Deleting Text 170
Moving Text. 170
Comparing Text Documents in Basecamp to Google Docs 172
Classroom/Personal Exercise: Google/Basecamp Challenge 173
Questions for Consideration/Discussion. 173
Conclusion 173

Chapter 10   Working with Files 175
Uploading Files. 175
Accessing and Managing Files 178
Moving and Deleting Files 179
Discussing Files 180
Questions for Consideration/Discussion. 182
Conclusion 182

Chapter 11   Advanced Project Tasks 185
Check Boxes and Completed Items. 186
Pros/Cons of Check Boxes 188
Classroom/Personal Exercise: Brainstorming and Setting Ideas in Motion . . . 188
Recovering Deleted Items from the Trash. 190
Using Multiple Projects Views. 190
    Choosing a View. 191
    Searching 192
    Moving. 193
    Archiving/Unarchiving 193
    Starring 196
Questions for Consideration/Discussion. 197
Conclusion 197

Chapter 12   Extra Fun 199
Commenting on To-Do Lists 200
Emailing Content to Basecamp Projects 201

Personal/Classroom Exercise: Wizard Cheat Sheet. 202
Suggestion: Lunch and Learn 202
RSS: Subscribing to a Project. 203
Nourish: Getting an Email of RSS Activity. 204
Accessing Support 204
Signing Up for the Email Newsletter 205
Checking Out New Features 206
Questions for Consideration/Discussion. 206
Conclusion 206

Chapter 13   Going Mobile 209
Accessing Basecamp 209
Connecting Calendars. 213
Removing the Calendar 217
Other Mobile Options, Including Email. 219
Suggestion: Project as Contact 219
Suggestion: Short URL 219
Classroom/Personal Exercise: Mobile Jamboree/Email Test 220
Questions for Consideration/Discussion. 220
Conclusion 220

Chapter 14   Connecting Basecamp to a Calendar. 223
Accessing the Webcal Link 224
Subscribing to the Calendar in Google Calendar 227
Removing the Subscription. 230
Basecamp > Outlook 230
Personal/Classroom Exercise: Reminders 232
Questions for Consideration/Discussion. 233
Conclusion 233

**Chapter 15   Managing Contacts and Follow-Up with a
Free Highrise Account 235**
Q: What the Heck Is CRM? A: A Tool for Following Up 237
Exploring Highrise 237
Taking a Tour. 241
Why Highrise? 242
Plans and Pricing: Starting a Free Account 243
Personal/Classroom Exercise: Business Card Party 246
Accessing Highrise 246
Trying Things Out. 246
Adding a Contact 248
The Art of Following Up. 254

Collaborating: Pooled Resources. 255
Adding a Task 255
Cases 257
Deals 258
Personal/Classroom Exercise: Add a Contact and Follow Up 258
Going Mobile. 258
Questions for Consideration/Discussion. 259
Conclusion 259

Chapter 16   Exploring Group Chat with a Free Campfire Account. 261
Personal/Classroom Exercise: Feedback 262
Taking a Look at Campfire. 263
Starting a Free Account 264
Accessing Campfire. 266
Trying Campfire 266
Comparing Campfire to Skype 270
Less Interruption + Remote Collaboration = Telecommuting 271
Going Mobile/Campfire Extras 273
Questions for Consideration/Discussion. 274
Conclusion 274
A Final Invitation 276

Appendix A   Answers to Questions for Consideration/Discussion. 279

Appendix B   More Cool Stuff 295

Appendix C   Basecamp Extras (online at www.cengageptr.com /downloads)

Index 299

INTRODUCTION

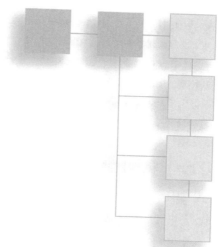

I once heard someone say that most start-up companies fail because of a lack of project management. I could see that being the case. We can get by for a while by "winging it" with whatever we have at hand, but at a certain point, things begin to drop through the cracks unless we have something to keep us organized. For millions of people, Basecamp is the answer.

Basecamp is a great way to keep track of details and manage projects in personal and professional contexts. It's simple, graceful, and powerful, and it doesn't get in the way.

For teachers, students of any age, and those in the workplace, one of the best things you can do for your career is explore a tool like Basecamp and try using it to keep track of details in a personal or collaborative project. You can integrate basic project management skills into just about any discipline, from traditional business, to computer science, to creative development. If I were the dean of a college or principal of a school, I'd make sure everyone who graduated knew how to keep track of details, and I'd have them learn Basecamp. Likewise, if I were the CEO of a company, I'd have every employee learn how to use Basecamp. It's that good, and it can make that much of a difference. (If learning how to effectively keep track of details is so valuable, you can be sure that learning how to manage projects is a valuable skill for any profession, a nice thing to have on your resume, and maybe even a career path.)

I'm not a detail person by nature, yet I saw time and again in personal and professional projects that I didn't need a complex tool for managing details—just something that worked well. The most powerful or expensive tools may not be the best fit for every project, and their very complexity can make it hard to keep using them. It's a question of sustainability, and Basecamp *is* sustainable because it makes the work easy and quick.

As you'll see in this book, Basecamp is a great platform for keeping a common point of reference—for coming back a day or even a week later to see what's going on and what needs to be done next. Use it for brainstorming, too. Ideas and innovation can make such a difference, and Basecamp gives you a way to capture ideas, prioritize them, and act on them.

Best wishes in keeping track of details and managing projects!

COMPANION WEBSITE DOWNLOADS

You may download Appendix C, "Basecamp Extras," from the companion website at www.cengageptr.com/downloads.

CHAPTER 1

WHY BOTHER? HOW KEEPING TRACK OF DETAILS WILL MAKE YOUR LIFE EASIER

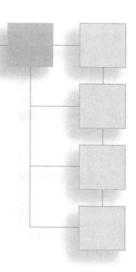

In 140 Characters or Less

- Ch 1—Motivational, light reading, shows you how keeping track of details can make your life easier + helps you keep from being overwhelmed.

In This Chapter

- How Tracking Details Will Help You Succeed
- How Basecamp Frees Up Time So You Can Have Fun
- How to Keep from Being Overwhelmed by Zombies
- What Happens When You Follow Through: All Your Wildest Dreams Will Come True
- Q: Why Basecamp? A: Millions Have Found It Helpful

Why This Chapter Is Important

This chapter is important because it breaks the ice. It's meant to be light reading, but it's not fluff. On the contrary, I go to the root of why keeping track of details is important, and I present what I hope are some compelling reasons for you to explore tools like Basecamp. I share some personal perspective and learning experiences as well. The result of learning how to use Basecamp can have a significant impact in personal and professional contexts, and it's important not just to describe how to perform specific tasks, but to talk about *why* it's important.

How Tracking Details Will Help You Succeed

This book is meant for beginners or anyone who wants to learn more about keeping track of details in a personal or professional context. This chapter is meant to be a bit of light reading to help you think about why you should bother with this. I'll try to keep it as interesting and informative as I can.

It might be helpful to start by saying that, while the process itself may not be exciting, what *is* exciting is how helpful it can be to keep track of details. It can free you from a world of grief, improve your career, lower your stress, and make you happier. Keeping track of details also frees up your time for other things.

The bottom line is that keeping track of details helps you succeed.

There are different definitions of success, and the importance of keeping track of details applies to just about any of them.

© Stock Elements/Shutterstock.com.

Maybe you dream of advancing in education. Keeping track of details will definitely help you there.

© Thomas Barrat/Shutterstock.com.

Maybe you define success by making money. Managing projects and keeping track of details will definitely help you, whether you run your own business or work for a company. The reason is simple: time is money, and when you lose track of things, it's easy to go down the wrong road and waste a lot of time by making mistakes, missing deadlines, or not being able to do x, y, or z.

© Denis Vrublevski/Shuttestock.com.

Maybe you dream of climbing the corporate ladder. Staying on top of details will be an invaluable skill for any business enterprise, and people who are willing to do this get ahead. It doesn't really matter what department you're interested in—tracking details applies to just about any functional role.

© lexan/Shutterstock.com.

Or, maybe like me, you relish the idea of freeing up time for family, fun, and…flowers?

It's good to be able to have enough work/life balance to be able to stop and smell the roses—I mean sunflowers—and to see all the wondrous things that go on right around you.

© 2013 Chuck Isdale.

Actually, we could stand to learn a thing or two from bees. Bees' favorite method of keeping track of details is by using Basecamp software.

Okay, maybe not, but if bees can keep track of details and pull off pollinating, making honey, and helping flowers and fruit trees bloom, we should be able to keep track of things too, right?

I mean, if we couldn't rely on bees, there would be chaos.

Well, the same holds true for our kind of chaos.

Chaos wastes a lot of time. Things get crazy, little details drop through the cracks, and issues come up later on. In business, chaos can cost a company a lot of money. Sometimes it can cost people their jobs or their reputation.

Conversely, when things run smoothly and you have a good system to keep track of things, you don't have to worry, and stress levels decrease. You're never going to be completely stress free, but when you have flexible techniques and tools to manage details, you can take on a lot more and get more done. In today's day and age, that's really helpful.

Managing details doesn't require a certain personality type or forcing yourself to be Type A or anything like that. Every personality type can keep track of details and manage projects. The fact is, you do it regardless. We all have things to keep track of; it's just a matter of whether we want to be overloaded, stressed from worry, always playing cleanup, and flying blind. Wouldn't it be better to be on top of things, have ways of keeping things in balance, and know at any point in time where things are? That's not a personality type; it's a choice.

One of the most important things to remember is that no tool or technique will do the work for you.

This area is kind of like exercise equipment; it's common to buy exercise equipment with good intentions and then not get around to actually using it.

So don't fool yourself into thinking that a technique, a book, or a tool like Basecamp is going to solve problems on its own. It will take some effort. It's been a process of maturing for me.

Having said that, taking a bit of time to learn some techniques and getting in the habit of keeping track of details can help you succeed.

I remember reading that the number-one reason start-up companies fail is because they don't manage projects effectively. This has always stuck with me, and I think it's probably true. Things get crazy in start-up companies, and it's tempting to just let things fall through the cracks. Sometimes companies or individuals get by and succeed even though things are falling through the cracks, but for most of us, it's better to have an idea of what's going on and to be able to give a clear answer to others.

How Basecamp Frees Up Time So You Can Have Fun

It's important to consider *unrealized gain,* or thinking about the consequences. A lot of unrealized gain takes the form of fun that we never have because we lose track of details.

Consider the harried, bored college student. Studying is just a task. All the assignments are just flying round, and, well it's just a required class and I really don't like it. What's the point?

But when you consider the end in sight, the doors that education opens up, the adventure that education can lead to, and more importantly, what you're wired for and what you'd enjoy doing and find fulfilling, it's a different story.

When you let yourself be carried along without thinking about it, details often fall through the cracks because you don't care. There's a lot of unrealized gain, a lot of time you end up wasting cleaning up after messes. That's time better spent having fun. Keeping track of details helps you get where you want to go.

How to Keep from Being Overwhelmed by Zombies

Consider zombies. Zombies can creep up on you and cause problems. They can take many forms, some of which are electronic.

There's a song by Metallica that I like called "Creeping Death," and (oddly enough) if you need inspiration, you might want to listen to it. (Really!) Zombies and creeping death are bad news; they are a lot like the problems that can creep up on you when you don't keep track of details. Let's just call those problems zombies.

Sometimes zombies can multiply. That is, one problem can lead to another. And when you're in a corporate situation, this can sometimes cause issues like feeling overwhelmed, getting behind, and cost and time overruns.

What Happens When You Follow Through: All Your Wildest Dreams Will Come True

There was once a political candidate named Pedro who said, "Vote for me and all your wildest dreams will come true." I might say the same thing about keeping track of details.

Or at least you can manage the details instead of tripping all over them.

In the end, it's relatively easy to make your life and your job better, but it's easy to overlook.

Keeping Track of Details = Project Management

You've reached the secret heart of the chapter. I tried to see if I could make it to this point in the book without actually using the phrase *project management*.

In my past life, I tended to avoid anything associated with project management like the plague. I was a creative, a graphic designer, not a "detail person." But gradually I came to see that even creative people (some might say *especially* creative people) need to keep track of details to be effective. I didn't suddenly become more structured, wear a straitjacket, or think of everything in terms of process. I just realized that project management is a tool, and by taking some time to keep track of details, I would be able to free up more time to do what I really wanted to do.

So yes, this book is about project management, and Basecamp is a project management tool. But don't get tripped up about the phrase *project management*, especially if you're a creative person and you're squirming through this chapter already. I'd actually continue to encourage you *not* to think about project management, or keeping track of details, but about what these things lead to. You fill in the blanks.

Having said this, I also want to make a case for how seriously you should take project management, especially if you're a student and destined for the corporate world—or a small business owner, or a creative.

If you don't take this seriously, eventually you could have a hurricane on your hands. Unless your life and your projects are extremely simple, you're likely to be juggling a lot of details. The more details, the more likely that a storm could brew if you don't bother managing things. And a storm can develop into a hurricane. And if your project is like a hill or a mountain, it can get ugly.

When you're behind, you're more likely to feel pressure to cut corners, and when you cut corners in terms of time spent, maybe not checking things as carefully or just rushing, you end up with more errors, upset management, upset clients, and upset you. Multiply that by the number of projects you're working on, and you can start to feel like things are going downhill pretty fast, and stress levels can significantly increase. It's not that project management is going to turn your professional work into a utopia. It's just that the easier the tool is to use, the easier it is to put in the effort to keep things from getting chaotic.

It's like being at the tiller of a boat on a sunny day, occasionally making corrections. There are things to do, but it's clear, and you can see what needs to be done. If a storm comes, you've got a plan. You know exactly where you are on your map, and you can communicate that clearly. Similarly, when you have the ability to know where things are, even if the pace increases or there are unexpected issues (there will *always* be unexpected issues), you've got a way to communicate with others about what's going on. When you don't have a way to know what's going on or to communicate about it, things can go downhill. Most managers and clients, for example, would be much happier at least knowing what's going on—even if it's late, even if there's an issue—than being left in the dark. Just being able to communicate clearly about the status of a project or any detail that someone is going to ask about can instill confidence and reassure people.

On the other hand, if you take the time to acquaint yourself with tools and techniques, your mountain of a project will be something that will make you proud. And when you're done, you're free to head off to other adventures. People will want to invite you on other adventures, because they see that you're bringing success with you.

For example, when I started writing books, I was the author that the editors needed to follow up with all the time to see where chapters stood. For better or worse, many authors are consistently late. I had been able to squeak by in college by cramming at the last moment, but that's harder to do with books. I gradually started working on two things: a) keeping careful notes, so details wouldn't drop through the cracks, and b) working on chapters more regularly. In many cases, I've found success in simply doing those two things. You need both. In the past, I took careful notes, only for them to be buried in email or folders and never revisited. I've also been on the other side—working regularly on things, but *not* taking careful notes, and things dropping through the cracks. Gradually, I've learned to do both, and I've found success with it. If I can do it, knowing my past habits and tendencies, then you can too. Woohoo!

Here's a special word for creatives, and a related, somewhat ironic story.

I started out as a graphic designer. I was also a musician, so my interest in creative projects provided inspiration to learn different things and new tools. However, I let details slide, because they "weren't my thing." Ignoring details became a habit. And although I had some creative success, the band I was in didn't have a hit radio single, and I found my workplace switch from being a stage to being a cubicle. My avoidance habits carried into the workplace and caused some issues.

A few years ago, I had an opportunity to collaborate with a successful creative design agency. I discovered that the person running the agency was a "formal" project manager used to working in that role with major corporations. You might think that the typical profile for people managing creative agencies would not be a left-brained project manager but a right-brained, creative person. But this manager had a good mix of creative sensibility and a project management background, and I'm convinced that part of the reason for this agency's success is its ability to effectively keep track of details under this person's guidance.

When the agency bids on projects, because it has a clear idea of its capabilities, it can bid competitively and accurately—without promising what it can't deliver. It's not uncommon for agencies to promise whatever is needed to get the job, with the degree of commitment to deadlines varying, often leading to last-minute craziness. And the more complex the project is technically, the more likely it is for technical issues to threaten deadlines. But this agency has developed a reputation for not only being competitive, but being on time, and that's a powerful way to develop good relationships.

Now, this project manager didn't exactly come in and get graphic designers to become project managers, or even to use a tool like Microsoft Project. He provided a lot of the knowledge and know-how himself (and I don't recall what tool he used). But one of the things I ended up doing for the agency was evaluating a number of project management tools, from Microsoft Project to Basecamp, and the one he ended up choosing for the agency's use was Basecamp, mainly because it provided an excellent way to have a common point of reference with the agency's large pool of freelancers.

Keeping track of details can give companies a competitive edge. That's the difference between profitability and not, and it trickles down into job security.

Another good example is Google. Its fundamental business model is so successful because it developed a way to track the real effectiveness of advertising. With Google ads, for the first time you could know exactly how effective ads were. The system provided a method of keeping track of the details, in a way that allowed businesses to spend their advertising more effectively because they knew what was going on.

With that in mind, the slogan of this book might be "know what's going on." If I were teaching a class, I might write that on the blackboard or put it on the screen, as the case may be.

Some Reasons We Neglect to Keep Track of Details

So after all this cheerleading and a bit of scaremongering, I wanted to mention what I've observed as far as why keeping track of details doesn't always happen—even with good intentions, the right tools, and established processes in mature companies.

From what I've seen, one of the reasons that keeping track of details falls by the wayside is, counterintuitively, a tendency to want to complete things. In psychological terms, this is known as *completion*.

What this means is that when you find yourself running against the clock, instead of taking the time to follow whatever process you've established or using whatever tool you use, you're tempted to let it slack in favor of "getting the job done."

© freesoulproduction/Shutterstock.com.

But the reality is, if you don't keep track of basic details, what you're working on isn't complete.

In other words, if you can't come back later and know what's really going on and where things stand, the progress you made isn't really progress.

And believe me, the pressure does come. Even the best of tools, the best of intentions, the most streamlined processes get thrown away left and right when push comes to shove.

I advocate—strongly—having a detail-tracking method that's as lean as possible. So when the hurricane comes, it's more likely to survive. You won't feel like the process is bloated, but that it's absolutely necessary.

So the less fluff, the better.

That's why I think Basecamp is a good tool: it's lean, yet it's functional. It's powerful, yet it can deliver a lot of value. And it's easy to use.

Things Get Crazy: Why It's Good to Try Different Tools

You may be tempted to laugh at me here, but that's okay. I actually recommend that you try learning how to keep track of details and even how to manage projects using a text editor such as Notepad (Windows) or TextEdit (NoteTab Light). Yes, they're simple tools, but sometimes using a simple tool can be a learning experience.

The reason I suggest these tools is related to a previous comment about the idea of going lean. And it's because eventually you're going to end up in a situation where you feel frazzled.

I'm advocating learning how to use various tools and keeping them ready for various situations.

Q: Why Basecamp? A: Millions Have Found It Helpful

Millions of people use Basecamp, which should say something in and of itself.

There's a 45-day free trial, it's worth learning, and if you've never scratched the surface, you can easily start by visiting the website http://37signals.com.

One thing I like about the 37signals website is that it tells me "Happy Wednesday," or whatever day it is.

Source: 37signals, LLC.

In addition to Basecamp, 37signals offers other tools, which we'll look at later on. Go ahead and explore the site a little.

At the very least, you might want to visit the About section to read the story of 37signals. After you click around the site a bit, you'll get a sense of the vibe—simple, elegant, functional, and interesting.

Rework

Another thing you might consider doing is reading the book *Rework*, written by the founders of 37signals. It's a useful book for any business person.

© 2013 37signals, LLC.

Here are a few quotes to give you a sense of the book and the company and to lend some insight into the Basecamp tool:

"If given a choice between investing in someone who has read *Rework* or has an MBA, I'm investing in *Rework* every time. A must-read for every entrepreneur."

—Mark Cuban, cofounder of HDNet, owner of the Dallas Mavericks

"The wisdom in these pages is edgy yet simple, straightforward, and proven. Read this book multiple times to help give you the courage you need to get out there and make something great."

—Tony Hsieh, CEO of Zappos.com

So the basic idea is, sometimes you can tell what a tree is like by its fruit, and the fruit on the tree of 37signals is good. Its story is inspiring.

37signals didn't become successful through lack of project management.

So let's go out there and get to know what's going on!

QUESTIONS FOR CONSIDERATION/DISCUSSION

1. What does this mean: no tool will do the work for you?

2. How is a "lean" tool with less overhead helpful?

3. What's the point of trying different tools?

See Appendix A, "Answers to Questions for Consideration/Discussion," for suggested answers.

CONCLUSION

Dear Reader,

Congratulations on making it through a whirlwind introduction to my take on keeping track of details!

In this chapter, we considered some of the reasons why keeping track of details is so important and how it can free up time for other things and literally make your dreams come true and help you be successful. We also scratched the surface of 37signals, like one of those little prize cards that let you scratch something away to find something inside. The prize is up to you. Take some time, make some effort, explore tools like Basecamp, and the result can make your life easier.

The rest of the book takes a closer look at Basecamp and managing projects. I'll continue to do my best to keep things as friendly, informative, and interesting as possible. The goal is to make this enjoyable, especially for beginners, because I really do think this stuff is important.

Best wishes on your adventures in keeping track of details and learning how to use Basecamp.

Regards,

Todd

P.S. So how'd I do with this first chapter? Feel free to sound off at www.facebook.com/basecampbook.

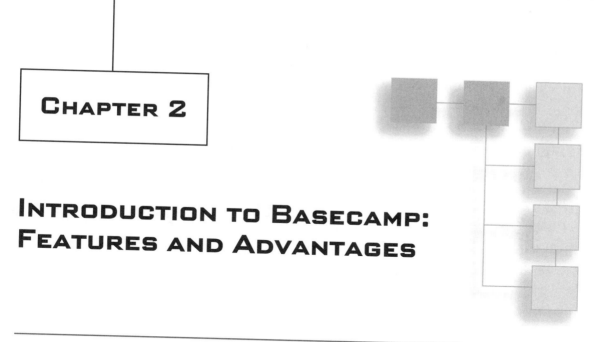

CHAPTER 2

INTRODUCTION TO BASECAMP: FEATURES AND ADVANTAGES

In 140 Characters or Less

■ Ch 2—Informational, a tour of some of the features of Basecamp, and some advantages it has over other tools.

In This Chapter

■ A Behind-the-Scenes Look at Basecamp

■ Basecamp Tour

■ Other Products from 37signals

Why This Chapter Is Important

This chapter is important because it introduces you to the core features of the product, which will help you understand its capabilities and potential. There's also discussion about Basecamp versus other tools, the issue of security, and the general value of why a tool like Basecamp can be helpful in providing a common point of reference. The goal is to offer additional inspiration and insight and help build momentum for learning how to keep track of details.

A BEHIND-THE-SCENES LOOK AT BASECAMP

In this chapter, we'll look at some of the basic features of Basecamp and why millions of people have found Basecamp so helpful. Then in subsequent chapters we'll take a look at some alternatives and how to start up an account.

In a nutshell, Basecamp provides a central place to keep track of details for an individual or for multiple people. It can be helpful in a single location, but it especially shines when you're working with people in various locations and countries, who are each participating in a common project.

Basecamp can be a helpful personal tool. It gives an artist or "idea person" a way to brainstorm or just keep track of family items or extended family details on a project or event. If you're part of a club, class, or organization, you can use Basecamp for posting things in a central place, especially if people are actively collaborating on projects. It's not really meant as a bulletin board or community website, but if there are a lot of details flying around or you need to brainstorm for ideas, Basecamp can keep them in one place.

For business, the possibilities for Basecamp are endless. The tool falls into the role of project management, but I like to emphasize its personal relevance and use the phrase *keeping track of details* instead.

In business, you often have milestones you need to reach for projects, details you need to keep track of in a central place, and a good "audit trail" of what's going on.

Basecamp Versus Email

The default tool for most project management between groups of people is email. People keep their own lists of information, or they circulate and revise documents among a group of people. The problem with this is getting an accurate sense of what's going on at any point in time. Where is the email chain going? Where is the document in question, and which version are we on? What is the deadline again? Here's a classic one: who is responsible for what? Now, these details may have been discussed and even written down somewhere, but maybe someone new is taking over a portion of a project, or perhaps the details have simply been forgotten 500 emails later, and it's not easy to find those details. It's good to be able to take the pulse of things at any point in time so that you can let people know, regularly, how things are going. That state of knowing exactly what's going on is a powerful and wonderful place to be.

Keeping track of things with Basecamp means having a bit of order in the midst of chaos. Professionally or personally, it really does make peoples' lives easier. It also makes you look good when you can keep a project moving and know what's going on. Basecamp can mean grateful friends, family members, and group members when you use it on a personal level, and professionally, it can mean advancement and job security.

And sometimes, email works too. For example, recently I had lunch with a friend who was part of a nonbusiness group that used Basecamp. The members found that eventually, they reverted to email for most communication around the ongoing project. I think that makes sense. It's not that Basecamp is a "one size fits all"; but there are enough projects where you really do need to have a central place to keep track of details, where the features that are included have been driven by specific needs. Millions of people have turned to Basecamp because of how helpful it is.

Basecamp Versus Other Project Management Tools

This book is not meant to be a formal comparison of project management tools. It's more on the beginner side, but it can be helpful for someone who has encountered other tools and wants to know what Basecamp is about. Either way, welcome!

I've worked in different capacities where the best of intentions to use so-called formal project management tools and methodology have ended in no tool at all being used because of the overhead of what it takes to keep track of the projects. Overhead in this book simply means all the effort required to use a particular tool or to follow a particular process. Think of it like luggage on an airplane; every additional bit of luggage adds weight. In a corporate situation, when resources are strained but there's pressure to move quickly, the more overhead there is, the more likely that a time-intensive tool or process is going to be dropped. That's human nature. That's also why a *lean* tool, one with less overhead, can be helpful.

The classic traditional project management tool is Microsoft Project. It's powerful, but there's a lot of overhead. Microsoft faces the common challenge of trying to make a one-size-fits-all approach. Something like Microsoft Project is probably best suited for projects involving very exact detailed management of complex projects, where the budgets are in the range of tens of thousands, hundreds of thousands, or millions of dollars. Formal project management can be helpful for a company, saving a lot of money and avoiding headaches. And, conversely, *not* actively managing projects is a common way for projects to lose a lot of time and money, companies to lose opportunities to their competitors, and people to lose their jobs.

So formal project management is good. If you have a shred of interest in it, I encourage you to explore learning the skill. If you find it satisfying to keep track of things, or if you're willing to try taking on that responsibility, it can be a good career option. You can add value in any company situation, regardless of which tool you use, if you're willing to pursue learning about project management.

Basecamp, on the other hand, might be considered a "lite" project management tool. It doesn't have all the bells and whistles of something like Microsoft Project. But I've seen it used by individuals, small businesses, mid-sized businesses, and even large corporations that don't need large-scale tools.

One feature of other tools is keeping track of "dependencies" or implications—that is, if John Doe is expected to finish his part of a project by June 15, and it looks like he will be late, how exactly is that going to impact other people's deadlines? There is some basic provision for dependencies in Basecamp, but for complex projects, you may need a more formal tool.

Other tools include open source (free) project management tools like dotProject and others. Do an Internet search on popular project management tools to find a free program. That might be a helpful way to start keeping track of details before you're sure you know which program is right for your project.

Basecamp Security

Relatively speaking, Basecamp is secure. Of course, any time you put something on the Internet, any time you email anything, there's a bit of uncertainty about the level of security. Even the most secure systems on the planet can be hacked. Think about how critical it is that information remains private before using an Internet tool like Basecamp. Should crucial corporate secrets, such as the date of new product launches, be entered into something like Basecamp? It depends.

Consider a typical corporate setup. You have an email system and a corporate network that are surrounded by what's called a *firewall*. In theory, this means that you'd have to have physical access to the network, or have very bad security measures, for someone to get in. Of course, determined hackers often find a way to get inside any network.

So would a typical corporate network, with traditional products like Microsoft Outlook and individual documents sitting on a corporate network, be more secure than a web-based tool that has secure sign-in but is transmitting things over the Internet? In theory, the corporate network is more secure. Some companies like to use Basecamp for some projects and not for others.

But is anything 100% secure? Not really. Defense department laptops can be left at cafes, mobile devices can be stolen easily, and the best-protected corporate networks can be hacked, from either the outside or the inside.

Basecamp is secure and fine for most applications, including many corporate situations. You can't purchase and install Basecamp behind a firewall, but you can *use* it behind a firewall. In other words, you can be on a corporate network, sign on to

Basecamp, and use the program, but the program itself will still be housed on the servers of 37signals—the provider of Basecamp.

Jason Fried and David Hansson are the cofounders of 37signals. I asked them about security.

> Todd: How secure is Basecamp? Has it ever been hacked?
>
> Jason: Basecamp is more than generally secure; it's very secure—far more secure than most people's internally hosted systems.
>
> David: We have a good breakdown of our security precautions at http://37signals.com/security. We have never (knock on wood) been hacked.

For people who really need to have something like Basecamp but insist on its being behind a firewall, you might want to look at Project Pier (www.projectpier.org/) or Jira (www.liventerprise.com/compare/Basecamp_vs_Jira/). Or you might try looking at some of the traditional tools like Microsoft Project or explore how you can use Tasks within Microsoft Outlook.

There's an interesting plug-in for Outlook called Taskline that can help manage individual tasks intelligently in conjunction with Outlook's calendar. See www.taskline.com. (This site also includes some dependencies management, such as shifting a calendar time that has been blocked out for a particular item if the deadline shifts.)

A Common Point of Reference

Having a common point of reference might be a good way to characterize both the value of project management in general and the value of looking at a tool like Basecamp in particular. Because Basecamp is easy to use, it is also more likely to be used.

Just remember that when push comes to shove, the more overhead you have with a project management tool, the more likely it is to be ditched completely when things get busy. And conversely, the leaner a tool is, the more sustainable it is, and the easier it will be for everyone to keep using it when things get busy. And they will get busy. Don't be alarmed; just be armed, with a tool like Basecamp, and you can face these situations with confidence.

BASECAMP TOUR

Welcome to Camp Basecamp! Please turn off all your mobile devices (unless you're reading this on a mobile device).

Today we'll take a quick look around and check out some of the things Basecamp can do. Remember, it's fine if you're not a project manager. And if you're like I was, and the phrase *project management* makes your eyes glaze over, just think of how such a tool can make your life easier and give you more time to do *x*, *y*, or *z*.

In fact, for fun, you might want to take a moment to actually write down some of the things you'd enjoy doing at work or at home if you had more time. Then post that list somewhere and let it help you remember how valuable keeping track of details can be. Time is precious.

Okay, the first stop on the tour is the login screen. I show this relatively boring detail to emphasize one cool thing about Basecamp: it's web-based.

Source: 37signals, LLC.

What? Isn't everything web-based now? Well, it's heading that way, but not every tool is yet. Plus, as mentioned earlier, even if you're using email that's web based, you still can't keep an email in a single location to serve as a common point of reference. Trying to manage any project through email conversations alone can get pretty chaotic; the more details there are to manage, the more deadlines there are. The next figure shows what you might see when you log in, which gives a bird's-eye view of what's going on, along with a sample "Explore Basecamp!" project.

Source: 37signals, LLC.

Then there's the calendar, which you can access from the link at the top.

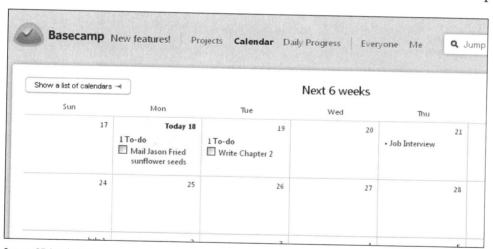

Source: 37signals, LLC.

The calendar shows you what's going on, such as upcoming events and to-do items. People usually use Basecamp for things that are related to a specific project, such as events where people meet to discuss the project, but you can put other things in there, too. For example, I need to go to the post office to send Jason Fried some sunflower seeds today, and tomorrow I need to finish writing Chapter 2. Then I have a job interview on Thursday.

Another nice thing about Basecamp is that you can assign to-do items to others. That is, you can assign a piece of a project to them and give it a deadline. It can be helpful to have a reference for following up with people and seeing how things are going.

We'll take a closer look at how to do these things later, but scheduling a to-do item is as simple as clicking on the to-do item, clicking on No Due Date, and choosing a date for it. Because of the way the software is programmed, No Due Date is telling you that there isn't a due date, so this is what you click on to choose a date.

Source: 37signals, LLC.

Basecamp is simple to use, yet flexible and powerful. You can use it for multiple projects.

Basecamp's calendar feature isn't meant to be a replacement for the calendar system you have in Microsoft Outlook, Google Calendar, or iCalendar, but you can synchronize Basecamp's calendar to other calendars if you like.

When you invite someone to participate in the Basecamp project, you'll be able to assign items to that person.

Source: 37signals, LLC.

Assigning an item is as easy as selecting a person's name from a drop-down list.

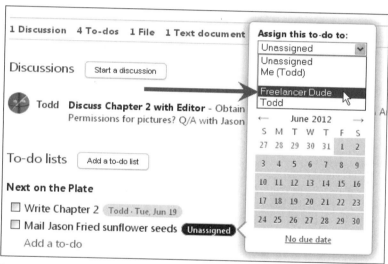

Source: 37signals, LLC.

After adding the item, you see a visual reminder in the calendar that summarizes things.

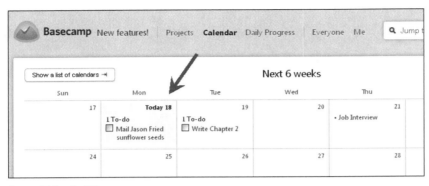

Source: 37signals, LLC.

Determining what needs to be done, allocating tasks to people, assigning deadlines, and being able to have a common point of reference are easy-to-use, helpful features of Basecamp.

But wait, there's more!

Each project in Basecamp can contain a variety of items, such as discussions, to-dos, files, documents, and dates. These features allow you to have greater flexibility when managing a project.

Source: 37signals, LLC.

So let's take a look!

Discussions

Discussions can be helpful when you need to talk about something in the project before you can move forward.

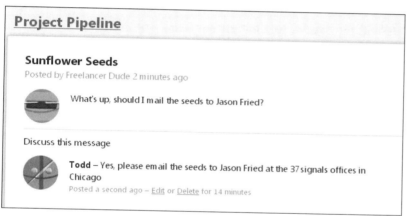

Project Pipeline ☆

Invite more people Catch up
2 people on this project on recent changes

1 Discussion   4 To-dos   1 File   1 Text document   Dates

Discussions   Start a discussion

Todd **Discuss Chapter 2 with Editor** - Obtain Van De Graaf Generator from American Science and Surplus Cost?
Permissions for pictures? Q/A with Jason Fried?   4:13pm

Source: 37signals, LLC.

Perhaps a freelancer is working on a project and has a few questions. The freelancer could start a discussion that could be carried on within Basecamp. You would receive email notification of her discussion, and you could respond by email, but an account of the conversation would also be kept in Basecamp. The value of this is that you end up with a common point of reference that you can check on later for details.

Project Pipeline

Sunflower Seeds
Posted by Freelancer Dude 2 minutes ago

What's up, should I mail the seeds to Jason Fried?

Discuss this message

Todd – Yes, please email the seeds to Jason Fried at the 37signals offices in Chicago
Posted a second ago – Edit or Delete for 14 minutes

Source: 37signals, LLC.

The discussion feature helps you move forward with a project, yet it also tracks discussions and resolutions so that anyone working on the project can know the decisions that have been made.

To-Dos

To-dos are probably my favorite feature in Basecamp. That's not because I'm a list person or because I'm Type A; in fact, I'm neither of those. Formal project managers might frown at me, but I've often managed projects using this feature alone. (Remember how more formal methods can break down when things get crazy?)

The great thing about to-dos in Basecamp is that you can create and rearrange them easily, and other people can add them.

Project Pipeline

To-do lists   [Add a to-do list]

Next on the Plate

☐ Write Chapter 2   Todd · Tue, Jun 19
☐ Mail Jason Fried sunflower seeds   Freelancer Dude · Mon, Jun 18
   Add a to-do

Brainstorming

☐ Picture of Editor touching Van De Graaf generator to show a frazzled person who is not using basecamp
☐ Include summary of chapter - 140 characters or less
   Add a to-do

Source: 37signals, LLC.

Rearranging is as simple as rolling over a to-do item…

To-do lists   [Add a to-do list]

Next on the Plate

☐ Write Chapter 2   Todd · Tue, Jun 19
🗑 Edit   ☐ Mail Jason Fried sunflower seeds   Freelancer Dude · Mon, Jun 18
   Add a to-do

Brainstorming

☐ Picture of Editor touching Van De Graaf generator to show a frazzled person who is not using basecamp
☐ Include summary of chapter - 140 characters or less
   Add a to-do

Source: 37signals, LLC.

…and dragging it into a different place on a list, or a *different* list.

To-do lists   Add a to-do list

Next on the Plate

☐ Write Chapter 2   Todd · Tue, Jun 19
   Add a to-do

Brainstorming

☐ Picture of Editor touching Van De Graaf generator to show a frazzled person
   who is not using basecamp

☐ Mail Jason Fried sunflower seeds   Freelancer Dude · Mon, Jun 18

☐ Include summary of chapter - 140 characters or less
   Add a to-do

Source: 37signals, LLC.

Voila!

For personal or business use, being able to easily capture tasks in a central place is great, because it's so easy to lose track of them. Like that idea for so-and-so to do such-and-such, and what was that again?

For business especially, I strongly recommend Basecamp to-dos as a great way to capture brainstorming, either during a meeting or when people have the time to add items during the regular workday. One of the best practices of a successful brainstorming meeting can be to jot down someone's idea without critiquing it. If you critique and offer feedback on ideas when brainstorming, sometimes you run out of time and don't hear everyone's ideas. It's much more helpful to write down all ideas while brainstorming and then come back to review them later. Brainstorming is one of the central points of this book.

I think of brainstorming as a three-step process:

1. Brainstorm, or capture ideas.

2. Prioritize those ideas.

3. Set the ideas in motion by assigning to-dos and creating milestones.

How many times have you been a part of a brainstorming session that had no follow-up? In the end, it's not about the tool, but about *using the tool effectively* in situations where it's helpful.

So Basecamp to-dos are an easy way to jot down ideas, and the drag-and-drop feature is an easy way to prioritize them.

Sometimes inertia keeps great ideas and projects from taking shape. Basecamp is a great tool for bringing them to life because it takes them from the idea stage into a stage where you have a framework for actually acting on them.

Files

Another helpful aspect of Basecamp is the Files feature. If you use email to manage details, join the club! But maybe you can recall a time when you were working on something and then couldn't remember where a file was. Or perhaps you were working on the project with other people, and you couldn't determine where the latest version was. Or maybe you sent the file to someone else for revisions and you didn't know what the status of it was. Problems like this sometimes happen at midnight, and the project is due the next day.

The Files feature can help with these situations by providing a shared directory: a simple, central place to put a project's graphics, word processing documents, PDFs, guidelines, details, rules, ingredients, works in progress, whatever.

The feature allows you to easily post files where they're accessible to anyone on the project.

Source: 37signals, LLC. © Gizele/Shutterstock.com.

Then you can discuss the image when you're logged into Basecamp or via email. The system manages all discussions so you don't even have to log in if you don't want to.

woman hair in wind.jpg
Uploaded by Todd 16 hours ago

woman hair in wind.jpg

Discuss this upload

Todd – In order to represent a frazzled person who isn't using Basecamp, I'd like the editor to touch a Van De Graaf generator and take a picture with their hair standing up. This pic is the closest I could find, on publicdomainpictures.net -- they don't look frazzled though.
http://en.wikipedia.org/wiki/Van_de_Graaff_generator
Posted a minute ago

Freelancer Dude – Totally awesome. I'll add some sparks shooting from the hair in Photoshop, and I'll post the latest file.
Posted a second ago – Edit or Delete for 14 minutes

Source: 37signals, LLC. © Gizele/Shutterstock.com.

Calendar

The next tab along the top in Basecamp is the traditional Calendar view.

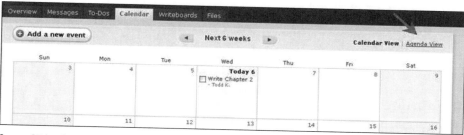

Source: 37signals, LLC.

You can also look at things in Agenda view. In Agenda view, instead of seeing things organized by day, you see a list of what needs to be done. Notice the check boxes in both the Calendar view (previous visual) and the Agenda view (next visual) that allow you to check off when things are completed.

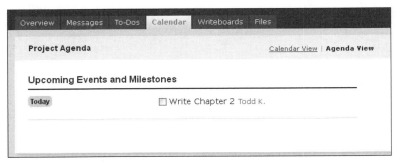

Source: 37signals, LLC.

Text Document

In Basecamp, text documents are central pages that multiple people can access and collaborate on. They're similar to Google Docs, a free feature in Gmail that allows you to create a word processing document online and invite others to collaborate on it.

Source: 37signals, LLC.

Text documents are helpful when you want people to review something. It might be easier in some situations to send an actual file, but that can get messy if multiple people are working on it. The file can become lost, buried, or forgotten, or you can end up with different versions of documents floating around.

A central text document can be a nice place to get things started.

Project Pipeline

See all text documents

Distinctives

| Bold | *Italic* | ☰ Bullets | ☰ Numbers | Quote |

This book rocks. It's written so well that people don't even have to read it.

Source: 37signals, LLC.

People and Permissions—"Everyone"

You can easily manage people and permissions in Basecamp.

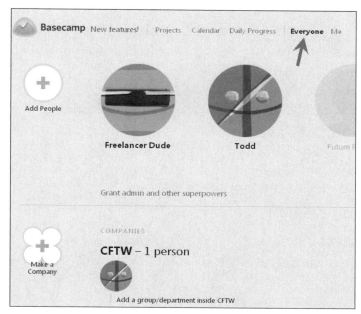

Source: 37signals, LLC.

For example, if you have a group of five people, you can create an account for each one. Then they can log in, and you can assign them separate projects.

Or maybe you're at a company using an agency with two freelancers. You can create a separate company in Basecamp for them and assign them to-do items. They can post files, and you can manage deadlines within Basecamp. This people and permissions feature allows you to monitor people's involvement.

Notification

On a related note, throughout Basecamp, you can choose to notify people when you've added something to a project. Let's say you're working on a project and you come up with a new idea. You can add it to the list and then notify specific people about it and invite them to comment. Or you can notify others that a task is complete. A group leader or manager might receive additional notifications about whatever's going on.

You can also click on a to-do list item and start a conversation.

Next on the Plate

☐ Write Chapter 2   Todd · Tue, Jun 19

☐ Mail Jason Fried sunflower seeds   Freelancer Dude · Mon, Jun 18

Add a to-do

Source: 37signals, LLC.

After the to-do item opens, you can discuss it.

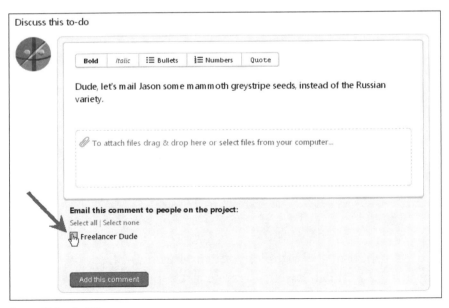

Discuss this to-do

Bold   *Italic*   ≣ Bullets   ≣ Numbers   Quote

Dude, let's mail Jason some mammoth greystripe seeds, instead of the Russian variety.

To attach files drag & drop here or select files from your computer...

Email this comment to people on the project:
Select all | Select none
☐ Freelancer Dude

Add this comment

Source: 37signals, LLC.

When you add comments, you can notify an individual person or a group of people.

A brainstorming meeting might lead to a series of ideas, or you might come across a to-do item and want to comment on it.

You can add your comment and attach files to it (such as "Hey, here's a mockup of the idea" or "Here's the Microsoft Word file"). Then you can actually subscribe people to receive notifications about the comment and subsequent discussion.

But can't you do all this with email?

Sure, and sometimes email is easier and more effective. But in other cases, it's helpful to have a common point of reference so that anyone on the project can easily see what's going on. That's what makes Basecamp shine. It allows you to keep track of files, thoughts, and ideas and then notify people when there's an update—all within one neat package.

The thing that happens in email inboxes is overload and things falling through the cracks. What if you want to make sure a tiny detail doesn't get lost in the cracks? What if someone emails you with requests or you have ten different people emailing you with requests, and you want to have a central place to jot them down to help you remember them? In those cases, Basecamp outperforms email.

OTHER PRODUCTS FROM 37SIGNALS

If you haven't already, you might want to go to http://37signals.com and click on the various icons for Basecamp and the other 37signals products that people often use in conjunction with Basecamp.

Source: 37signals, LLC.

For example, some companies find it helpful to have a dedicated chat room for live communication related to a project, and Campfire can help do the trick. Highrise can be a helpful way to manage contacts, such as following up on them, and Backpack can be helpful for sharing documents.

You can think of the suite of 37signals products as a set of powerful tools for remote collaboration, especially helpful when different people and even companies collaborate from different locations. But these tools are also helpful when everyone is in the same location.

Another thing that's important to note is that these tools are integrated. In Chapters 15 and 16, we'll see how you can use Highrise and Campfire with Basecamp, and how to conveniently access them from an integrated menu.

QUESTIONS FOR CONSIDERATION/DISCUSSION

1. How does a project management tool provide a common point of reference? What's the purpose?

2. How can you use a to-do list to reprioritize ideas?

3. In what situation would it be helpful to be able to carry on a discussion based on an uploaded item? Why would people want to be notified?

4. What's the point of having a log of discussion and activity kept in a central place? Why not just use email?

5. What kinds of things could you do with all the time you free up from managing a project effectively?

See Appendix A, "Answers to Questions for Consideration/Discussion," for suggested answers.

CONCLUSION

Dear Reader,

Congratulations on making it through your second chapter!

In this chapter, we reviewed the basic features and advantages of Basecamp.

In subsequent chapters, we'll look at some simple alternatives to Basecamp, which can help you get a sense of tools you might like to have "at the ready." We'll also create a free Basecamp account.

The goal is to make this as enjoyable as possible, especially for beginners. Best wishes on your adventures in keeping track of details and learning how to use Basecamp.

Regards,
Todd

P.S. So how'd I do with this chapter? Feel free to sound off at www.facebook.com/basecampbook.

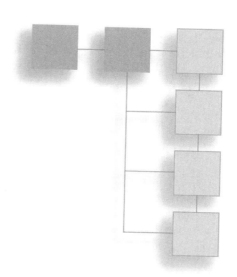

CHAPTER 3

SIMPLE ALTERNATIVES TO BASECAMP

In 140 Characters or Less

- Ch 3—A look at some tools for keeping track of details, which can also help the beginner to understand some project management basics.

In This Chapter

- Notepad/TextEdit
- NoteTab Light
- Google Docs/Tasks
- Excel
- Charting Progress
- Waah Waah, Boo Hoo, Yawn; This Is Boring, and I Want My Xbox/iPhone

Why This Chapter Is Important

It's always a good idea to consider alternatives to any tool you use, especially in project management. There's nothing wrong with using one tool and sticking with it, but in some situations it's helpful to know your alternatives. Besides, one company might use Basecamp while another uses a different tool, so one theme of this book is that it's not about the tool, per se, but about what a tool can help you accomplish. When you think of it this way and expose yourself to different programs and methods, you can develop transferable skills that aren't limited to a particular tool.

In this chapter, we'll look at some simple but powerful alternatives to Basecamp. You might come across a situation in which you don't really need Basecamp, but one of these other tools might be helpful. Or, if you're new to the world of managing projects and keeping track of details, starting as simple as possible can help you get through your project as well as beginning to imagine what a more powerful tool could do. Official project managers might struggle to keep a straight face at first, but I will show what something as simple as a text editor tool or a Microsoft Excel file can do for project management.

Part of the reason I cover some of these basic options is that I've seen how they're used as fallback options when the overhead required by other project management tools breaks down. In some cases, using a project management tool is required because there's no other choice. Basecamp comes the closest of many of the tools I've seen to being a lean, sustainable solution, offering a lot of power while remaining easy enough to use without the necessity of a fallback tool.

Next, we'll look at some free, powerful tools from Google that you can use to work on collaborative projects. It's useful to consider entirely free tools, such as the kind offered by Google, so that you can have a backup if paid tools aren't available. Basecamp has a 45-day free trial, which is great, but until Basecamp is free beyond 45 days, you might want to consider alternatives.

One thing worth mentioning about the Google tools is that anyone with a Gmail address can use them for free (see http://mail.google.com). Google also offers a paid version, Google Apps, for companies and colleges, which lets you use all the same Google tools, but in a customized format. In other words, your email address would be something like todd@sunflower.edu, instead of tekelsey@gmail.com or todd@mycompany.com. It's like having your own private Google. An increasing number of companies and colleges are using this paid service from Google, which offers a powerful alternative to traditional Microsoft and other systems. The advantage is that Google manages the servers, and all the software is "in the cloud," so it can be an efficient solution. It's also collaborative. For more information on that line of thought, see http://www.google.com/enterprise/apps/business/, http://www.google.com/apps/intl/en/edu/, or even http://www.google.com/enterprise/apps/government.

There really is no one-size-fits-all tool; the tool you should use depends on how complex the project is. If projects are more complex than Basecamp can handle, then maybe Microsoft Project or some other tool is the answer. Or, if you're in a club and you don't need a Calendar function, perhaps a Google Doc is all you need.

Looking at other tools can help you learn how to learn. This is a shifting landscape. Tools change over time, and new features are added, but if you know what to look for, you can use the best tool for what you need, when you need it. Toward that end, I've asked some questions at the end of the chapter, suitable for a class or an individual, to help you think critically. See Appendix A for suggested answers.

After that we'll move right along into starting a Basecamp free trial account, in Chapter 4.

NOTEPAD/TEXTEDIT

Okay, project managers, stop snickering. Be honest: has there ever been a time when you opened a text editor to jot down details? Raise your hand. Or, has there ever been a time when you were using _____ at your company, but you didn't want to take the time to open and configure a file, so you went to Notepad (PC), TextEdit (Mac), or a Notes feature (mobile device)?

So for better or worse, you've used Notepad, TextEdit, and similar tools to keep track of details, and you still will. As with any other tool, they have advantages and limitations.

You need to get started somewhere, so you might open and save a file and start by titling the project based on what you're planning to accomplish; in this case, call it "Growing Sunflowers."

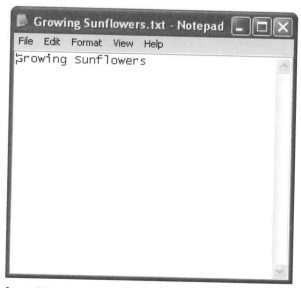

Source: 37signals, LLC.

To start breaking a project into its component parts, you might think about a timetable. Are there any deadlines for the project? How long might the project take? What are some of the milestones?

Source: 37signals, LLC.

You also might start to jot down individual tasks that need to be accomplished, so that either you can do them, or you can assign them to someone else. In some cases, person A's completion of a task might have implications for person B. These are called *dependencies*.

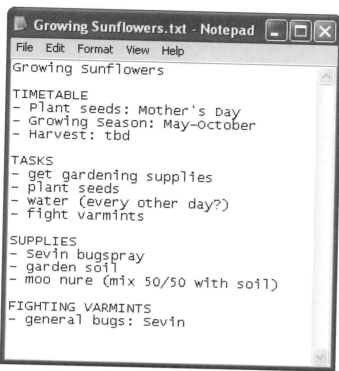

```
Growing Sunflowers.txt - Notepad
File  Edit  Format  View  Help
Growing Sunflowers

TIMETABLE
- Plant seeds: Mother's Day
- Growing Season: May-October
- Harvest: tbd

TASKS
- get gardening supplies
- plant seeds
- water (every other day?)
- fight varmints

SUPPLIES
- Sevin bugspray
- garden soil
- moo nure (mix 50/50 with soil)

FIGHTING VARMINTS
- general bugs: Sevin
```

Source: 37signals, LLC.

For example, let's say I'm planting sunflowers as part of a club, and the task of getting gardening supplies and seeds is given to Jake. If I'm the one who is going to do the planting and watering, I depend on Jake to get his task done first.

In a corporate situation, this is one of the central things you end up dealing with, especially if you're the person managing a project. It could be that you're involved with some tasks in the project, but you might also be assigning tasks. And if one of your team members is relying on another person, you definitely want to keep track of the status of the project. But what if someone doesn't get something done on time, or there are unforeseen circumstances that lead to delays? This is where a tool that can keep everyone apprised of status can come in handy. As you'll see later in the book, a tool like Basecamp provides a way for each participant to log in and "keep things going" by posting files, notes, or discussion so that everyone can see what's going on, at any point in time.

To return to our example, as we're taking notes for this project, the list of notes might expand, but you might add a set of "global" notes at the top, such as a list of general questions or strategic questions, that might require discussion. Should we go organic this year in growing sunflowers? Will the price of our widgets affect the final outcome of the project? What are the consequences if the project isn't done on time?

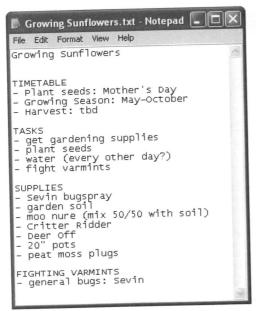
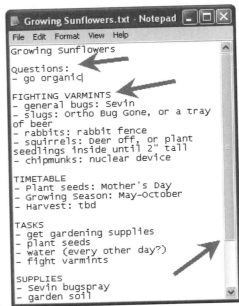

Source: 37signals, LLC.

The second arrow shows how the set of notes on "fighting varmints" has been relocated (through cutting and pasting). We might call this *reprioritizing*. When you are brainstorming or working on individual parts of a project, it can be helpful to have a flexible way of elevating the most important things to get done. Some personality types might prefer to clearly and logically lay out a set of tasks for a project, plan them, review them, and just follow them to the letter. Unfortunately, there are often outside factors, especially in corporate projects, in which you have to be able to adapt to changing situations and changing priorities. Therefore, *reprioritization* is a critical skill. It's partly why I like the drag-and-drop to-do lists in Basecamp so much, because they offer such an easy way to reprioritize notes, especially for brainstorming. But here in the text editor, you can simply cut and paste to reorganize your list.

I put the third arrow in the diagram to show how the list of notes is expanding. In the case of a text editing document, this means having to scroll through the document. The big question when keeping track of details is, how do you add information to a project and keep it accessible, so that things don't drop through the cracks?

Now, if you're just starting out, or teaching a class, it might be good to begin by creating a project and trying to manage it in a text editor program to see what happens.

One of the immediate things you'll encounter is that, for the file to be useful, you need to *keep revisiting it*. And that principle holds true no matter what tool you use. Even if you have a calendar and reminders, no tool is going to manage a project for you. The sooner you accept this fact, the better off you'll be in the long run.

One thing that's good to do from the beginning is to ask yourself how you are going to remember to check in with your tool and see how things are going. For some people, this might mean simply developing the habit of "checking in" with their chosen tool in the morning or at lunch. It could mean setting reminders in your calendar program. It might mean that you leave a browser window or Notepad window open on your screen. Or maybe it means that you figure out how to have your computer automatically launch that window when the computer restarts, so that when your computer crashes at an inconvenient time, and you're doing 10 things, the computer remembers to open that critical window—even if you don't. (In Windows, you can have a file or program automatically run when Windows starts up by placing a shortcut in the Startup folder. There are ways to do this on a Mac, too. On a mobile device, I suppose you'd just need to set a reminder or keep the icon for your given program on your home screen and develop the habit of consulting it.)

NoteTab Light

If you want to have an easy way of taking notes for capturing details or meetings, one option I've come across that's modestly better than a text editor like Notepad or TextEdit, is NoteTab Light. It has a lot of features, windows, and panels, but you can turn them off so that it looks more like Notepad.

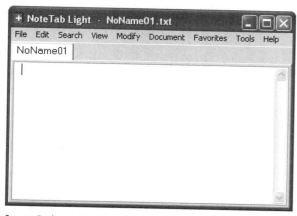

Source: Fookes Holding Ltd.

One of the nice things about NoteTab Light is that you can set Options to automatically save files every ___ minutes as desired. AutoSave is a feature I typically set up in any program that has it, such as Microsoft Word. I've been through enough grief over working on something and then having the battery die or the power fail or the computer crash, and we all know how frustrating it can be to lose all of our work. This also serves to highlight one of the strengths of web-based tools, which constantly save updates so you generally don't have this issue.

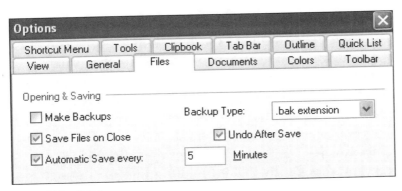

Source: Gridinsoft, LLC.

Another thing that's nice about NoteTab Light is that you can open multiple documents in tabs, as you can in the most recent versions of Firefox, Chrome, and Internet Explorer. This allows you to have more information at your fingertips.

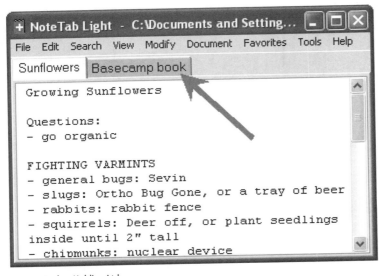

Source: Fookes Holding Ltd.

When you click on a tab, notes on various items are accessible within a single window.

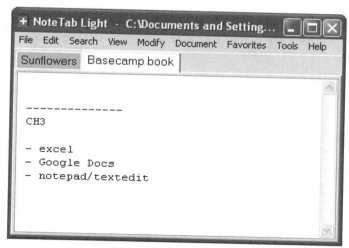

Source: Fookes Holding Ltd.

Project managers, don't worry. I'm not advocating that people manage projects in NoteTab Light; it's just serving as an example of a helpful tool. For some people, NoteTab Light might serve as a helpful alternative to taking handwritten notes in meetings. If you're like me, it's hard to keep up with taking notes by hand because people tend to talk quickly, but taking notes on a laptop helps ensure that details don't fall through the cracks. Maybe you can take notes in a simple text editor and then use your favorite project management tool to translate these notes into something else.

For those interested in NoteTab Light, visit www.download.com and look in Windows software. If anyone has a similar tool or other tools they've found helpful on Mac, Windows, or mobile device apps, feel free to post info to the Facebook page www.facebook.com/basecampbook. I can also post links to the "companion page" for the book at www.toddkelsey.com/books/basecamp.

Google Docs/Tasks

Google Docs is a feature included free within Gmail (sign up at http://mail.google.com). If you want to use an existing email address instead, you can click the Sign Up link shown here to create a Google account, which uses your current email address. I recommend that you try Gmail. I used AOL back in the day, and then Microsoft Outlook, but I gradually developed the opinion that Gmail is the best, most helpful, most spam-free email system out there. Using Gmail also makes it easier to sign in to the many helpful tools Google offers that come free with the account.

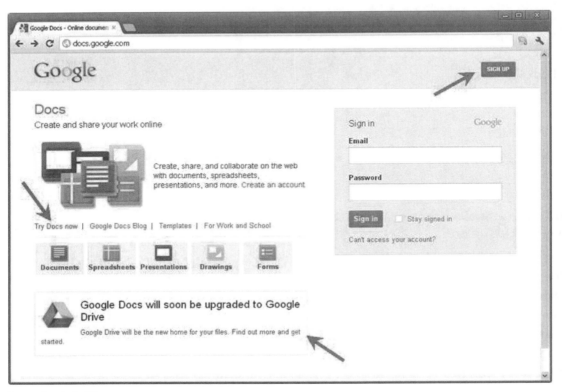

Source: Google.Org™.

Google Docs is basically a suite of online collaboration tools. You can think of Google Docs as a free, online, collaborative version of something like Microsoft Office. Office is gradually coming online, but Google Docs has been doing it for a long time and has some pretty advanced features while remaining easy to use.

For example, you can create word processing documents online in Chicago and invite people in California or Shanghai to participate. Google Docs is helpful in classroom settings, in personal settings, and in corporate settings. (I consider Google Docs secure, but a company or college could also use Google Apps, mentioned earlier, for a private Google experience that includes Gmail functionality with your own website name, such as todd@mywebsitename.com.)

But wait, there's more! You can also create online presentations, online spreadsheets, drawings, and even forms.

An important thing to remember about Google Docs is that you have the choice of making your documents private or publishing them to the web. In fact, a Google Doc is the simplest way to make a quick web page, and updating the web page is as easy as saving the document. If you want a short link for your page, you can always take the long link Google gives you and shorten it at http://bit.ly or http://tinyurl.com.

Another thing that's important to remember (and try) is that Google Docs are embeddable, which makes them powerful. You could use another free Google tool called Google Sites (http://sites.google.com), which happens to be the easiest, free way to make websites, and insert a Google Doc or a presentation into your site. Then, when you want to update the presentation, you just open it; because the presentation is embedded into your site, it updates automatically.

Remember that Google Docs are collaborative. Any way you use them, you can invite other people to update them or participate in them. Google offers a helpful suite of tools to use and experiment with, and I highly recommend that you investigate them and become familiar with them. Even if you don't use them to keep track of details, they're just helpful, period.

Okay, there's one more thing I have to mention. In addition to the "standard" Google Docs tools, there's also Blogger (see www.blogger.com), which is the easiest way to start a blog. But as an example of integration, you can easily insert Google Docs as widgets into a blog post. For example, I have a blog to showcase an idea I had called RGB, so I made a simple blog post about it and inserted a Google Presentation. Then I took the long link to the blog post and shortened it at http://tinyurl.com so that the link would be easy for me to remember. If you want to see an example of it, visit http://tinyurl.com/aboutrgb.

Docs

Okay, it's time to wake up! There's fun ahead!

If you want to try out Google Docs or invite a friend to, Google has made a demo version available. You don't even need to sign in.

Visit http://docs.google.com and click the Try Docs Now link. If you want, you can always sign in with a Gmail account created at http://mail.google.com, or click the Sign Up link on the docs.google.com page as previously mentioned; if you access Google Docs this way, the user experience might be different, but if you're in Gmail, just look for the Documents link at the top of the screen. However, to keep things simple, you might just want to sign out of your Google account, sign out of Gmail, and visit the link http://docs.google.com so you can follow along with the rest of this section.

When you click the Try Docs Now link, a screen opens and defaults to Document, as shown in the next graphic, but you can always click Spreadsheet or Presentation or Drawing to try out the other types of features.

Source: Google.Org™.

As the Google Doc says, you can click and just start typing. You can also copy the link (see the arrow in the previous graphic) and email it or send it via instant message to a friend so that she can collaborate on the document, too.

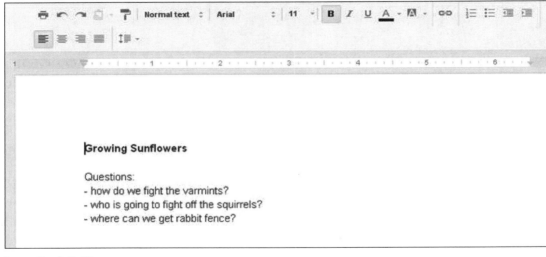

Source: Google.Org™.

In the context of this chapter, the idea is to consider Google Docs as a way to collaboratively take notes on a conference call, for example, or a way to collaboratively build a document as part of a project. Google Docs functions similarly to a conventional word processing program and even includes a fair amount of formatting capability. In the full free version, you can also download into various formats, such as PDF, OpenOffice, or even Microsoft Word. Google Docs isn't perfect, but it's easy to use and powerful.

Another thing you can do is to simultaneously work on the document with someone else. In the previous graphic, the question is posed, "How do we fight the varmints?" I sent the document link to another person, who logged onto the document and added the answer that follows.

Growing Sunflowers

Questions:
- How do we fight the varmints?
A: maybe we can establish a truce

- Who is going to fight off the squirrels?
A: |

- Where can we get rabbit fence?

Source: Google.Org™.

So the power of remote collaboration is not only that it is remote, but that it can be *asynchronous* (that is, people working on the document at different times, as in different time zones, or at different times of the day), or it can be in real time, such as on a conference call. I've had conference calls with people in California before with us both logged on to the same Google Doc, and it did a pretty good job of updating things in real time, including popping up little markers to show who had just added something.

Google Doc Exercise

For a classroom or personal exercise, you might like first trying the Google Doc demo as described, and then signing up for a Gmail or Google account, opening a Google Doc, and trying the full version, including inviting other people into the document using the Share button. If you want to get crazy, you might even like to try publishing your Google Doc to the web, converting the link into a "short" URL using http://bit.ly, or http://tinyurl.com/, and claiming victory over technology by developing a collaborative web page in 60 seconds or less.

So the project management benefits of collaborative documents are many. And, by the way, Basecamp has a similarly helpful feature called "documents," which is integrated right within the project management workflow.

Now, when you're experimenting with using Google tools to keep track of details, you can access Docs under the Documents link at the top of the Gmail screen. (You might also like to try the Calendar link as well.)

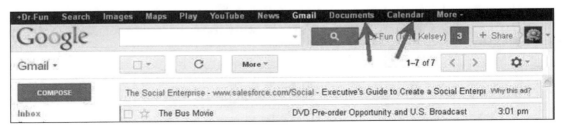

Source: Google.Org™.

The Calendar feature allows you to set up reminders for yourself (ding ding ding—to check your project management tool, for example, or for meetings). Reminders can be sent via email, or even to a mobile device, and they can take the form of conventional invites for meetings as well. While the Calendar feature is not integrated into project management workflow like it is in Basecamp, it's still worth knowing about as an alternative to Basecamp and Outlook.

Source: Google.Org™.

Events/reminders can be set to be repeating, they can be color-coded, and you can "add guests" as well.

Source: Google.Org™.

Tasks

Another helpful feature in Gmail is Tasks. To try them, click the Gmail menu and choose Tasks.

Source: Google.Org™.

A little window pops up in the browser window.

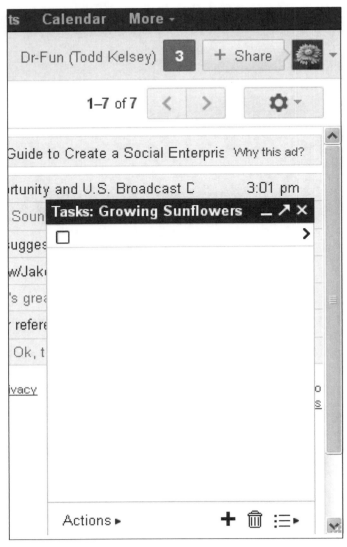

Source: Google.Org™.

And, if you like, at the top of the Tasks window, you can click the little Pop-Out icon.

Source: Google.Org™.

And then you get an entirely separate Tasks window, which can be helpful.

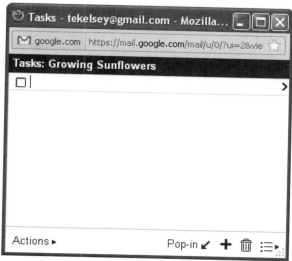

Source: Google.Org™.

Tasks can represent an easy way to enter in notes as part of a brainstorm session; this feature most notably compares to to-dos in Basecamp. It can be helpful for brainstorming.

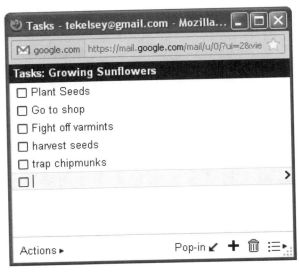

Source: Google.Org™.

And as with Basecamp to-dos, you can roll over an individual task, and when you get the grabber icon, you can click on a task...

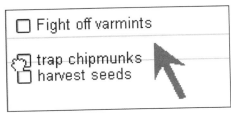

Source: Google.Org™.

...and drag the task into a different position.

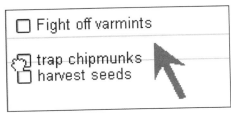

Source: Google.Org™.

And you have a reordered list. Voila!

Tasks: Growing Sunflowers

☐ Plant Seeds
☐ Go to shop
☐ Fight off varmints
☐ trap chipmunks
☐ harvest seeds

Source: Google.Org™.

Why is this cool? Because reprioritization is a fundamental skill in managing projects, during which a list of priorities or ideas might need to change from time to time. Also, in brainstorming, you might like to meet with people and follow the best practice of capturing all ideas without critiquing so that everyone's voice is heard. *Then* you can do the work of prioritizing.

Another nice feature of tasks in Gmail is that you can press the Tab key to indent them. Other similar features are available in the Actions menu, including the ability to email the task list to someone.

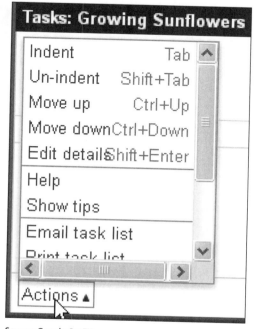

Tasks: Growing Sunflowers

Indent	Tab
Un-indent	Shift+Tab
Move up	Ctrl+Up
Move down	Ctrl+Down
Edit details	Shift+Enter
Help	
Show tips	
Email task list	
Print task list	

Actions ▲

Source: Google.Org™.

The ability to indent helps you organize the information.

Tasks: Growing Sunflowers

☐ Plant Seeds

☐ Go to shop

☐ Fight off varmints

  ☐ trap chipmunks

☐ harvest seeds

Source: Google.Org™.

Another feature is the pop-up menu from the icon in the lower-right corner of the Task window, which allows you to create a new list.

Source: Google.Org™.

You can also go into individual tasks by rolling over them and clicking the rightward triangle/bracket.

Source: Google.Org™.

You can add notes or click the little calendar icon (to the right of Due Date), and choose a due date for the item.

Tasks: Growing Sunflowers

‹ Back to list

☐ Plant Seeds

Due date   📅

Notes

Move to list ▼

‹ Back to list

Actions ▸   Pop-in ↙ ➕ 🗑 ☰▸

Source: Google.Org™.

Then the due date reminder can appear alongside the task.

Source: Google.Org™.

Similar to other tools shown in this chapter, as an individual learning experience or classroom experience, it might be good to try using Gmail Tasks to manage a project, as a way to learn some of the basics, such as gathering details, establishing a timeline, creating a list of priorities, and brainstorming.

And then when you're finished with a task, you can click on it to mark that it's done. Woohoo!

I was tempted to leave this for you to discover, but I might as well say that one limitation of the current version of Gmail Tasks is that they're not collaborative—that is, you can't share an individual task list so that more than one person can work on the same list. You could do that in a Google Doc, but not with the same drag-and-drop functionality. Although sharing an individual task list is not available in the current version, it's always possible that Google might add the function; it always seems to be adding new features to Google Docs. At the time of writing, the newest feature of Google Docs is Google Drive, which would be a space for storing online files, including ones that you upload, such as a graphic. This would be equivalent to the Files feature in Basecamp.

EXCEL

Last but not least, we come to Microsoft Excel, also known as a spreadsheet program. Back in the day, especially in my early days as a graphic designer, about the last thing I thought I'd ever do is use Microsoft Excel for anything. It was financial, weird, and better left to its own devices.

Since then, I've encountered a number of situations in which Excel is helpful, including for setting up a detail-tracking file. We'll take a look at a few simple examples here, as well as at how to upload an Excel file to Google Docs for collaborative use (and how to download a Google Spreadsheet in Excel format).

For keeping track of details, the easiest way to think of the value of an Excel file is that it allows you to have a lot of information in a relatively small space. Let's say you had to write a book, and it had 16 chapters. Then, in each chapter, you had to take about 10 pictures, and then had to keep track of obtaining legal permission to use those pictures. You could keep track of this in a conventional word processing document, but by making a table of 16 rows, and 20 columns, you could store all the information in a convenient place and also be able to see it in a single glance.

Excel is designed primarily for numbers, but you can type text into the cells.

Formulas

The other thing that you can do in Excel is to use formulas. Special props to my older brother Mark, who showed me years ago how to work with formulas. The nice thing about formulas is that they can do math for you automatically. Let's say you are entering in how many hours it takes you to work on a piece of a project, and you want to have a "running total" that is automatically updated, at the end of a series of each rows. Excel can do that. I've seen Excel files emailed back and forth, or stored on a network, where a "shared" Excel allows multiple people to work on it. As we'll see a bit later in this section, you can also create spreadsheets online.

This section is not meant to be a tutorial on Excel; it's just meant to show you some of the things you can do in the context of project management. Chances are at some point you might be keeping track of details and realize that it might be helpful to have a little chart to check off what the status of things are. What has generally driven me to learn new tools is reaching the limit of my current tools or needing a more advanced tool because I'm trying something more complex.

Excel is like that for me. I never touched it until I realized I needed to keep exact track of particular details at a job. In that situation, I needed to know exactly what was going on so I could respond to my manager's questions at any point in time. I quickly realized I couldn't remember everything. Microsoft Word was unwieldy, but an Excel spreadsheet proved helpful.

Gradually, I learned how to use formulas. Perhaps you'd like to try using Excel (or the spreadsheet function in openoffice.org's equivalent to Microsoft Office) or Google Spreadsheets so you can keep track of some details. Learn just the basics of formulas, because you might find it handy to be able to make your own tools. Plenty of people make their own tools, digital and otherwise.

Rescoping

An example of a tool you could make would be a rescoping tool, which is also an example of something to consider in project management; it's a kind of holy grail that is always out there ready for some adventurer to pursue.

A rescoping tool reflects a situation you might end up in at some point, in which you have limited hours to work on your personal or corporate project, and then you need a way to add things to a pipeline. The most common way to respond to this is to just do the best you can. But the more pressure there is, the less sustainable this approach is. And in corporate situations, there's sometimes a classic tension between doing what you can with the resources you have and making a case to either reduce the workload or to hire additional help, freelance or fulltime. Or you might simply need to say, "Well, I'm happy to add this to my pipeline. It looks like this project will push the deadlines for x, y, z. An alternative is that we can hire some temporary help to cover the hours, which I've estimated to be a or b."

So if you're catching the drift, being able to play with formulas might allow you to add, subtract, and multiply. You might do those calculations with a calculator the first time, but why not try them in a spreadsheet?

For example, here's the corner of an Excel spreadsheet.

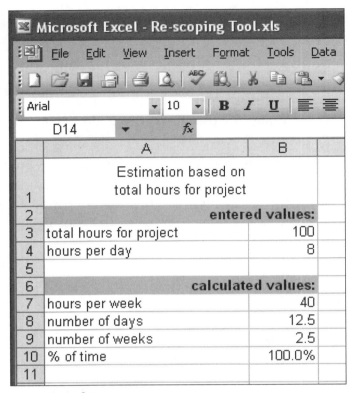

Source: Microsoft® Corporation.

So toward the top, you can type in values, and the numbers below are calculated.

For example, if the total project is 100 hours, and you estimate spending 8 hours a day, at the bottom you see how many days it would take.

If you could only spend 2 hours per day on the project, it would take 50 days to complete.

	Estimation based on total hours for project	
1		
2	**entered values:**	
3	total hours for project	100
4	hours per day	2
5		
6	**calculated values:**	
7	hours per week	10
8	number of days	50.0
9	number of weeks	10.0
10	% of time	25.0%

Source: Microsoft® Corporation.

Another type of tool you could make would be based on weeks.

Estimation based on deadline (number of weeks)	
entered values:	
number of weeks	0.0
hours per day	0
calculated values:	
hours per week	0
number of days	0
% of time	0.0%
total hours for project	0

Source: Microsoft® Corporation.

You might say that you are going to spend 4 weeks, 2 hours per day on the project. At the bottom, Excel tells you the total hours and the percentage of your time.

Estimation based on deadline (number of weeks)	
entered values:	
number of weeks	4.0
hours per day	2
calculated values:	
hours per week	10
number of days	20
% of time	25.0%
total hours for project	40

Source: Microsoft® Corporation.

What's going on behind the scenes is that a formula in a specific cell (calculated values) is taking numbers you've entered and multiplying them or adding them any way you specify.

It doesn't take too much work to learn how to enter a simple formula so that a calculated cell can, well, calculate. The letter and number scheme for identifying cells is a bit like the game Battleship. In Battleship, you indicate what quadrant you want to make a move in by giving a letter and number to represent a position on a grid (see http://en.wikipedia.org/wiki/Battleship_game or http://tinyurl.com/batship).

Okay, so we see in the next graphic that in cell E10 (letter first, representing the column, then the number, which is the row), there is a formula. In cell 10, it is taking E7 and multiplying it by E3.

Source: Microsoft® Corporation.

Piece of cake. You've sunk my Battleship!

Excel Exercise

What's the point again? The point is to remember that Excel can do your work for you. Yes, you can use a calculator, but once you've calculated a bunch of numbers and made estimates, and then one tiny thing changes, you realize how nice it would be to have a more flexible tool. So build it! Try it as a personal or classroom exercise. Then if you'd like to look at the one I made, email me at tekelsey@gmail.com, and I'll post the Excel file I created to the book page at www.toddkelsey.com/books/basecamp. Check the page first to see if anyone has emailed yet.

Having little tools like this at your fingertips can help you respond to dynamic situations; and depending on your situation, it might be helpful to have a tool that allows you to rescope so you can express the limitations of your pipeline. If you just go to someone and say, "I'm getting a little busy, can this wait?", the response might be, "No." And if we're still in troubled economic times when you're reading this, you might not necessarily want to push too hard on your company to hire more resources; management is going to want you to be more productive no matter what.

But everyone has limits, and having a tool to express the implications of a management decision can be helpful, even if it's just for your own planning. And it might enable you to at least *try* to say something like, "Okay, the deadlines will have to push out to this specific date _____," and see what happens, or "Okay, I think we'd need to get 100 hours more resource time on this project to make the deadline," and see what the response is. And, depending on the deadline and project and company, you might be doing everyone a favor by showing what the real status of the project is.

You can strengthen your case when you've shown that you can generally predict with accuracy how long a task will take you. But that's the beauty of tracking your own details: Excel can help you know your capabilities and let other people know them, too.

You can see how a simple tool can have a big impact. Maybe it's allowing you to go home earlier to watch *24* on DVD, play Frisbee with your dog, or at least get more sleep. So when your eyes glaze over while reading this book, remember that all this is helping you have more time to do other things. It's also likely to impress your employer, clients, coworkers, and fellow volunteers because you're freeing up time to get more done. And that can mean promotion and job security. Put in a little effort, and reap the rewards.

CHARTING PROGRESS

Now we'll move on to a more conventional chart use of Excel that is fairly common and that you might like to try even if you're not wearing a suit or working in a cubicle.

I created a spreadsheet when I needed to progressively work through a series of items. It was for a product feature that was going to be added to the website for particular countries. It didn't need to be added to all of them, and people didn't necessarily know which ones it should be added to. It was a work in progress, or what some would call a dynamic work environment. I called it chaos.

I wasn't an analyst at the time. In fact, I had barely made it off the tour bus as a professional musician at that point. But if I could dive into Excel, so can you. Do a cannonball dive if you have to.

Okay, so there were, let's see, about 20-something different environments for which I had to update material. And then there were other features that needed updating. It got pretty complex, but this little Excel chart made it really simple. First, I needed to ask someone, for a particular country (for example, UK) and a particular feature (for example, row 4/5—SSI coverage), whether it needed to be updated. Then I would just add little Xs and keep track of progress. So when my manager popped out of the blue and asked, "What's up?", I could respond. And when I arrived each morning, I knew where I had left off.

	Cascade Worksheet			Main					Channel		International - active							Misc		
Project			US	NN	EH	W2	CV	QW	CO	BH	UK	AU	DE	NL	BE	FR	PL	IN	KR
Consolidated Guide	applies to	X																	
> SSH - PPD - SSI coverage	done	X																	
SiteMail Guide	applies to					X													
> sync coverage removal	done					X													
Advanced Email	applies to	X																	
> upgrade note in email config	done																		
120406 parking page update	applies to	X	X	.	.	.	.	.	.	.	.	.	.	.	.	.	.	.
	done																		
Exchange Update	applies to	X	X	.	.	.	X	.	.	X	.	.	.	.	.	.	.	.
	done																		
Authorization Code FAQ	applies to												X					
	done																		
Domain Name FAQ update	applies to	X																	
	done	X																	

Source: Microsoft® Corporation.

Spreadsheets are pretty simple to set up. Just type in the text, and ask a friend who has used Excel to help you with formatting.

Charting with Excel is a handy skill to have. Chances are you will run into Excel at some point. It can be your friend, so don't be afraid of it.

Collaborative Tracking

Here's a feature that's a bit more fun. I used this spreadsheet when I was volunteering for the One Laptop Per Child project (www.laptop.org), and we were working on translating some documentation into a number of different languages. We had translators from around the world volunteering. We needed to know what the status of the translating was, and the translators needed to know some information, too. So we made a list of the different versions and added columns with notes like Name of Translator and TimeZone as a reference for Skype calls. You could try to keep track of something like this via email, but in a collaborative situation, you would probably quickly have a nervous breakdown. In other words, a spreadsheet can save your sanity.

Microsoft Excel - xodoc_translation_matrix.xls

File Edit View Insert Format Tools Data Window Help Adobe PDF

E19   *fx* liz

	ty	lang	status	appropriate	name of translator	TimeZone
1			NOTE: only volunteer project managers should send translations out. Others could "nominate" translations they know are coming and make notes in notes column.			
2						
3						
4	ty	lang	status	appropriate	name of translator	TimeZone
5	1	es=Spanis	delivered		June Greever	?
6	1	pt=Portugu	delivered		Claus Aranha	?
7	1	hi=Hindi	delivered	indLinux.org	IndLinux members	
8	1	am=Amhar	delivered		Elias Muluneh	?
9	2	ARABIC	todd handling			
10	2	ar=Arabic	getting quote	Lingo	tbd	
11	2	ar=Arabic	querying		tbd	
12	2	ar=Arabic	in conversation			
13	2	ar=Arabic	Todd; will		Khaled Hosny	
14						
15	2	th=Thai	delivered	iTeach.org	David M. Bucknell	?
16	2	he=Hebrew	11/27 for free;		Dov	?
17	2	fr=French	delivered		Ancelin Gauthier	?
18	2	ru=Russia	delivered		Alexandra Maier	?
19	2	ru=Russia	nominated		liz	CST
20						
21	2	n/a	n/a		Greg DeKoenigsberg	?

xodocv3-en-102007

Ready

Source: Microsoft® Corporation.

We ended up importing this document into Google Docs and inviting everyone to collaborate on it so people could update info as needed. Then we had a view of things at a glance and knew what was going on.

That spreadsheet brings up another benefit of Google Docs and collaborative editing—a real-world implication. As I was writing this chapter, I wondered, "Hmm…do I still have that spreadsheet around?" It had been a few years since I had worked on it, yet finding the file was as easy as logging into Gmail, going into Documents, typing "translation" into the Search box, and sifting through the short list of documents with the word "translation" in the filename or contents. The search capability allowed me to easily find documents I'd worked on in the past. Don't underestimate the value of having a central, online place to organize your documents and files, whether in Google Docs, Google Drive, or the file feature in Basecamp. It's really helpful.

Source: Google.Org™.

Of course, the other nice thing about having the spreadsheet online is that you can just click the Share button and invite someone on the other side of the world to visit the spreadsheet and provide details.

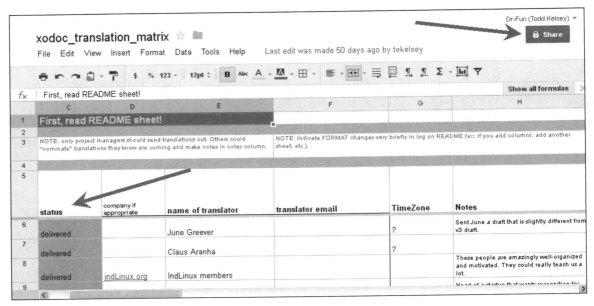

Source: Google.Org™.

Another column is marked Status. It's a perennial feature of keeping track of details, whether you're working on a personal project or a corporate one, or volunteering for One Laptop Per Child or your local organization. At some point, one or more people are going to want to know how things are going, and having a way to track status, in a central location, is handy.

The other arrow at the bottom of the previous graphic is pointing to tabs. Like Excel, Google Spreadsheets has tabs, which allow you to have a lot of information that's easily accessible.

Another way spreadsheets can make your life easier is their ease of access of information reference. You could list any kind of information in a scrollable word processing document. But then how would you find the info you're looking for? You could search for it, but what if you didn't know what you were looking for? The advantage of a spreadsheet is that you can have a lot of information within a few clicks, and it can be dynamic information that changes regularly. That's when the online version of a spreadsheet is nice—when people are logging in and updating a status.

Here's another view, this time of the File menu in a Google spreadsheet. As we saw earlier in this chapter, not only can you save to a number of file formats on your computer, you can publish to the web. In other words, you can convert a Google spreadsheet to a live web page, public or otherwise. This is a marvelous capability that's part of Google Docs, Google Presentations, and Google Spreadsheets. It's the quickest, easiest way on the planet to publish web content, and it's free!

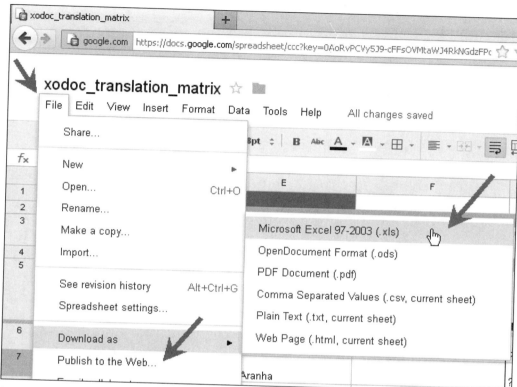

Source: Google.Org™.

Visual Aid

Even though this section is just a simple introduction to spreadsheets and is not meant to be a tutorial, I'm also going to include a chart, just for grins. There are myriad charts you can make in Excel or Google Spreadsheets that are meant to provide a simple way of visually representing things. For example, you might have a pie chart to show that 30% of the project is done, and 70% remains. It's easy, at a glance, and something you can email or print out. Instead of wading through numbers, you can look at a visual.

When you use formulas and you update information, the chart updates, too. Spreadsheets can save you a lot of time.

Here's an example of a simple spreadsheet created in Google Docs, which I log into on a regular basis, and enter my weight. Hopefully this disclosure will inspire me to get into the gym more often!

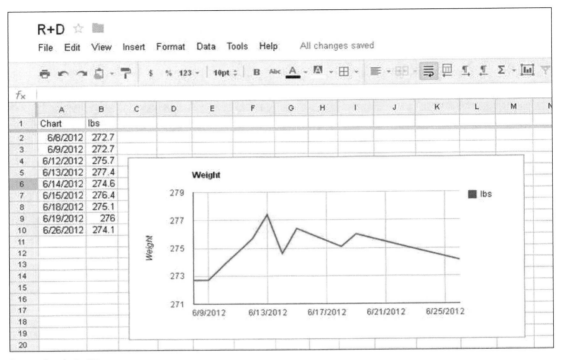

Source: Google.Org™.

This example is designed to demonstrate that keeping track of details can extend to personal life. It's also an example of a clear visual and the way a diagram can provide information quickly, with a single look. You know at a glance how you're doing, whether you're charting revenue, and how many hours you've spent on a project. This particular type of chart is a line chart, which shows a *trend*. Trends are impressive ways of showing information, because they can tell you what direction you're headed in.

But one reason for having a chart and data as part of a project is to be able to make a convincing case. If you're getting really bored at this point, think about something you might want to convince someone of. Now think about the fact that telling them a story or being passionate will help, but what if you could *show* exactly what you mean? Sometimes when you're working on a project, you need to demonstrate progress visually. The visual helps you get what you want—more time, more resources, or even a course change. If you see where things are headed and make a chart showing the trend, you can show that if x change were to be made, the chart would look like y. In simplistic terms, this is known as *forecasting*.

If I, a graphic designer turned goatee-toting, tattooed, earring-wearing rock 'n' roll musician, can step off a tour bus, gradually face the real world, and learn about these detail-oriented tools, you can too!

Final Considerations

If you have any doubts about using simple tools for project management, now I'd like you to consider that a Google Spreadsheet is a web publishing platform. Imagine being able to display an embedded chart in a blog or website that automatically updates when you update the data. Can you imagine that being useful? Heck yeah! Try it.

Exploration Exercise

Or, if you've been following through this chapter like you're visiting Willy Wonka's Chocolate Factory—a bit dazed, but interested—I suggest going back through the chapter, as a personal or classroom exercise, and just trying things. Think of it as exploration. Have some fun, and be creative. Creative? Yeah. Whether in corporate pursuits or personal ones, creativity is important—even in project management.

Here's a creative idea: Find someone else who would like to learn how to do some of these things, and teach that person as soon as you learn them yourself. Showing someone else how to do something is an excellent way to learn.

Try a Notepad project. Then morph that project into Google Docs. Explore Google Docs and Google Presentations, and publish your text documents and presentations to the web. Then try Google Spreadsheet. Try regularly tracking some information, even if it's simple information such as this: How many emails did I get today? How many times did I check Facebook? How many times did I pick up my mobile device and look at it? Then, as an experiment, try changing your behavior, tracking it, and making a chart.

If you're ready to work on your project, track something in the project, like hours spent, or divide hours spent into different kinds of tasks and show what percentage of your time is spent in meetings. Then track that over time.

Charts and spreadsheets offer accountability. This is important in project management, because it can show that you, or whoever is working on things, is accountable. You can demonstrate that you're making progress or that something needs changing. Then you can work together and encourage each other to make some progress on the project.

I don't have plans to make the earlier weight chart any more public than it already is, but you're certainly welcome to follow my little www.twitter.com/toddkelsey account, where I do post my progress. Or you can friend me on Facebook and cheer for me when I reach my goals. Or go to the Facebook page and post a link from a Google Doc you've published, claim victory over Excel, or find a group on LinkedIn and ask for help with Excel. Or form a Facebook group for readers of this book, post it on the Facebook page, and invite people to join you. Mutual encouragement works for learners. Viva la social!

Waah Waah, Boo Hoo, Yawn; This Is Boring, and I Want My Xbox/iPhone

You've nearly made it to the end of the chapter. I'm going to guess that you've picked up your mobile phone a few times over the course of reading this chapter, and that your eyes glazed over at least once. It's okay. I picked up my phone a couple of times, too.

But hopefully between the examples and commentary, you've seen not only some alternatives to Basecamp, but some fundamental reasons why project management can make your life easier. However, if you're not convinced, I invite you to file this book away until you do get into a situation in which you need to keep track of details. In fact, if you don't think any of these techniques will ever be useful to you, I *dare* you to file this book away. I bet you one Facebook comment (1 F.C.) that you will eventually run into a situation where these things are helpful and doable. ::handshake::

If you're thinking of the world of managing details, and your spirits are low, remember that I'm not suggesting you should be a professional project manager. After all, I'm not one. But I honestly believe that if you try learning some of these things and then go on to scratch the surface of Basecamp, it can make your life easier. Again, this might be more valuable when you've run into a nightmare and need backup, but I'm trying to make it personal and tell stories to reinforce the value early on. Please feel free to go on the Facebook page and tell your story—the good, the bad, or the ugly.

Learning how to keep track of details was a process of maturity and discipline for me, and it might be for you, too. Try to think of how to make it fun. If you're managing a project and it's not the ideal job, try to make it fun by tracking your performance and working to beat your goals. You might be surprised at how this can help.

Corporate work can be exciting when you have the opportunity to access education and opportunity to pursue what you like. If you can find that freedom to pursue education and to think of what kind of occupation would be a good fit for you, I highly encourage you to work on it. Go check out the book *What Color Is Your Parachute* from your local library.

Am I anti-Microsoft because I haven't mentioned Microsoft Project? No, I like what Bill Gates has done with his money in making the world better, and I think there's a place for tools like Project. But I've been in a number of situations where there were the best of intentions, including the best of tools—like Project—but there wasn't enough organizational maturity, enough commitment, to carry things through. New processes, endless meetings, and proposals are all good things, but without the maturity to follow through, they can all fall apart. And that's where I think that the official role of project manager can be so helpful. You can save a lot of money, make a lot of money for yourself or your company, and help people keep their jobs.

So how many times did your mobile device interrupt you while you were reading this chapter? Mine interrupted me a number of times while I was writing the chapter. It's a lot like managing a project—you end up getting interrupted a lot, depending on the project and the organization and company. And a good project management tool sometimes is the most helpful in simply allowing you to accurately make a note of how things are going and return to it later to pick up where you left off, with all the details you need.

Mobile Exercise

In case you're wanting more commentary on how mobile devices fit into this, then as an exercise, try the variation of doing all the suggested items from a mobile device. Try your iPhone or Android device, or find a library that has tablet computers. Even Google Docs works on mobile devices, kind of. And throughout the book, try Basecamp on a mobile device. The developers have gone a long way toward making it mobile friendly. Or if you have an iPhone and need a place to get started, try an app called Dropkick. Yes, I'm all about the reorderable to-do items.

QUESTIONS FOR CONSIDERATION/DISCUSSION

1. What are the strengths of Notepad and TextEdit?

2. What are Notepad's and TextEdit's limitations? What can't you do with these tools?

3. What are some advantages of NoteTab Light?

4. What are the strengths of Google Docs?

5. What are the limitations of Google Docs? What can't you do with it?

6. What are the strengths of Excel and Google Spreadsheets as project management tools?

7. What are the limitations of Excel and Google Spreadsheets? What can't they do?

8. How can you make sure to revisit whatever tool it is that you're using?

See Appendix A, "Answers to Questions for Consideration/Discussion," for suggested answers.

Conclusion

Dear Reader,

Congratulations on making it through your third chapter!

I tried to pack a career's worth of perspective and roll it up into this chapter.

As you've no doubt noticed, this book is not just about managing details with Basecamp. I'm trying to help readers consider alternatives, because tools change all the time, and transferrable skills are important. I encourage you to explore what you're interested in, have fun with it, and show someone how to use it so you can remember it better. Even if you never use any of these alternative techniques again, you might notice in later chapters how they relate to things you can do in Basecamp.

In the next chapter, we'll run through how to start a free trial for Basecamp, and then we'll launch full bore into Basecamp.

The goal is to make this process as enjoyable as possible, especially for beginners. Best wishes on your adventures in keeping track of details and learning how to use Basecamp.

Regards,

Todd

P.S. So how'd I do with this chapter? Feel free to sound off at www.facebook.com/basecampbook. If you thought something was silly, maybe it can be changed in the next printing; or if you really liked something, maybe it will help me defend myself from the editors. Carpe diem!

CHAPTER 4

CREATING A NEW BASECAMP ACCOUNT

In 140 Characters or Less

- Ch 4—Walks through the process of creating a new Basecamp account, and some basic configuration.

In This Chapter

- Starting an Account
- Exploring Basecamp

Why This Chapter Is Important

Whether you have a paid Basecamp account or just a free trial, it can be helpful to know where some of the basic settings are. As an example, I can almost guarantee that you'll want to know how to disable the Daily Recap feature, which is explained in this chapter.

In this chapter, we'll take a quick look at how to start an account and some of the basic configuration, including making a new project.

STARTING AN ACCOUNT

Starting an account is easy; all that's needed is an email address. You'll be off and running in no time!

Choosing Among Pricing Options

To start a free 45-day trial account, visit www.basecamp.com.

It's always possible that details such as terms, length of trial, and pricing may change between the time I wrote this and when you read it. For example, Basecamp may go from a 45-day free trial to being free, period. If you notice a change to the software, links, or any other part of the Basecamp website, feel free to post the change to http://facebook.com/basecampbook. You might look at www.toddkelsey.com/books/basecamp for potential updates, too.

At basecamp.com, you'll find information about pricing and starting the 45-day free trial. Try clicking on the Find Out Why link to learn more about Basecamp, or you can just click the 45-Day Free Trial link at the top.

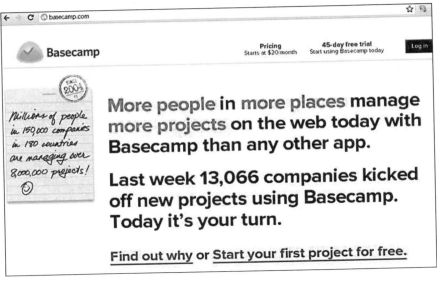

Source: 37signals, LLC.

If you click on the Pricing link at basecamp.com, you'll get a list of the current pricing.

The general tiers of pricing depend on the amount of storage space you get. You can economize by sharing your account with several people.

Signing Up

When you're ready to sign up, go to basecamp.com/signup, or click on the 45-Day Free Trial link on basecamp.com.

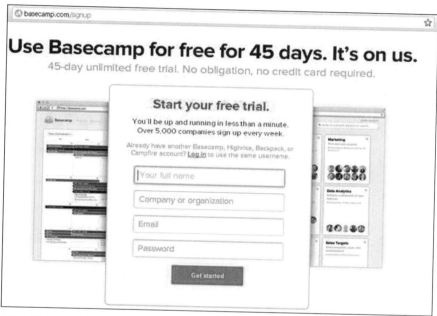

Source: 37signals, LLC.

Then just fill in your information, choose a password (remember to write it down!), and click the Get Started button.

Next, you'll get a confirmation message, and you can click the Explore Your New Basecamp Account button.

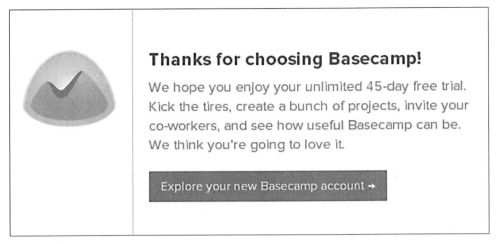

Source: 37signals, LLC.

The next thing you see is the home screen for Basecamp. It shows an overview of your projects and contains a variety of links, allowing central access to the various features of Basecamp.

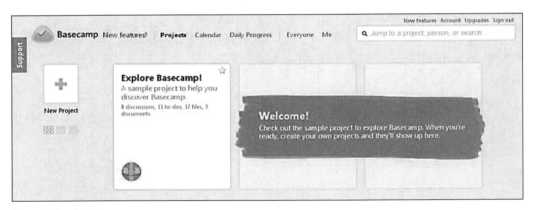

Source: 37signals, LLC.

- **Projects**—Brings you back to the home screen, with a view of your projects.
- **Calendar**—Allows you to look at Calendar view, where you can schedule events and keep track of scheduled items.
- **Daily Progress**—A quick way to see what happened on a given day.
- **Everyone**—For inviting new people to a project and managing permissions.
- **Me**—A view of your own profile. It allows you to upload a profile icon and adjust the notification settings.

- **New Features**—An ongoing announcement stream of new features. 37signals continually works to improve the project, and new features are announced there.

- **Account**—As discussed in this chapter, this is where you can adjust some of your account settings and upgrade your plan.

- **Upgrades**—Describes a more direct route to learning about the different price levels and upgrading your plan.

- **Sign Out**—When you want to log out, click here.

You might also want to visit www.basecamp.com and look for the Help and Email Newsletter links at the bottom of the screen. To get announcements, you can sign up for the email newsletter. Also, it's useful to know how to consult the Help section in case you need to search for an answer or contact the support department, which is really responsive.

EXPLORING BASECAMP

In the previous section, we saw the overview screen with a list of projects. Your new account comes with a sample project already started: an "Explore Basecamp" project that contains several sample items and a helpful explanation. I invite you to click on that and check it out before you create your first real project.

In general, I recommend clicking through the links at the top, which represent the main types of project elements you can work with: Discussions, To-Dos, Files, Text Documents, and Dates. You might also like to try clicking on the Invite More People link.

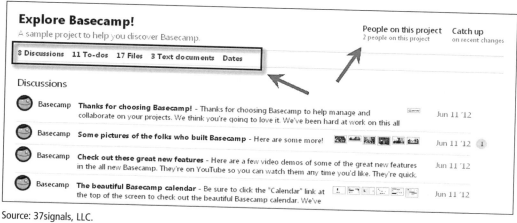

Source: 37signals, LLC.

Remember that you can always click on the Basecamp logo or the Projects link at the top of the screen if you want to return to the home screen.

Source: 37signals, LLC.

Creating Your First Project

To create your first project, go to the Projects screen in Basecamp, and click the New Project icon.

Source: 37signals, LLC.

Then you can type in a name and description for the project, which you can change later.

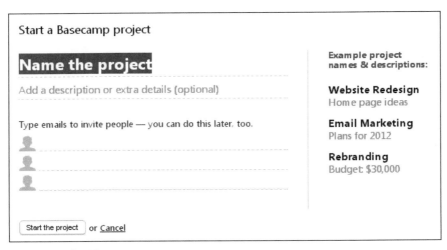

Source: 37signals, LLC.

If you know of anyone you want to invite to the project, you can send an invitation right from that screen if you like.

Start a Basecamp project

Project Pipeline

A sample project so I can learn Basecamp

Type emails to invite people — you can do this later, too.

👤 freelanceguy@website.com   ✖

👤 myfriendjohndoe@gmail.com   ✖

👤

👤

[Start the project] or Cancel

Source: 37signals, LLC.

When you're ready, click the Start the Project button.

The Project View screen opens, with links across the top for working with basic project elements: Discussion, To-Do List, File, Text Document, and Date.

Project Pipeline ☆

Invite more people   Catch up
1 person on this project   on recent changes

Add the first: Discussion To-do list File Text document Date

Welcome to your project!
Basecamp is great for all kinds of projects, large and small. Kick things off by starting your first discussion, creating a to-do list, or writing a new document.

Source: 37signals, LLC.

Exploring Project Settings

Keep in mind that there's a Project Settings link at the bottom of a Project window.

Source: 37signals, LLC.

The Project Settings link allows you to change the overall status of a project. You can change a project status to Archived so that no more changes can be made to it but you have a record of it. Archiving also saves space. For example, if you have a 10-project plan, you can free up space for new projects by archiving old ones.

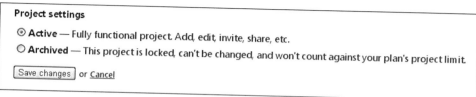

Project settings

○ **Active** — Fully functional project. Add, edit, invite, share, etc.

○ **Archived** — This project is locked, can't be changed, and won't count against your plan's project limit.

[Save changes] or Cancel

Source: 37signals, LLC.

When you have archived projects, an Archived Projects link appears on the main Projects screen.

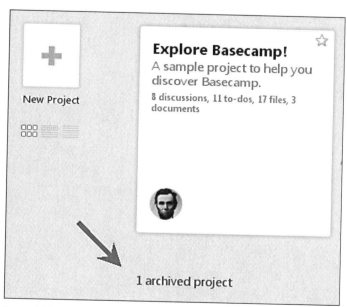

Source: 37signals, LLC.

To the right of the Project Settings area is a link for deleting a project. The Account link at the top-right side of the main window shows your account details and allows you to adjust some basic settings.

Source: 37signals, LLC.

From here, you can change the name of your account, export data, or cancel the entire account. It also provides one way to access upgrade options.

Your account details

RGB Green Change your account name
Member since June 26, 2012

Current package: Trial
You currently have 2 active projects and are using 5.13 MB of file storage.
You are currently on a trial subscription. Your trial runs until August 11, 2012.

Choose your plan

Export your data

- Copy all of your Basecamp data to a downloadable HTML archive you can view in your web browser.
- Exports can take a few hours to process.
- You'll get an email when it's done

Start export

Need to cancel?
We'll be sorry to see you go. You won't be charged again once you've cancelled.
Your data will be permanently deleted after 30 days.

Cancel your account

Source: 37signals, LLC.

Configuring People

Chapter 6, "Managing People: Inviting Collaborators," covers in more detail working with people you invite to an account. This section introduces the feature, including showing you how to upload a profile icon. Uploading a profile icon allows you to easily see who is working on a particular project by looking at the profile icons on the general Project screen.

To configure people, click on either Everyone or Me.

If you went through the Everyone link, click on the icon of the account you created (for example, for me, it was Todd Kelsey).

This brings up the Me screen, which gives an overview of any activity you've been involved with on the project. (If you clicked the Me link instead of Everyone, you'll go directly here.) On the left side is a link taking you through easy steps for inviting someone else to the project. On the right side are options for updating your personal info and adjusting My Basecamp Settings.

First, click the Update Your Personal Info link.

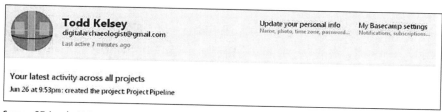

Adjust the settings as desired, and click Save Changes when you're done.

Edit your account

Upload your photo…
[Choose File] No file chosen

First name   **Todd**

Last name   **Kelsey**

Email address   **digitalarchaeologist@gmail.com**

Time zone   (GMT-06:00) Central Time (US & Canada) ▼
                The time zone setting only applies to Basecamp.

Username   **digitalarchaeologist@gmail.com**

Password   ••••••••••••••••••••••
                6 characters or longer. Add at least one number for extra
                safety.

Confirm   ••••••••••••••••••••••
password

[**Save changes**] or *Cancel*

Source: 37signals, LLC.

One thing you can do right away is personalize your profile icon, also known as an *avatar*. You can change it from the colorful but generic one automatically assigned to you. Click the Choose File button. For new users, this might say Browse instead.

When you're done uploading an image you want to use, click Save Changes.

It may take a few minutes before you see the profile icon throughout Basecamp, but when it does appear, it will provide a helpful visual of people who are involved in a project. If you don't want to upload a picture of yourself, you can choose any image out there, as long as it is in the public domain (see www.publicdomainpictures.net) or is not the property of someone else.

Note

See "Profile Image Fun: PicResize.com" in Chapter 6, "Managing People: Inviting Collaborators," to learn about a tool that can come in handy when you're working with uploaded pictures.

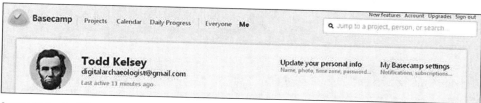

Source: 37signals, LLC.

Now your image will appear for others to see.

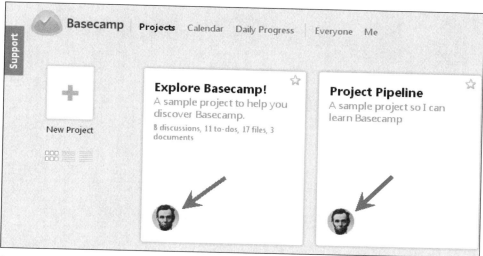

Source: 37signals, LLC.

Next, from the Me screen, click My Basecamp Settings.

Source: 37signals, LLC.

This screen allows you to adjust where notifications are sent. If you like, you can disable the Daily Recap from Basecamp.

I can almost guarantee that you're going to want to remember this option, and you'll probably want to let anyone you invite on a project to know about it, too. I'm not sure why On is the default setting for this option. Perhaps the Basecamp creators will change that.

Note

You can also change the notification option via a link in the recap email.

Todd Kelsey

Basecamp settings

Email notifications
Send all Basecamp email notifications to this address:

digitalarchaeologist@gmail.com   Save

Subscribe to the Daily Recap
☑ Send me an email every morning showing what happened yesterday in all my projects.

Source: 37signals, LLC.

If you uncheck or check the Daily Recap feature, Basecamp automatically saves this setting.

Questions for Consideration/Discussion

1. What does the Me link do?

2. How do you delete a project?

3. Why would you want to archive a project instead of delete it?

4. Where can you turn off the Daily Recap email?

5. What are some techniques you can use to keep your eyes from glazing over while learning about project management?

See Appendix A, "Answers to Questions for Consideration/Discussion," for suggested answers.

CONCLUSION

Dear Reader,

Congratulations on making it through your fourth chapter!

In this chapter, we covered how to get an account going and do some basic configuration. Coming up next, we'll learn how to use some of the central features in Basecamp, such as managing projects with to-dos; managing conversations (comments and email notifications); and managing people (inviting collaborators, adjusting permissions).

Best wishes on your adventures in keeping track of details and learning how to use Basecamp.

Regards,

Todd

P.S. So how'd I do with this chapter? Feel free to sound off at www.facebook.com/basecampbook.

CHAPTER 5

Super Basic Project Management with Basecamp To-Dos

In 140 Characters or Less

- Ch 5—Jumps into basic project management, shows how to create and schedule to-do items in Basecamp, and view them in a list or calendar.

In This Chapter

- Categories of To-Dos
- To-Dos as Project Development
- The ADDIE Approach
- Nuts and Bolts: Creating a Project and Adding To-Dos
- Basic To-Do Functions: Rearrange, Delete, Edit
- Accessing/Discussing a To-Do Item
- Due Dates
- Filtering and Reordering Lists
- Viewing To-Dos on the Calendar
- Classroom/Personal Exercise: Creating To-Do Lists
- Classroom/Personal Exercise: Prioritizing To-Dos

Why This Chapter Is Important

To-do items are the basic building blocks for managing projects in Basecamp. They have several features that allow you to manage your project quickly and flexibly; learning how to effectively add them will build a solid foundation for your project structure.

In this chapter, we'll take a close look at to-do items and some of their special features. You can keep things as simple as you like or schedule to-do items so that you can begin to create a timetable for your project. Project management could start with something as simple as creating a brainstorming meeting, getting a to-do list started, and inviting other people to add their own items to the list. But the magic of project management is setting it in motion—taking the pieces and thinking of them over time. Even if you end up changing the deadlines, just the act of scheduling can help you develop momentum and provide accountability. Sometimes that's all you need for managing a project effectively.

Categories of To-Dos

You can think of to-do items in several categories: ideas, tasks, milestones. For example, if your project has three parts, you might decide that the milestones are Finish Part I, Finish Part II, and Finish Part III. You might schedule these milestones at the end of each month, and then schedule individual tasks that allow you to reach each milestone incrementally.

To be clear, you don't need to schedule everything, but doing so can help you keep moving, especially if you tend to do a number of things at once.

To-Dos as Project Development

Managing a project could be part of creating it. In other words, a process like brainstorming might allow you to help define what it is you want to do. In other words, project management isn't necessarily about planning things; it can also be about brainstorming and design. You might give yourself a week to brainstorm the tasks that go into designing your product or report.

It can be helpful to think of going from the general to the particular. If you're not sure where to start in terms of details, try asking yourself or your team what you want to accomplish. What are your goals? Then you might discuss the general steps needed to reach your goals.

As an example, I'm going to take a general project that I've been working on and give a behind-the-scenes view using Basecamp. I'll start by following some of the suggestions I've made, so you can see how project management might look in practice.

If you do develop an interest in project management, you might like to review what Wikipedia has to say about project management. See http://en.wikipedia.org/wiki/Project_management.

THE ADDIE APPROACH

A simplified form of the traditional approach to project management, ADDIE pursues a project in five parts:

- Analysis
- Design/planning
- Development
- Implementation
- Evaluation

This approach is chiefly used in instructional design, but you can apply it generally. Not all projects require each stage, but there are some universals. See http://en.wikipedia.org/wiki/ADDIE_Model.

Unless you've already analyzed and figured out what you're doing, the analysis stage can be a good place to start your project on Basecamp. This might be where you're asking questions, discussing challenges, and figuring out how to answer them. In fact, many projects start not with a product or a plan but with a question or a problem: Our problem is x. The Analysis phase focuses on this question: How are we going to fix x? How are we going to respond to x situation?

Similarly, brainstorming might involve ideas on how to solve a problem or how to approach it, but it could also involve coming up with questions. A company might say, "Our goal is to improve quality," and the analysis phase might involve brainstorming and asking, "How can we improve quality?"

During design or planning, you fill out as much information as you can while you discuss the project with others and conduct research. For example, you'll figure out what kinds of resources you need to accomplish the project and what the costs will be.

Development might involve creating first and then testing, asking people for reactions, or validating what you are trying to accomplish. Implementation involves launching—setting things into motion publicly—or getting people involved to spread the word.

Evaluation doesn't always happen. Often companies or organizations launch projects or products and then move on to the next project, without fully evaluating the impact of what they just did. When you're managing a project, you can help your organization or company grow towards excellence by suggesting something as simple as budgeting time for project evaluation: How did things go, what did the audience think, and how can it be better next time?

NUTS AND BOLTS: CREATING A PROJECT AND ADDING TO-DOS

Here I'll demonstrate the ADDIE model on Basecamp by planning a sample project. Of course, you're welcome to try out the software by typing in exactly what you see in my example, which I'll call NPOEx, but consider thinking of something that's personally relevant instead. If you have something directly applicable now—a vacation to plan or a house project to tackle—go for it. If not, just have some fun. Pretend you just won a million dollars, and you're planning project Build Dream Home, or whatever other project you'd undertake with the cash. If you're a parent or would like to be some day, try out project Raise a Child. Hey, you could even think of finding a life partner as a project: Find "The One." (Crazier things have been tried!)

Whatever project you decide to practice with, just sign into Basecamp and create a new project by clicking the New Project icon.

Source: 37signals, LLC.

Then you can give the project a name and description.

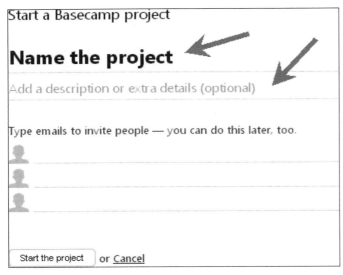

Source: 37signals, LLC.

Once you're ready, you can click Start the Project. (Before doing that, you can enter email addresses here to invite people to the project if you already have collaborators in mind, or you can wait to do this when you get to Chapter 6, "Managing People: Inviting Collaborators.")

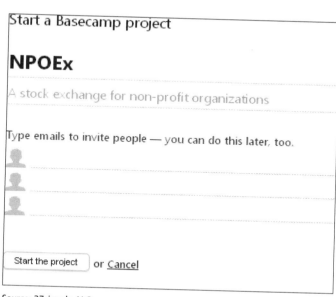

Source: 37signals, LLC.

Next, click the To-Do List link to create the first to-do list.

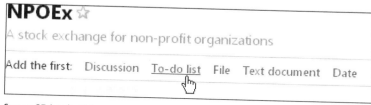

Source: 37signals, LLC.

I'm going to make a to-do list for each ADDIE phase, each stage of my project. You can name your lists whatever you like, of course; this is just one approach.

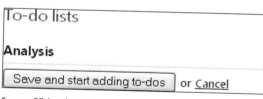

Source: 37signals, LLC.

After you name your list, click Save and Start Adding To-Dos. A blank to-do item appears (Add This To-Do). You can just start typing an individual task there.

After you've added as many to-do items as you have in mind at the moment for this list, you can click I'm Done Adding To-Dos.

Source: 37signals, LLC.

Basic To-Do Functions: Rearrange, Delete, Edit

Now that you have a few to-do items, it will be helpful to know about the most common things you're likely to want to do with them.

To rearrange a to-do item, just roll over the item until you get a grabber hand.

Source: 37signals, LLC.

Then click, drag it into a different position, and let go of the mouse button. Here, I've moved the Write Book to-do up one position.

Source: 37signals, LLC.

Note

When you have more than one to-do list, you can also drag items from one list to another.

To delete a to-do item, roll over it, and click on the little trash icon on the left.

To edit a to-do item, roll over the item, and move the mouse over to the left until you see the Edit link.

Analysis

☐ Develop description for non-profit stock exchange

☐ Write book - decide on title

🗑 Edit ☐ Consider stages (Unassigned)

☐ Post ideas on http://facebook.com/npoex, ask for feedback

Add a to-do

Source: 37signals, LLC.

Change the item's text, and click the Save Changes button.

Analysis

☐ Develop description for non-profit stock exchange

☐ Write book - decide on title   (Unassigned)

[Save changes] or Cancel

Source: 37signals, LLC.

ACCESSING/DISCUSSING A TO-DO ITEM

In addition to editing a to-do item, you can access it by simply clicking on it in the to-do list.

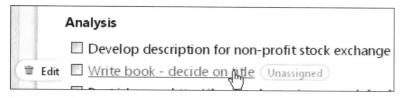

Analysis

☐ Develop description for non-profit stock exchange

🗑 Edit ☐ Write book - decide on title (Unassigned)

Source: 37signals, LLC.

Accessing an item allows you to add a comment and even a file to it. Note that adding a file in this context is considered adding a comment, so that's how you'll get here: through the Comment field. As part of my project analysis, I want to add a file to the Write Book—Decide on Title item. First, I access that to-do item, which brings up the Edit and Delete links on the right, a history of activity below, and a field for adding a comment.

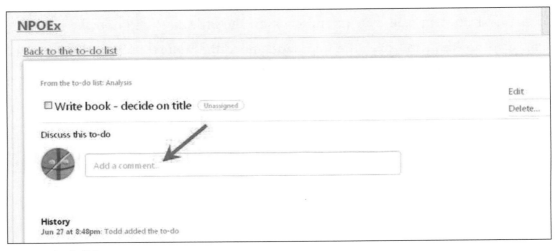

Source: 37signals, LLC.

When you click Add a Comment, the window expands; from there you can click the Select Files from Your Computer link (or drag files into the window).

Source: 37signals, LLC.

In this case, I've uploaded two files to the comment: a cover image idea, and a text document with a synopsis of the book idea. I added these at the analyzing stage, but you can do this at any stage of your project. (This is just one way of working with files in Basecamp. We'll look at other ways in Chapter 11, "Advanced Project Tasks.") When you're finished adding files and typing in anything you'd like to mention in the Comment area, click the Add This Comment button.

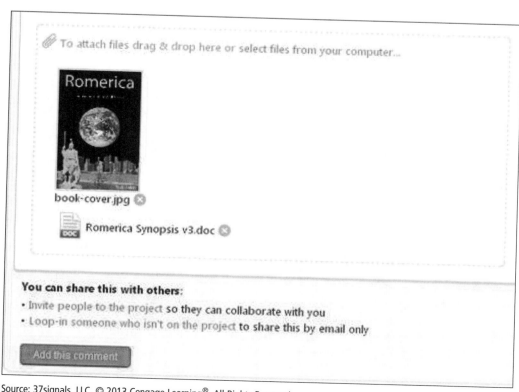

Then, when other people access that to-do item, they can see the files, access them, and add more comments.

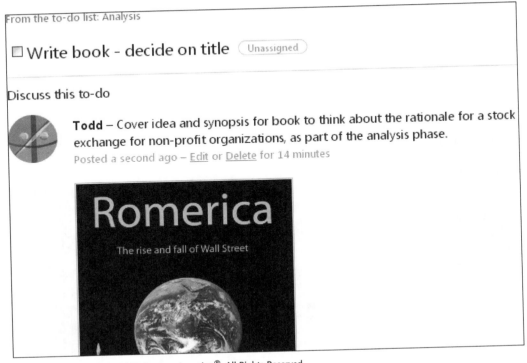

From the to-do list: Analysis

☐ **Write book - decide on title** (Unassigned)

Discuss this to-do

Todd – Cover idea and synopsis for book to think about the rationale for a stock exchange for non-profit organizations, as part of the analysis phase.
Posted a second ago – Edit or Delete for 14 minutes

Romerica
The rise and fall of Wall Street

Going back to the to-do list, you can see that wherever a comment/file has been added, the item shows the presence of the comment.

Analysis

☐ Develop description for non-profit stock exchange
☐ Write book - decide on title (1 comment)
☐ Post ideas on http://facebook.com/npoex, ask for feedback
   Add a to-do

DUE DATES

So far we've been working within one to-do list. Let's add another to-do list. Go to the to-do lists area in your project and click the Add a To-Do List button.

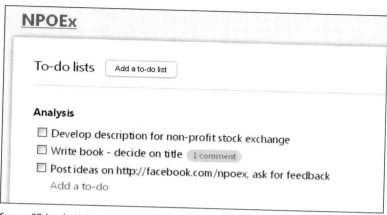

Source: 37signals, LLC.

Now add a few items. I'm going to think about the design phase of the project, so I've called my list Design. On the first item, I'm going to set a due date. You might have noticed by now that items come with an automatic status of Unassigned and No Due Date. Clicking Unassigned allows you to change that default status.

Source: 37signals, LLC.

A little calendar pop-up window appears. You can click on the date desired or click on the right and left arrows above the calendar to select a different month.

Source: 37signals, LLC.

The date appears below the to-do item. When you're done setting a due date, be sure to click the Add This To-Do button, or you might lose your last item.

Source: 37signals, LLC.

Note

When working within to-dos, always click Add This To-Do. Sometimes I click I'm Done Adding To-Dos instead, but then Basecamp doesn't add the last to-do you're working on, so be sure to click Add This To-Do first.

FILTERING AND REORDERING LISTS

As you're working on to-do lists, you can click on one of the drop-down menus on the right to show only items that are assigned to a particular person or that are due at a particular time.

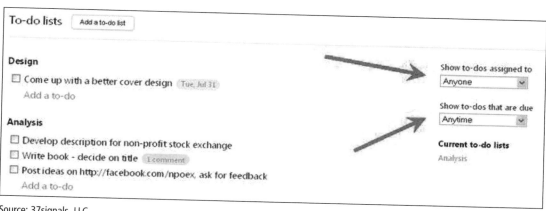

Source: 37signals, LLC.

You might also want to reorder lists. To do that, click on a list.

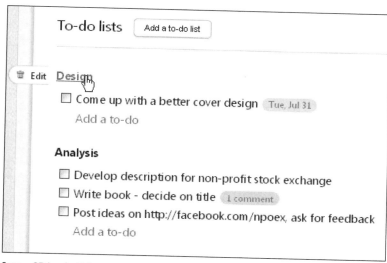

Source: 37signals, LLC.

Then drag the list into the desired new position and let go of the mouse button.

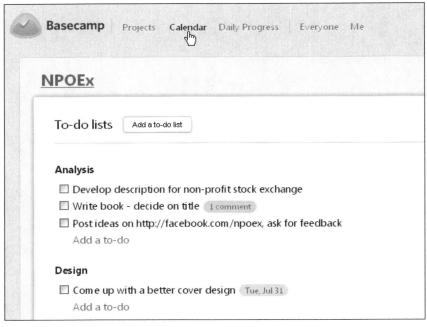

Source: 37signals, LLC.

VIEWING TO-DOS ON THE CALENDAR

The more lists you have, full of items with different due dates, the easier it is to lose touch with the overall project timeline. But you can always click on the Calendar link at the top of the screen to get a bird's eye view of all to-do items with due dates assigned.

Source: 37signals, LLC.

My to-do item appears on July 31, with a small text preview. You can hover over the preview to see the full item description, or you can click on it to see any related comments. It also comes with a check box, so you can check items off from right there.

22	23	24	25
29	30	31	August 1
		1 To-do ☐ Come up with a better...	

Source: 37signals, LLC.

The calendar is flexible. It shows to-do items due on the same day for multiple projects, and you can click the Show a List of Calendars button if you'd like to adjust what is showing.

A list of projects and calendars appears, and you can check or uncheck which calendars appear as desired, somewhat similar to the way the Google Calendar and other systems work.

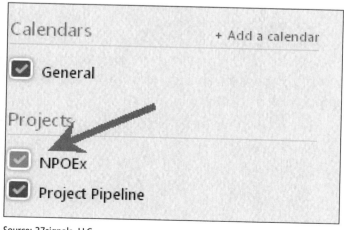

Source: 37signals, LLC.

There's also some color-coding at work. In this example, the NPOEx project has been assigned a general magenta color to distinguish it from other projects, so items on the calendar from NPOEx show up in magenta.

From the calendar, there are two ways to return to the to-do lists. You can click on a to-do item on the calendar, or you can click on the Projects link at the top of the screen.

Basecamp   Projects **Calendar** Daily Progress │ Everyone Me

Source: 37signals, LLC.

And from there, select your project, and click on the To-Dos link.

NPOEx ☆

A stock exchange for non-profit organizations

1 Discussion   4 To-dos   3 Files   Dates   │   Add the first: Text document

Source: 37signals, LLC.

CLASSROOM/PERSONAL EXERCISE: CREATING TO-DO LISTS

If you'd like to follow along, I invite you to complete a simple exercise in working with to-dos. If you haven't already, start a project, maybe using one of the ideas mentioned earlier, and create a series of to-do lists. You could set them up according to the stages of the project or different aspects of the project—any way you'd like to organize it. If you like, try making ADDIE lists, for the phases of analysis, design/planning, development, implementation, and evaluation.

Then try setting a due date for an item and even attaching a file. When you finish, you might end up with something like this.

Analysis

☐ Write book - decide on title `1 comment`

Add a to-do

Design

☐ Come up with a better cover design `Tue, Jul 31`

Add a to-do

Development

☐ Determine Costs

☐ Create a mock up of the game board

☐ Create requirements document

Add a to-do

Implementation

☐ Launch the Alpha version

Add a to-do

Evaluation

☐ ask for feedback on http://facebook.com/npoex

Add a to-do

Source: 37signals, LLC.

What you've done is lay the foundation for managing a project. Congratulations!

CLASSROOM/PERSONAL EXERCISE: PRIORITIZING TO-DOS

If you feel like tackling another exercise, you might simply develop a to-do list with ideas for new projects, products, people you might want to ask out on a date, ideas for surprising your spouse or boyfriend/girlfriend, gift ideas for people, whatever—and then try prioritizing those items. And, of course, you can assign due dates.

Welcome to the world of keeping track of details on Basecamp! You've already mastered some important skills.

QUESTIONS FOR CONSIDERATION/DISCUSSION

1. What does ADDIE stand for? What's the point of that concept?

2. What's the difference between editing a to-do item and accessing it? What can you do when you select/access a to-do item?

3. How do you assign a to-do item?

4. How do you make a due date for a to-do item?

5. How do you get a to-do item to show up on the calendar?

6. What's the point of assigning due dates for to-do items?

7. What's the airspeed velocity of an unladen swallow?

See Appendix A, "Answers to Questions for Consideration/Discussion," for suggested answers.

CONCLUSION

Dear Reader,

Congratulations on making it through the fifth chapter!

In this chapter, we tried out some of the basic actions with to-dos; considered how to approach developing a project in phases, with to-do lists for each phase; and assigned some due dates. It wouldn't be surprising if you're asking yourself, "Is that all there is to it?"

The answer? It's just the beginning. After a project gets rolling, sometimes deadlines change, as do the people involved in the project. There are discussions and issues that need resolving.

Along these lines, in the next chapter, we'll take another close look at inviting collaborators into a project. As I mentioned in an earlier chapter, working with other people on a Basecamp project can also help you learn how to use the program, not only because you can explain some of the basic steps to them, but because others' interaction will show you implications of those steps for yourself.

Best wishes on your adventures in mastering to-dos.

Regards,

Todd

P.S. So how'd I do with this chapter? Feel free to sound off at www.facebook.com/basecampbook.

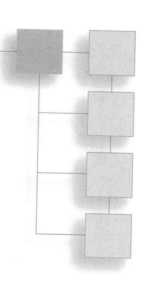

CHAPTER 6

MANAGING PEOPLE: INVITING COLLABORATORS

In 140 Characters or Less

- Ch 6—Takes a closer look at how to manage people, adjust permissions, invite people into Basecamp, and organize them into companies.

In This Chapter

- Adding People to Your Project
- Adjusting Permissions
- Deleting Collaborators
- Managing Expectations
- Profile Imagine Fun: PicResize.com
- Creating Companies

Why This Chapter Is Important

This chapter covers some of the important skills for working with others on a project, including inviting them and adjusting what they can do. Granting and revoking the privileges of your collaborators are important capabilities as you stay on top of your project's details. In fact, Basecamp calls them your superpowers. Go you!

It's also helpful to know how to organize people into "companies." This feature can refer to actual, distinct organizations or to groups of people. You can invite an entire "company" (a department within your company, or a group of your own creation) to participate on a project.

One of the reasons I like the software developed by 37signals so much is that it's flexible and easy to use. With Basecamp, for example, working with people on a project is just as easy as it is powerful. You can type in people's email addresses, directly invite them to your project, organize them into meaningful groups (companies), and grant them access to various projects at the same time—easily. You can also be selective by granting someone access to certain projects but not others. You might be the only administrator, or you might grant complete access and control to others.

But it's important to think about those options. You don't necessarily want to grant everyone complete access to everything, such as the ability to delete not just individual items but entire projects. So it's good to learn the basics, and, thankfully, it's pretty easy to manage. (Thanks, 37signals!)

When you do invite people, one thing to think about is preparing them for what to expect. Basecamp is easy enough to use, but you might want to make a simple cheat sheet or think of what you want to ask them to do, just to be safe.

ADDING PEOPLE TO YOUR PROJECT

As we touched on in Chapter 5, "Super Basic Project Management with Basecamp To-Dos," there are a few different opportunities in Basecamp for inviting others to join your Basecamp project. One occurs as soon as you create a new project.

Sending Invitations

Once a person is "in the system"—that is, already a Basecamp user—you don't have to reinvite him to sign up for the Basecamp login. You just have to invite him to connect to the new project.

For example, my sample Basecamp account has two people: me, and the Freelancer Dude. Gosh, looks like I need a shave. So does Freelancer Dude.

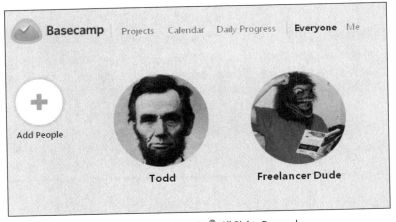

Because Freelancer Dude is already in the system, as soon as I start typing his name when I create new projects, his full name pops up as an option. Then I can select him and invite him to the project.

Source: 37signals, LLC.

Eventually you'll want to add people into the system the "traditional" way. To do that, start by clicking on the Everyone link at the top of the screen.

On the Everyone screen, you can add people and organize them into companies. Let's start by adding a few people. I'll go through the adding process from your perspective as well as theirs—to see what they will see.

Click the Add People button.

Source: 37signals, LLC. © 2013 Cengage Learning®, All Rights Reserved.

Enter their email addresses.

Source: 37signals, LLC.

Then scroll down to step 2.

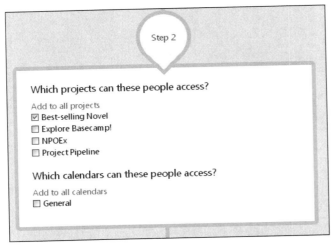

Source: 37signals, LLC.

Check the boxes next to the projects you want to add someone to, as well as the calendars he can access. Add to All Calendars is a safe bet, unless you want to limit access. Basecamp maintains a General calendar, which shows all your projects' tasks and timelines simultaneously, but there are also calendars for each project. In theory, adding people to a project also adds them to the correct calendar. But you might create additional "global" calendars to keep track of separate events, so you might end up with more calendars than appear in the list in the previous graphic. In that case, the Add to All Calendars link would be helpful to have checked.

Next, scroll down to step 3.

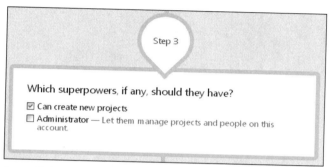

Source: 37signals, LLC.

The powers you grant depend on the situation. You might be adding team members who should have the ability to create new projects; check the box as I've done here. You might be inviting a comanager who should have complete capabilities; in that case, check the Administrator box. You can adjust these settings later here and elsewhere on Basecamp.

Now, if your account only allows 10 projects, multiple people with the ability to make projects can eat up that 10-project limit pretty quickly. But one benefit of granting the power to create projects is the learning experience and excitement it can generate—which is especially valuable if you're trying to get Basecamp buy-in from colleagues. (And you can always upgrade your account.)

Once you've made those decisions, scroll down to step 4, and click Send the Invitation.

Source: 37signals, LLC.

After you send out invitations, the Everyone screen shows profile icons—just place-holders at this point, unless you've invited someone who already has a customized icon. Here, too, you'll see the Grant Admin and Other Superpowers link.

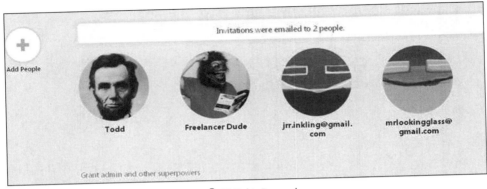

Source: 37signals, LLC. © 2013 Cengage Learning®, All Rights Reserved.

This is like the Hall of Justice for Superheroes. It's helpful to remember where this is, in case you need to switch things in the future.

What Invitees See

People you invite to a Basecamp project get a friendly little email. Your profile icon is embedded into the invitation—another reason it helps to customize your profile picture (especially if it's more personal than mine is here).

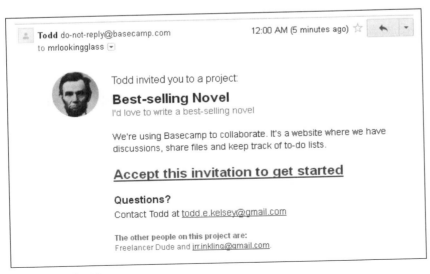

Source: 37signals, LLC.

When friends click on the Accept link in the email, they're brought to a screen where they can enter in basic information and upload a profile icon.

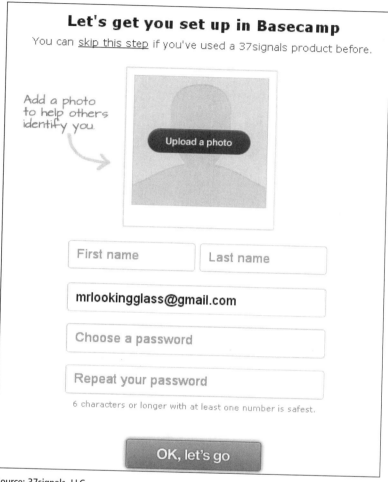

Let's get you set up in Basecamp

You can skip this step if you've used a 37signals product before.

Add a photo to help others identify you.

Upload a photo

First name   Last name

mrlookingglass@gmail.com

Choose a password

Repeat your password

6 characters or longer with at least one number is safest.

OK, let's go

Source: 37signals, LLC.

Note that if someone has used Basecamp in the past, he might be presented with this screen.

Sign in to get started with Basecamp

Since you already use Basecamp Classic, you can sign in to Todd's Basecamp using your existing username and password.

Enter your username or email

Enter your password

Forgot your username or password?

OK, let's go

Source: 37signals, LLC.

When a new collaborator signs in, he will see pretty much the same thing you see, and he can access the Me link at the top of the screen to update his info.

Clicking on the Me link takes someone to his personal screen.

Source: 37signals, LLC.

ADJUSTING PERMISSIONS

To adjust access and permissions for someone in the system, go to the Everyone link in Basecamp, click on the icon for the person you want to adjust, and click on [Member]'s Superpowers and Access to Projects.

Source: 37signals, LLC. © 2013 Cengage Learning®, All Rights Reserved.

Then check and uncheck the options as desired.

Freelancer Dude

Freelancer's superpowers

☐ **Can create projects** — Let Freelancer create and share new projects.

☐ **Admin** — Allow Freelancer to create projects, see all people on the account, delete people, and grant admin powers to other people.

☐ **Billing liaison** — Freelancer can upgrade, downgrade, and update billing details.

Remove Freelancer completely from Basecamp

Projects Freelancer can access

Add to all projects | Remove from all projects

☐ Basecamp Book
☑ Best-selling Novel
☐ CFTW
☐ Ideas co-developed with SHU Interns
☑ NPOEx
☐ Now

Calendars Freelancer can access

Add to all calendars | Remove from all calendars

☑ General

Source: 37signals, LLC.

There's no Save button at the present time; you just choose what you want, and it automatically saves.

DELETING COLLABORATORS

You can remove someone from a project at any time. You access that screen in the same way you access the power-adjusting screen: go to Everyone view, click on the person's icon, and click on [Member]'s Superpowers and Access to Projects.

Then click Remove [Member] Completely from Basecamp.

MANAGING EXPECTATIONS

When you invite others to join your project, remember that they might not already understand how Basecamp can help them work on the project more efficiently. In fact, they might see it as a time waster, not a time saver. So anything you can do to encourage them to give it a try is a good idea.

Along these lines, you might like to consider sending a little cheat sheet that you send out to collaborators. Yes, Basecamp is easy enough to use that you might not even need it, but a little direction can go a long way.

Instead of just creating a cheat sheet, I'll make some notes here, but I invite readers to try making one for my project page. First look at www.toddkelsey.com/books/basecamp to see if any other notes have been posted yet. Whether they have or not, feel free to send yours to me. Now how's that for collaboration? Or if you'd like a special challenge, start a Google account or a Gmail address, go to http://sites.google.com, and discover how easy it is to create a website. Then make your cheat sheet on the site or in a Word doc, attach it to a page, and then go to the Facebook page and post the link. Woohoo!

Some things to consider mentioning in your cheat sheet:

- You can access Basecamp from a mobile device.
- Please upload a profile icon to help make it easier for people to identify each other.
- If you'd like an easy tool for cropping/resizing a digital picture for a profile icon, try http://picresize.com.
- We'll send a follow-up document with plans for the project.
- Feel free to check out the to-do list and add ideas to the Brainstorming area.
- We'll be using the project to assign to-do items.
- You might like to try creating a to-do item and then adding a comment to it. The comment feature allows us to carry on conversations around to-do items. You can also attach files to comments.
- Feel free to add a comment to a to-do item, attach a file, and click Notify Me to try things out.
- Feel free to create a text document to get some notes started.
- You might want to visit the Me link at the top of the Basecamp screen, click on the My Basecamp Settings link, and uncheck the Subscribe to Daily Recap link.
- When you upload or change a profile icon, the modification might take a few minutes to show up in the system; until it does, there's a placeholder icon. Don't be alarmed. All is well; your profile icon will show up soon.
- Feel free to email if you have any questions.

■ I read this really great book on Basecamp by Todd Kelsey (Amazon link). It's written so well that you can use it as a pillow; just sleeping on it will allow you to learn everything you need to know.

Note

I've noticed that when uploading profile pictures, the picture doesn't always immediately become visible in the system; sometimes it takes a few minutes to refresh. Until the icons are updated, there are little placeholder icons, like the third one over from the left in this graphic.

PROFILE IMAGE FUN: PICRESIZE.COM

Time for a break. Go to picresize.com. Try uploading an image there and cropping it into a profile icon.

Click Browse to select the picture from a list of your image files. Then click Continue.

Place the cursor on the picture, and click and drag down and to the right. If you want to constrain the selection to be square, hold down the Shift key as you're dragging.

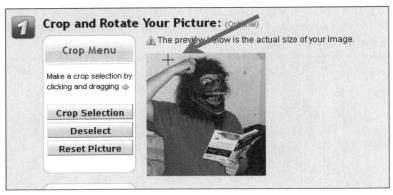

Source: 37signals, LLC. © 2013 Cengage Learning®, All Rights Reserved.

After you have the picture the way you want it, click again to set the selection. Then click the Crop Selection button, and your image is cropped.

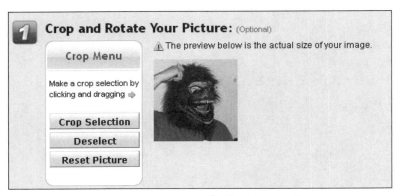

Source: 37signals, LLC. © 2013 Cengage Learning®, All Rights Reserved.

Next, select No Change, a percent change, or a custom size. Some sites have specific size requirements for profile pics; 150 × 150 will probably work. Play with it and have some fun.

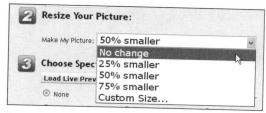

Source: 37signals, LLC.

When you're done playing around, click I'm Done, Resize My Picture!

Then click Save to Disk, if you can resist the temptation to try one of the other options.

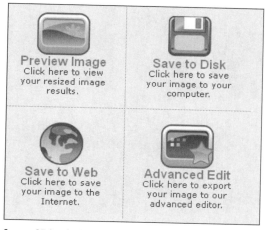

Source: 37signals, LLC.

You're done! PicResize is cool; you might want to tell people about it when inviting them to upload a profile icon.

CREATING COMPANIES

The last feature on this chapter's agenda is companies. Let's say we've invited some people into Basecamp, and we'd like to organize them into companies to make it easier to invite them as a group in the future.

The first step is to click the Make a Company icon on the Everyone screen.

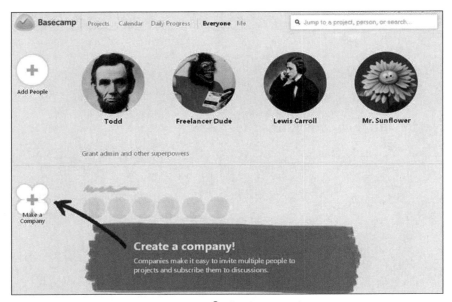

Source: 37signals, LLC. © 2013 Cengage Learning®, All Rights Reserved.

Next, type a name for the company, and start typing the names of the people you want to add.

Source: 37signals, LLC.

Then click the Create the Company button.

Once you've created a company, you can subdivide it into departments by clicking the Add a Group/Department link.

To create the group or department, you just type the name, check who you want to add to it, and click the Create the Group button.

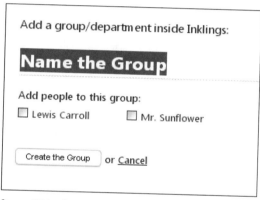

The group name appears.

In the future, if you want to add people to the company, remove them, or delete the company, just click on the company name in the Everyone screen, and make changes as desired.

Of course, putting collaborators into companies isn't just for your own organization. It's also handy when you want to add a company, or group within that company, to a new project. You just click the Invite More People link.

Then start typing the name of a company or group to select it.

After the company is added to the invitation list, click X to the right of anyone from a company or group that you don't want to add.

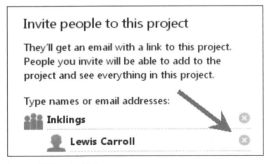

Then click Send Invitation.

Note

Even though you can add a company, you don't manage superpowers at a company level. If you want to fine-tune anything, you have to go to the Everyone screen, click on the specific person, click the Superpowers and Access to Projects link, and make adjustments on that screen.

Mr. Sunflower

Mr. 's superpowers

Remove Mr. completely from Basecamp

☑ Can create projects — Let Mr. create and share new projects.

☐ Admin — Allow Mr. to create projects. see all people on the account. delete people, and grant admin powers to other people.

☐ Billing liaison — Mr. can upgrade, downgrade, and update billing details.

Projects Mr. can access

Add to all projects | Remove from all projects

☑ Basecamp Book

☑ Best-selling Novel

☐ CFTW

☐ Ideas co-developed with SHU Interns

☑ NPOEx

☐ Now

Calendars Mr. can access

Add to all calendars | Remove from all calendars

☐ General

Source: 37signals, LLC.

Note

An individual can be invited to more than one Basecamp account. For example, Joe Freelancer might be invited to join an IBM account as well as an Apple account. If both IBM and Apple invite Joe using the same email address, he will sign in to Basecamp, and then each Basecamp account may show up at the top of his screen. In other words, an individual person, with a specific email address, may have a single sign-in but be able to access multiple accounts. The company feature is also distinct from this. The company feature is a container for organizing people, with a specific Basecamp account. So IBM may create a company for Joe Freelancer, and Apple may create a company for Joe Freelancer, but they're separate, because they exist in separate accounts.

QUESTIONS FOR CONSIDERATION/DISCUSSION

1. How do you add people to Basecamp?

2. What kinds of permissions and access can you grant?

3. What are companies in Basecamp?

See Appendix A, "Answers to Questions for Consideration/Discussion," for suggested answers.

Conclusion

Dear Reader,

Congratulations on making it through your sixth chapter!

In this chapter, we reviewed some important things to know about working with people and adjusting their access. I do think it's helpful to send people some kind of cheat sheet, but you're certainly welcome to tell them about this book, too! (By the way, all royalties are being donated to nonprofit research.)

In the next chapter, we'll look at how comments, discussions, and conversations can help a project stay on track and keep everyone apprised of how things are going. Sometimes communication is the key to a project's success, and there's a reason why so many millions of people like Basecamp—it helps with project-based communication. Email can and should be used for communication, but Basecamp can wrap it into the project itself, so anyone working on the project can log in and see how things are going. Leaving communication to people's individual email inboxes is a recipe for disaster. Conversely, using Basecamp is a recipe for success. Woohoo!

Best wishes on your adventures in keeping track of details and learning how to use Basecamp. I hope you're starting to see how cool the tool is and starting to daydream about all the things you can do in the free time you'll free up by using Basecamp. Or maybe you're seeing how much value you can add to a group or company by being willing to help out with detail tracking.

One way to get into this is to start with brainstorming; everyone can participate, and it's a way of introducing people to Basecamp. You can ask people to meet, log in on a conference call, and open up the to-do list. Then you can start capturing ideas. Don't critique; just capture. Then everyone will feel engaged and appreciated. Defer any criticism. Then come back, after all the ideas are captured, and prioritize. You'll end up with a valuable tool that can keep valuable ideas from falling through the cracks.

This brainstorming could lead to projects or maybe even a promotion! Woohoo!

Regards,

Todd

P.S. So how'd I do with this chapter? Feel free to sound off at www.facebook.com/basecampbook.

CHAPTER 7

MANAGING CONVERSATIONS

In 140 Characters or Less

- Ch 7—A look into discussions in Basecamp, including the use of comments and notification to carry on communication about a project.

In This Chapter

- Starting a Discussion
- Notification
- Participating in a Discussion
- Editing/Deleting Comments and Discussions
- The Move Feature
- Cross-Pollination: The Power of Collaboration
- The Most Awesome Feature in Any Program, Ever
- Comment-Based Discussion
- Commenting on Text Documents
- Breaking Gridlock, Unlocking Paralysis, Setting Things in Motion

Why This Chapter Is Important

In this chapter, we'll look at Basecamp's discussion feature, which is a tool that can help you keep track of things in a central place. Basecamp can be valuable even if you never use the discussion feature, but discussions can be a nice way of posing questions and taking care of loose ends. This feature allows you to discuss to-do items or files, post a comment about them, and then notify people automatically. You get direct notification via email and can respond that way if you like; but you or anyone else on the project can also just join the discussion right within Basecamp. And if you come back a day, a week, a month later, you can pick up right where you left off.

So it's good to know how you can use the feature, which has a high probability of helping to make your life easier.

STARTING A DISCUSSION

Posting a comment on a to-do item, which was covered in the previous chapter, starts a discussion. Then you can view the discussion either through the to-do item or through the Discussion link at the top of your project.

You can also create a standalone discussion, which we'll try here.

To begin, access a project, and click Discussion.

Source: 37signals, LLC.

A simple window appears, similar to a comment window. You can click in the subject line or within the body to type in information as desired. You can also attach a file.

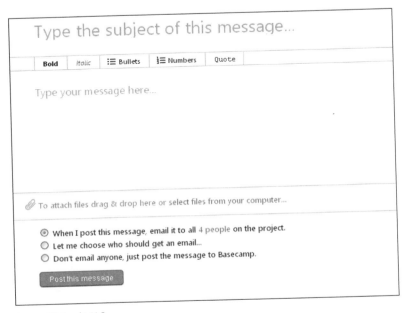

Source: 37signals, LLC.

In this example, I've started a sample discussion. It's similar to the way I might send an email to get a discussion going, but because I'm doing this in Basecamp, it will keep the discussion in a central place, so everyone can see what's going on.

In this case, I've created the subject, Marketing Plan, entered a simple message, and attached a word processing document.

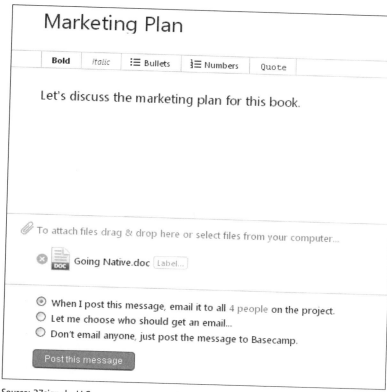

Source: 37signals, LLC.

NOTIFICATION

There are several options for choosing who you want to send the message to.

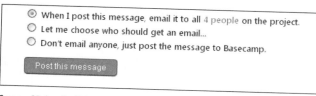

Source: 37signals, LLC.

When you're done, you can click the Post This Message button.

Going back just a bit, if you click the Loop-in link, you can enter in a name or email address before clicking Post This Message. (The name function here is for people who are within your Basecamp instance "somewhere" but not already added to this specific project.)

Loop-in someone who isn't on the project to share this by email only:
They'll see the whole discussion, and they can reply via email, but they can't see anything else in the project.

Type a name or email address...

Post this message   or Cancel

Source: 37signals, LLC.

After the message is posted, it appears under Discussions in your project, along with a preview of the message. A small icon appears toward the right if you've added a file.

Best-selling Novel ☆
I'd love to write a best-selling novel

Invite more people   Catch up
4 people on this project   on recent changes

1 Discussion   1 File   Add the first: To-do list   Text document   Date

Discussions   Start a discussion

Todd   **Marketing Plan** - Let's discuss the marketing plan for this book idea. Please review the short story, attached below, and let me know what you think.   10:32pm

Source: 37signals, LLC.

PARTICIPATING IN A DISCUSSION

As soon as you post the message, whomever you chose to notify receives an email similar to this one, which gives a few different options. This is a view of a sample email. The exact way it looks depends on the recipient's email system, but it will always contain several options. When you reply to a Basecamp "notification" email, it channels what you say back into the discussion and notifies other people.

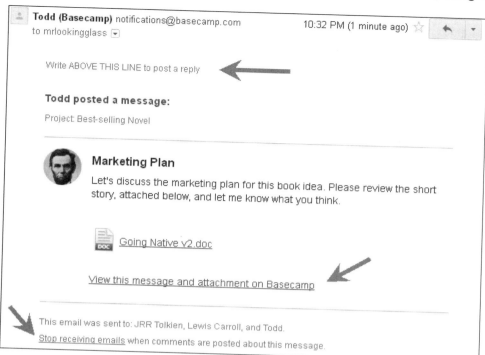

Source: 37signals, LLC.

The recipient of a notification can reply to the email, and it will feed it back into the system. When the recipient receives the email, he can also click on the View This Message and Attachment on Basecamp link. Clicking on the icon for the file (for example, Going Native v2) will take him back to Basecamp as well, but the file attached to the original comment in Basecamp will not become an attachment to the notification email.

People might choose to read or reply. If someone who has been notified does not want to continue receiving notifications, he can click the Stop Receiving Emails link at the bottom of a notification email. This feature alone is an advancement over the endless number of emails that people end up getting as a result of Reply Alls, especially in corporate environments. Thanks, 37signals!

Next, we see what happens when a person replies to a notification email. His icon appears in the discussion, and his comment is brought into Basecamp.

Source: 37signals, LLC.

This is another example of how nice it is to have everything in one place. As you can see, email is involved, but you can also delete the emails you get without having to worry about where to file them or find them. You know that the discussion will always be right there in Basecamp.

Another nice thing is that you don't have to forward an email to someone and make him scroll down for several minutes to find a tiny detail and catch up on things. With the discussion system in Basecamp, if someone wants to know what's going on, there's a clear place to go and find out what's up.

In the discussions area, when someone has responded, there is the preview of the comment, as we saw in the previous graphic, but you can also click on the title to the discussion to access it directly.

Source: 37signals, LLC.

This allows you to access the complete discussion.

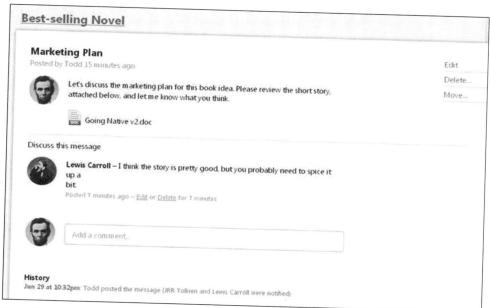

Source: 37signals, LLC.

EDITING/DELETING COMMENTS AND DISCUSSIONS

If you look at the previous graphic, you'll see that the comment, "I think the story is pretty good" has Edit and Delete links under it. There is a limited period of time in which a comment can be edited or deleted, but only the person who is managing the project/discussion can do so. Currently, commenters can't delete their own comments.

There is also a way to edit or delete an entire discussion item. Once you access the discussion, you see an Edit/Delete link at the top right. Again, only the person managing the discussion can edit or delete.

THE MOVE FEATURE

Another interesting feature in discussions is the Move feature. You can see this option below the Edit and Delete options. Move is pretty cool, because it allows you move a discussion to a different project or create a new project around it.

To move a discussion, just click Move.

Then you decide whether to start a new project, or move the discussion to another project.

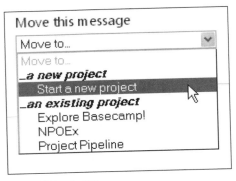

Source: 37signals, LLC.

That's pretty powerful. Say you're working on a project and you start a discussion. People respond, and the discussion takes on a life of its own. Then you can create a new project around it. Super cool.

CROSS-POLLINATION: THE POWER OF COLLABORATION

This magic of having things in a central place and "one thing leading to another" is also known as cross-pollination. It's kind of like a conference where people get together and work on solving a challenge or work on exchanging ideas. So you could think of the value of collaborative project management as a conference.

Yes, traditional email can be collaborative. But when you bring people together for a conference, there's something special about that dynamic. Sparks can fly.

I was struck one time visiting a scientific conference with a friend who is a nanoscientist. One session involved the scientists bringing their posters representing their research and ideas into a big room. You could just walk around the room and talk to people. The format wasn't strictly organized, because you could go wherever you liked and talk to whomever you liked. That kind of thing can lead to powerful connections—people exchanging contact details, talking about collaborating on research. It's really cool.

It's kind of like, well, the "real" kind of cross-pollination.

Not only can a tool like Basecamp be used to "just manage projects," which is a valuable thing, but it can create a powerful platform for collaboration. It does this by providing a good tool—the to-do list feature—for capturing ideas and brainstorming. Basecamp also provides tools like discussions, where you can say, "Hey, what about this?" And it allows a discussion to spawn a new project with the Move feature. I might go so far as to call Basecamp an innovation platform.

The other analogy that might come to mind is social networking. Basecamp is kind of like a social network. In a social network, there's some cross-pollination—an exchange of thought, pictures, ideas—that can lead to things. The result can be revolutionary, quite literally (see http://facebook.com/freedomsongs). But the thing about Basecamp is that it doesn't just provide a place where you can share things; it provides the tools to do something concrete and set it in motion.

That's partly why to-dos are exciting. They are an easy way to capture things, but they also allow you to bring something to life through collaborating. And no, I'm not an email hater, but email has its limits. I've experienced those limits, one of which is the ease with which ideas, discussions, and collaboration of every kind can get buried. It's like a constantly filling quicksand hole. We need email, but a tool like Basecamp can take things out of the chaos and simplify and coordinate communication. With Basecamp, ideas and projects can be lifted out and preserved, and crucial ideas can be protected, given a place to go, and brought into being.

So yeah, cross-pollination is really cool. Viva la Basecamp!

THE MOST AWESOME FEATURE IN ANY PROGRAM, EVER

Here's something cool. When you're using some features in Basecamp, like Edit, Delete, and Move, you can click Nevermind if you decide you don't actually want to take the action.

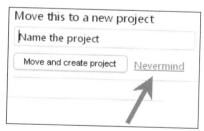

Source: 37signals, LLC.

I love it. Instead of Cancel, you can say, "Nevermind."

Okay, I'm easily amused. Maybe the Nevermind link will go away, but I hope not. I love it almost as much as the 37signals website wishing me "Happy Friday."

Okay, back to the serious stuff.

COMMENT-BASED DISCUSSION

We've looked at comment-based discussion before, but we'll take a different look here. When you enter comments on a to-do item, which might be the most common place to carry on a discussion, the comments are fed back into a central discussion.

This is another example of Basecamp lifting out bits and pieces of things you say and keeping track of them. It's kind of like having several personal assistants. For example, you might comment on a to-do item, and your "personal assistant" (Basecamp) puts that comment into an official discussion. This makes it easier for you, or someone else, to come back into the project and know what's going on. For example, a person might be added to the project later and not know to look at to-do item 24 in list number 6, but they can look through the discussions to see what's going on.

To review, you can comment on a to-do item by selecting the To-Do link in a project.

Source: 37signals, LLC.

Then, you can access the to-do item by clicking on it.

Source: 37signals, LLC.

The to-do item appears, and you can click in the Add a Comment area.

Source: 37signals, LLC.

This can lead to a discussion, in the same way creating an official discussion happens. When you comment, you can add a message and notify people. In this case, it's an invitation to come onto Basecamp and add ideas to a to-do list.

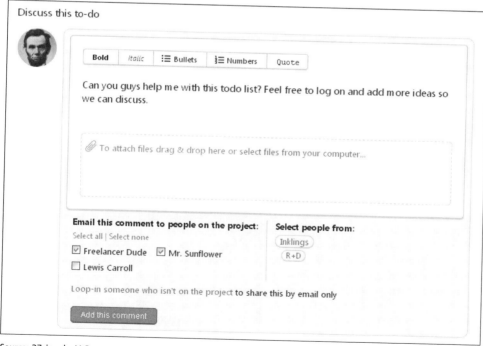

Source: 37signals, LLC.

This is an example of inviting collaboration through the comment feature. You could email people and pose the question and get Reply Alls, but why not invite people in for some cross-pollination. Woohoo!

As you're working on to-do lists, having in-person meetings can be nice, especially for brainstorming. The feedback is immediate, and there can be a kind of energy and inspiration as you feed off each other in a live situation. Similarly, a live conference call in which everyone's looking at a to-do list might be nice. But using comments and to-do lists can be another realistic way to gather information and even brainstorm, as people have the time. It's especially helpful if you're on different schedules in different locations.

COMMENTING ON TEXT DOCUMENTS

As with other project elements, you can enter comments at the bottom of text documents if you like. We'll take a closer look at text documents in Chapter 9, "Working with Text Documents." Basically, you can collaborate on and comment on a word processing document in Basecamp. In other words, you build a document together and discuss it along the way.

Discuss this document

Add a comment...

History
Jun 29 at 11:09pm: Todd created the document

Source: 37signals, LLC.

And that wraps things up for this chapter...

But wait, there's more!

BREAKING GRIDLOCK, UNLOCKING PARALYSIS, SETTING THINGS IN MOTION

Live conversations and meetings can be great, but sometimes meetings go nowhere. The energy dies down, things fade away, and opportunities are lost. This sometimes happens because it can be hard to take the first step. Basecamp is nice because it's so simple to take that first step.

Having a tool for discussion can provide you with an opportunity to collaborate. If you know something needs to be done but needs some help to get there, you can start a discussion. Getting the ball rolling by thinking conversationally can be a way to take an idea, get feedback, or think about next steps. How many times have you been thinking about a "formal project" and didn't make progress but found it easy enough to generate an email to people. Maybe that email is still somewhere in your email inbox. Having that discussion feature can help you take the step, but take it in a central place.

It's easy to get things rolling if you have a conversation in an environment where you can easily start working on it. For example, perhaps you need to create a requirements document or project plan. That might not sound exciting, but if you start a conversation, it creates some energy or at least some momentum. And in Basecamp, you can go back and look at a discussion and then start working on a text document. You've got everything you need, close together, and that makes it easier to take the next step. Once you have some momentum in a discussion, it becomes easier to develop a document, which can often be required in business for the formal part of bringing something about.

Conversations are like the mixing bowl—they provide a place to stir things up.

Okay, now on to the questions.

QUESTIONS FOR CONSIDERATION/DISCUSSION

1. In what kinds of scenarios could you start a discussion as part of a project?

2. What's the value of having a web-based project management tool like Basecamp gather information in a central place? How does it compare to email?

3. What is cross-pollination?

4. How would you invite discussion by commenting on something in Basecamp?

5. How would inviting someone to brainstorm in Basecamp keep ideas from "falling through the cracks"?

6. How would the Move feature help you start a new project? What's the point?

7. How is it valuable to have tools to "set things in motion," as opposed to just capturing ideas?

8. What are some ideas for projects you could do or brainstorming lists you could make that you could discuss with others and might motivate you to use Basecamp?

See Appendix A, "Answers to Questions for Consideration/Discussion," for suggested answers.

Conclusion

Dear Reader,

Congratulations on making it through your seventh chapter!

As you can see, I've tried to slip some ideas into the middle of the instructional material to show how valuable a tool like Basecamp can be. Discussions are the building blocks of any project. In Basecamp, it's simple to capture them and to involve people. Discussions in Basecamp provide strength in numbers, but without the chaos.

In the next chapter, we look at another aspect of setting things in motion—scheduling events, working with dates, and using the calendar. It's like time travel—going into the future to decide what's going to happen, and then holding yourself accountable to get there.

Best wishes on your adventures in keeping track of details and learning how to use Basecamp.

Regards,

Todd

P.S. So how'd I do with this chapter? Feel free to sound off at www.facebook.com/basecampbook.

CHAPTER 8

TIME TRAVEL WITH BASECAMP: USING DATES AND THE CALENDAR

In 140 Characters or Less

- Ch 8—Going forward and backward in time, assigning due dates, creating events, establishing milestones to help a project run effectively.

In This Chapter

- Estimation Versus Allocation
- Internal Estimation
- Creating Events on the General Calendar
- Using Events as Milestones
- Assigning Due Dates to To-Do Items
- The Most Exciting Thing in This Book: Project Management = Telecommuting
- Classroom/Personal Exercise: Estimate/Evaluate
- Classroom/Personal Exercise: Check In/Touch Base

Why This Chapter Is Important

This chapter is important because time travel is important. Have you ever seen the television show *Dr. Who*? Dr. Who's pretty good at getting around in time and space. Why am I talking about him? Because, let's face it, time travel is more exciting than establishing deadlines and maintaining accountability in project management—and that's what this chapter is about. Now before they cart me off to looney land, I might be able to escape punishment by mentioning gamification.

Gamification involves using game design techniques, game thinking, and game mechanics to make technology less intimidating and more engaging. In other words, just make things fun. Gamification can be general, like keeping a scoreboard of how well people do hitting their deadlines, or it can be a personal thing, like monitoring how productive you are. It can also be something as simple as asking everyone to assign a score in different categories to some aspect of the project when it's done. You can use a tool like www.surveymonkey.com to do that; in fact, I recommend exploring SurveyMonkey for the evaluation phase of any project as a good way to solicit feedback. Soliciting feedback on people's participation in a project and seeing some anonymous scores might motivate people and be a form of gamification. You can ask people to rate you on various things on a 1 to 10 scale so you can do better the next time. To make it really interesting, offer prizes, incentives, and rewards. With incentives and celebration, you can make just about anything fun. Sometimes achievement goes by unnoticed because of the pace of the business world, and gamification might be a simple way to offer some recognition. Maybe you could start a Basecamp project around this idea of gamification at your company or organization.

Granted, equating Basecamp with time travel might be stretching things a little bit, but play along with me for a minute.

Dr. Who has a vehicle that is bigger on the inside than it is on the outside. Well, a well-managed project is like Dr. Who's vehicle. It doesn't look very big on the outside, but there's a lot going on inside. It's not hidden, necessarily, but it's running so smoothly that you don't notice it. A badly run project is more like Dr. Who's vehicle exploding. But instead of a mess of wires and smoke, people barely know what's going on, and they don't communicate well.

(It's a bit like Hermione's purse in the *Harry Potter* series. Anyone want to make some analogies about project management in *Harry Potter*?)

But when the project is run well with Basecamp, you can bend time and space (oooooh, ahhhh) by compressing it so that you can have more time to do things you enjoy.

ESTIMATION VERSUS ALLOCATION

I experienced two ways of working with projects at a company I once worked for: estimation and allocation.

The classic way projects are developed, and the way they were developed at this company, was this: management sets more or less arbitrary deadlines, you are asked to accomplish something by a certain date, and you allocate time and do your best to meet the deadline. At this company, instead of basing the timing of the project around estimation, we just launched into things. At that point in my life, I was reading a book about the concept of a company's maturity level. In many of the companies the author had worked with, there were superstars who would pull out all the stops to make deadlines happen, which brought about unrealistic expectations on the part of management. Relying on superstars is not sustainable: they can move on or burn out, and not everyone can become one. The alternative is to work toward a higher degree of organizational maturity, in which you take some time for estimation and basic project management. Doing this across the board allows you to have a more reliable foundation to manage projects because things are more consistent, and you can estimate better.

INTERNAL ESTIMATION

Let's look a little more into how you get your part of a project done in that situation. If you find yourself in a situation with arbitrary deadlines, you might try to figure out a way for things to work better. You might not be in a position to set policy, but if you're responsible for anything against an overall deadline, you can work on internal estimation. That is, you might work backward and allocate blocks of time for various aspects of the project so you can meet the deadline.

Even in this situation, you might want to estimate how long it will take you to do certain tasks and then keep general track of how long it takes you in terms of hours or days. Doing so can provide you with some gamification by working to improve the accuracy of your estimation, which can be fun. But it can also build the crucial skill of estimation. The more accurate your estimation is, the more likely you can move from allocation to estimation.

In other words, if you can demonstrate that you've been developing the ability to estimate tasks and you can show that your estimated time spent and actual time spent are getting closer, management might be more likely to allow you to get more involved in the process of helping to create deadlines. You might even help to inspire confidence by being a source of estimation. It's not easy, and it takes some effort, but by working at it, you can provide some value.

Even if you don't have any choice in the matter and you end up having to work late to get things done with the arbitrary deadlines, there's an easy way to track the overall hours you spend. (Ding ding ding—Basecamp.) This can help the organization grow in maturity. Instead of having to constantly play catch-up and stay late all the time, you might be able to establish realistic deadlines when there's confidence that the estimation is accurate.

And if you're tracking the hours spent and can estimate fairly accurately, you can respond to allocation with estimation. It's not necessarily that you're pushing back, but you might review the project and come up with an estimation of how many hours it will take. Some of you might remember in Chapter 3, "Simple Alternatives to Basecamp," that little rescoping tool I had been trying to make, a tool that would allow me to respond to things being dropped in the pipeline.

There's value in showing the true cost of a project in terms of hours—even if you have no choice but to spend them. If the pattern in the company or organization you are working at is to push employees until they burn out or push back, which is pretty common, thinking about estimation can provide you with a more convincing case to say, "I estimate this project will take __ hours to complete." If you are protecting work/life boundaries, you can say, "The impact is that we'll need to push out these other project deadlines or add more resources to the project."

And even if it's a stressful situation, having a clearer idea of what's going into projects could help you to approach it all with a positive attitude and tone of voice because at least you have a better idea of what's going on, instead of just feeling buried and keeping your head above water.

It might be politically that you'd just want to track things in this situation and then at some point turn up the heat; all I'm saying is that having a clearer idea of what's going on can help you improve how things are done, which can mean you don't have to burn out. The economic downturn has meant that many employers are pushing employees for ever more productivity with fewer resources, and this makes lean project management even more critical—as little overhead as possible, but just enough project management to keep things from getting chaotic.

In an environment where arbitrary, assigned deadlines force you to allocate from available hours, estimation can help you face the reality of needing to set aside time sooner rather than later to complete a project. Waiting until the last minute can add stress, which can be unhealthy. In some ways, this book is about looking at a tool that can help remove excess stress from your work life.

One more thing before we get into the actual Basecamp software. If you're not that excited about "getting into a calendar" or "blocking out time," don't forget that I started out hating the idea of planning anything. I felt that just about any process or planning was a waste of time and effort. I associated it with bureaucracy and the attempt to control me; I didn't want to cage myself in. But I gradually realized that it could be pretty suffocating and stressful to face deadlines in the professional world, and just "winging it" was not going to cut it. I also saw that taking some time to keep track of things wasn't really limiting myself; it was freeing myself up to get things done.

So yeah, I'd say that if you have any hesitancy about "getting into a calendar" or "blocking out time," especially if you feel like you are not a detail person by nature, then from one nondetail person to another, I'd say that there are some situations where you do need to keep track of details, and if I can do it, you can do it, too. I still look at a calendar sometimes and think that the more I put on the calendar, the more I'm directly removing my freedom. But I also recognize that the "empty calendar" is an illusion. There are things that need to get done, and taking the time to plan them out a bit can actually have a direct impact on stress. Subconsciously, you know everything. You know all the loose ends, and this bubbles up as stress. It can also translate into avoidance. Let the cloud form behind you, and it drives you; it owns you.

Conversely, when you get things down on paper or start putting things down on a calendar, it can actually be encouraging, because you get the feeling that you're making concrete progress. You recognize that you are not caging yourself in but freeing yourself to get things done, with your eyes open instead of closed. It can be encouraging, and yes, it can even be exciting.

I don't look down my nose at people or companies who aren't organized well. Did I say that I was well organized? I'm better than I used to be, but I have room for growth. I think it's human nature. And I don't want to scare anyone either, especially students who might be freaking out that the corporate world is crazy. It's not crazy; it's just human.

And for every company that has ad hoc deadlines handed down to stressed out employees, there are also companies, jobs, and roles where you do have the freedom to estimate. You end up being asked to set a deadline. And it's just as important and helpful in this situation to learn how to estimate and work with calendars and deadlines on projects, because you can establish confidence by setting realistic deadlines and delivering projects on time. However, you can also cause issues if you don't bother to learn how to do it and you simply overpromise and then work like crazy to meet your unrealistic deadlines. Sometimes you might get lucky, but other times not.

So I hope you're at a mature company or organization or that you're willing to approach things with a bit of planning if it's just a personal project, your own company, or freelance work. But don't be surprised at some point if you end up in a more difficult situation and you can think of it positively even then; you might have an opportunity to help make everyone's lives easier.

CREATING EVENTS ON THE GENERAL CALENDAR

The general calendar in Basecamp is the one that you can access and see regardless of which project you are currently in. If you are creating an event, the easiest thing to do might be to create an event in the general calendar instead of a project-specific one. Perhaps you'd be more interested in creating project-specific events when you have more projects to work with or when you investigate the idea of using events as milestones, discussed in an upcoming section.

But just to get familiar, to access the calendar, click the Basecamp logo to get back to the home screen, outside of any particular projects, and click the Calendar link at the top of the Basecamp screen.

A simple calendar appears. To create an event, just click on a day.

Show a list of calendars ↵		Next 6 weeks				◄ ►
Sun	Mon	Tue	Wed	Thu	Fri	Sat
6	7	8	9	Today 10	11	12
13	14	15	16	17	18	19
20	21	22	23	24	25	26

Source: 37signals, LLC.

A pop-up window comes up, where you can enter a name for the event and an optional note. If you check the Send Other People check box, you can select who to send it to.

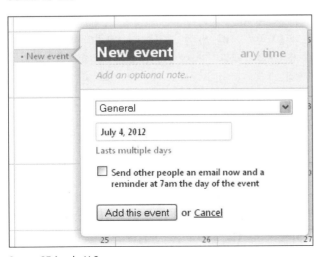

Source: 37signals, LLC.

Then you can click on the drop-down menu and choose whether to place the event on the general calendar or on a project-specific calendar.

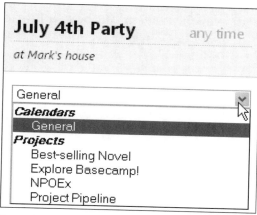

Source: 37signals, LLC.

Then when you're ready, you can click Add This Event.

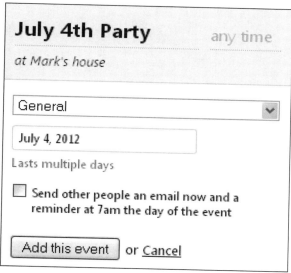

Source: 37signals, LLC.

The event shows up on the calendar.

Pretty simple. The Basecamp calendar is not meant to be a full-fledged calendar system to replace Outlook or Google Calendar. It's just meant to complement a calendar like that, to focus on deadlines and due dates and events for the project. However, as we'll see in Chapter 14, "Connecting Basecamp to a Calendar," it's possible to "feed" your Basecamp calendar into another calendar system.

An interesting thing happens after you create an event. When you click on the event in the calendar, a Discuss This Event link becomes available, which can be helpful for discussing an upcoming event or a milestone (discussed later in this chapter).

July 4th Party   any time

at Mark's house

General   ⌄

July 4, 2012

Lasts multiple days

☐ Send other people a reminder at 7am the day
   of the event

Discuss this event...

[Save changes] or Close   🗑

Source: 37signals, LLC.

The other thing that appears is a tiny trash icon, which allows you to delete an event. If you click to discuss the event, it opens and has the standard comment function.

From the calendar: General

Wednesday **Jul 4**   July 4th Party
                       at Mark's house

Discuss this event

Add a comment...

Source: 37signals, LLC.

USING EVENTS AS MILESTONES

There is no one "right" way to manage a project, but setting milestones is one thing that people do to keep things moving. Think of milestones as a goal or a stage. Remember the ADDIE model from Chapter 5, "Super Basic Project Management with Basecamp To-Dos"? If you think in terms of analysis, design, development, implementation, and evaluation, Analysis Complete might be an example of a milestone you can set.

On a calendar, you might set an event to represent a milestone. I recommend creating a project and breaking it down into a few stages. It might be an imaginary new fashion line, a particular widget, a new robot, or the next iPhone model. Imagine some of the milestones you'd have to reach, have a team of people on the same project, and make each milestone into a to-do list. What tasks are required to reach that milestone?

You might also want to include the date of the milestone in its title, just to reinforce it. Then, in working on the to-do items, assign due dates to those (as discussed in the upcoming section).

For example, let's say we have a project called The Next iPhone. Apple has asked us to help plan how the next iPhone is going to be developed and rolled out. (Lucky us!) We're in Basecamp, with the project selected.

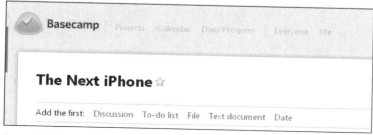

Source: 37signals, LLC.

We can click the Date link, which is another way to create an event. In this case, it creates the event on this project's calendar.

We could call this milestone Design Complete.

Milestone: Design Complete   any time

Add an optional note...

June 30, 2012

Lasts multiple days

Email this event to people on the project:
Select all | Select none
☐ Freelancer Dude

Loop-in someone who isn't on the project to share this by email only

Add this event or Cancel

Source: 37signals, LLC.

We could click on the date and navigate using the right and left arrows on the calendar to get the desired month and set the milestone there.

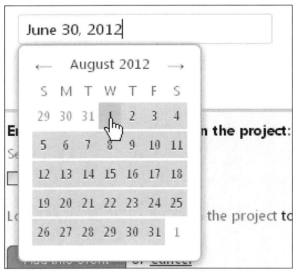

June 30, 2012

←   August 2012   →

S M T W T F S

29 30 31 1   2   3   4

5   6   7   8   9   10 11

12 13 14 15 16 17 18

19 20 21 22 23 24 25

26 27 28 29 30 31 1

Source: 37signals, LLC.

Then we can click Add This Event to complete the process.

The Dates section shows as a list, so this is a nice way to establish milestones.

The Next iPhone

Dates [Add a new event]

Upcoming events

August

Wednesday **1** Milestone: Design Complete

Source: 37signals, LLC.

If you're following this as an exercise, you might want to come up with two or three milestones, each about a month apart, and then try working with to-do items that build up to those milestones.

Source: 37signals, LLC.

If you want to be consistent, use the Milestone prefix. It can help distinguish these events as, well, milestones. (To edit an event, just click on it on a calendar or in this Dates view in a project, and click the Edit link on the right.)

Ah, much better. Feels like the project is coming together! Milestones can be established in a brainstorming session in a to-do list, in a meeting, or during login. Then someone might create them as milestone events, with tentative dates.

Assigning Due Dates to To-Do Items

The next steps in the process might involve making to-do lists representing each milestone, filling in tasks that need to be accomplished to reach the milestone, and assigning due dates.

For example, the flow could go like this:

1. Brainstorming (to-do list)—Think of what the milestones are.
2. Create milestone events in the project calendar.
3. Create to-do lists for each milestone.
4. Brainstorm the tasks required to complete each milestone.
5. Assign tasks and due dates to people.

I'm approaching it somewhat simply here, but if you're following along and doing something like this, you might also want to work dependencies into your to-do items. For example, if you are painting a building, you might have part of that item indicate "dependent on finding a painter." Including dependencies can help you look at a project globally and see how the pieces fit together. Or maybe it involves placing the to-do items in sequential order, if one step has to happen before another one. Reordering to-do items can help you plan tentative dates.

Along those lines, I'm going to go ahead and create three to-do lists in the project, based on these three milestones.

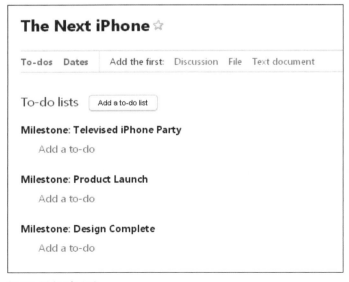

Source: 37signals, LLC.

The only problem is that the lists are out of order. That's okay; it's easy to reorder them. Just click and drag the milestones into the correct position.

Source: 37signals, LLC.

I could place the date of the milestone in the title of the to-do list if I wanted to emphasize it. To change the title of a list, just roll over it and click Edit.

Source: 37signals, LLC.

Ahh, that's nice.

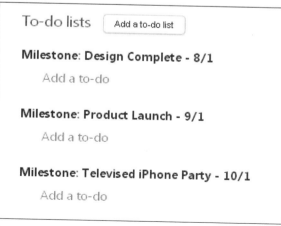

Source: 37signals, LLC.

Some people prefer to organize things in stages, such as design, launch, and promotion. Instead of having a list based on the milestone you're working toward, it might just be a stage that takes place from such and such date to another. There's no right or wrong way to handle this. Experiment!

But having a milestone approach, and including dates in the titles and in to-dos, can help you as you are filling in tasks required to work toward specific milestones.

If you're on a team, you might get someone to be the calendar maestro to keep track of and coordinate dates. It wouldn't hurt to do some role playing and pretend that one of your dependencies is late with his portion of the project, forcing you to adjust the dates that come after that. The point is to simulate a real-world situation involving deadlines that need to shift. It serves as a good fire drill.

In a classroom situation, you could start by plotting out homework assignments and setting the milestones of assignments that are due throughout the course of the class. Or you might plot out the remaining chapters of this book as milestones across a particular number of days or weeks. The world is your oyster. Experiment and have fun!

All right, so back to the to-dos.

You might think of tasks that are necessary to reach the next milestone. Add them.

To-do lists   Add a to-do list

Milestone: Design Complete - 8/1

- ☐ Design case
- ☐ Design screen
- ☐ Add new funky functions
- ☐ Get rid of the annoying function that makes Siri pop up all the time
  - Add a to-do

Milestone: Product Launch - 9/1

- ☐ Send invitations to press
- ☐ Ask U2 to play at the product launch
- ☐ Order 5,000 glow in the dark wigs and lots of glowsticks
- ☐ Rent out a stadium
  - Add a to-do

Milestone: Televised iPhone Party - 10/1

- ☐ Ask Conan O'Brien to host a televised party
- ☐ Think of zany iPhone segments for the show
- ☐ Issue press releases and get the word out on social media
  - Add a to-do

Source: 37signals, LLC.

Now, if you review this list and play along, you can see that you don't necessarily have to plan things so that one thing is required before you get to the next thing. But in your exercise, you might experiment with including notes about what an item is dependent on.

> **Milestone: Product Launch - 9/1**
> ☐ Send invitations to press | Dependent on Freelancer dude writing press release
> ☐ Ask U2 to play at the product launch
> ☐ Order 5,000 glow in the dark wigs and lots of glowsticks
> ☐ Rent out a stadium
>   Add a to-do

Source: 37signals, LLC.

As often is the case, as you start thinking about a project, you might realize additional things that need to happen. Or you might create separate to-do lists or offload entire tasks to people with due dates. The point here is to get comfortable with jotting things down as they occur to you. Don't forget that part of the experiment and the real world of Basecamp is remote collaboration. You might convince a long-distance friend to practice having phone calls, logging in, and adding comments or to-do items.

In this case, I'm going to add another to-do item to my list.

> **Milestone: Product Launch - 9/1**
> ☐ Write press release
> ☐ Send invitations to press | Dependent on Freelancer dude writing press release
> ☐ Ask U2 to play at the product launch
> ☐ Order 5,000 glow in the dark wigs and lots of glowsticks
> ☐ Rent out a stadium
>   Add a to-do

Source: 37signals, LLC.

Now we might get to the point of assigning items and due dates.

To assign an item, roll over it and click the Unassigned button.

Source: 37signals, LLC.

If you are following along and haven't done it yet, create a dummy email address, like Gmail. Invite a freelancer or team member to the project so that you can practice assigning. You can also assign yourself.

This is part of the art of project management. It depends on your situation and the timelines.

Source: 37signals, LLC.

As you think about assigning due dates, you can imagine how it might be helpful to have the dates of the milestones in the title of the to-do item. As an example, if your product launch is September 1, and if sending invitations to the launch depends on writing the press release, when do you want to have the press release complete? You decide that 30 days before the launch party would be good, so you assign a due date of August 1. You're starting to set a project in motion!

Milestone: Product Launch - 9/1

☐ Write press release   Wed, Aug 1
☐ Send invitations to press | Dependent on Freelancer dude writing press release
☐ Ask U2 to play at the product launch
☐ Order 5,000 glow in the dark wigs and lots of glowsticks
☐ Rent out a stadium
    Add a to-do

Source: 37signals, LLC.

When you're working with different people, having a way to keep track of due dates and assign them is really helpful. So is having a central place to manage them.

For example, let's say you establish the due date that you need a to-do item by. You might need to assign it if the person reports to you, or you could first ask when he could get it done by, keeping in mind your overall date. So having an easy way to look at the project while negotiating or planning can be helpful. Then let's say you want to assign the item. To do that, roll over whatever appears at the right of your to-do item (a date, or Unassigned), and click.

Milestone: Product Launch - 9/1

🗑 Edit ☐ Write press release Wed, Aug

Source: 37signals, LLC.

Then choose someone to assign it to.

This system can make communication and keeping track of things pretty straightforward. It provides you with a way to make things clear to everyone involved.

If you've assigned a to-do item, when the stakeholder logs into Basecamp, he has a list of what he needs to do. He has a central place to track what he needs to work on and what it's related to.

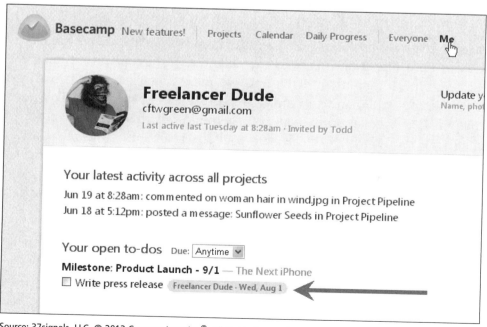

He also gets an email notification.

These straightforward building blocks can allow you to build a project, start working with dates, and then have a dynamic way of keeping track of things and responding to changing conditions.

If you haven't been involved in managing projects before, it might be helpful to emphasize that point. The point of project management isn't so much to plan every detail, but to establish an overall outline while assuming that there are going to be changes, surprises, challenges, and delays.

There are different philosophies of project management. I suppose I lean heavily toward "lean" project management, for the sake of making it more manageable. That's partly why I appreciate Basecamp so much, because it makes it easy to respond to changing conditions.

Another phenomenon that's worth mentioning in the midst of assigning due dates and assigning items to people is accountability. If you manage a project by making a list of things that need to be done in Microsoft Word, for example, and then you send emails assigning tasks to people or sit in a meeting and make notes of who is going to do what, it might work. But there's a lot of room for human error and for confusion. In this scenario we're only talking about a single project, and the reality is that most people are doing many things at the same time. So the clearer you can communicate, the better. Instead of having *your* list of deadlines and 10 other hand-written lists or a series of emails spread out among different computers, it can be helpful to have a point of common reference in a central place.

Part of the reason I keep using that phrase "point of common reference" is because of how stressful it can be when things begin to fray at the edges. People are human: we skimp on sleep, we type things incorrectly, and we make mistakes. Things can get confused by the best of people, and the more pressure there is, the more likelihood that things can pop up. A collaborative spirit is helpful, and the common point of reference provides everyone with a clear way to keep track of things. Freelancer Dude might be juggling 20 different things, but he has an easy way to see exactly what's going on with a specific item on that project. And if there's date slippage, the person who is relying on the press release to be written can access the project, see who's working on it, and trace things easily and immediately.

Basecamp provides tools for clear communication and straightforward accountability. It doesn't do the work for you, but it can be really, really helpful. Woohoo!

If you're following along, I recommend working through your milestone to-do lists, assigning due dates, and branching out from there. At this point in the book, you might have enough to work with to try doing an entire project, carrying on some discussion around items, and simulating communication about deadlines and more. Or you might want to wait until you get through Chapters 9 and 10. Your choice.

THE MOST EXCITING THING IN THIS BOOK: PROJECT MANAGEMENT = TELECOMMUTING

To add variety, I've been trying to sprinkle in interesting things here and there. Now I'd like to take an opportunity to talk about a philosophy I have about project management and telecommuting.

I equate project management with telecommuting because companies have a significant opportunity to enable more telecommuting by leveraging realistic but powerful project management tools like Basecamp in a way that provides accountability for productivity. These days, depending on the industry and region, there's more and more remote work.

So if we think of a team of graphic designers, about the last thing they're probably going to want to do is engage in any form of project management. "I'm a creative person, not a project manager!" But if you've been reading the entire book, you might remember mention of the interesting creative agency run by a formal project manager and how he ended up choosing Basecamp after I evaluated a number of options. If I can do it as a former graphic designer, you can too. And if that agency can do it, so can you. So can anyone.

One of the things graphic designers would probably love to do is telecommute. And these days, depending on the industry and region, there's more and more remote work. It might be because a freelancer is hired remotely by an agency to work on a project for a client, or an employee might be lucky enough to work for a company with a flexible telecommuting policy.

And there are, of course, a lot of different philosophies about it. But I think that project management equates to telecommuting because there's a significant opportunity for companies to enable more telecommuting by leveraging realistic but powerful project management tools like Basecamp, in a way that provides accountability for productivity.

Said more simply, a record of proven productivity and a clear audit trail of activity and met deadlines, demonstrated through project management, can build confidence. It can also establish reliability and consistency without being a straightjacket limiting creativity. Some employees' first reaction to project management, especially if they're in the creative field, might be to resist it like the plague, just like I used to feel about any kind of process. So management might have the desire to get more organized, to be more efficient, to be able to be more consistent and reliable in producing material or whatever it is. And management might try to establish process and project management with varying levels of success.

In the case of graphic designers, the rationale to work with a "lean" tool could partly be to establish confidence, reliability, and consistency, without it being a straightjacket, and to realize that it's going to help the business relationship (significantly). Ideally, the incentive could be more telecommuting.

So there's a big opportunity for companies of every size to look at this, to try experiments, and to look at the significant benefits of project management, including going to the extent of tracking estimated and actual hours.

Another thing in my experience is that, when it comes down to it, about the last thing employees realistically want to do is to track hours. For most roles, it's just too hard; how can you track hours when you're working on so many things at once? There's little motivation to even try. Managers, however, want to know that every hour is being used productively.

Project management might provide carrots to both managers *and* employees. If management is resistant to the idea of telecommuting because they're afraid people are just going to nap all day, what if there was a way to make employees significantly more accountable for their time than they are currently? What if productivity significantly increased? Most companies would probably allow more telecommuting if there was more accountability. And project management does equate to accountability, so it lends itself to telecommuting naturally.

In spite of any reservations you might have about tracking time and being straightjacketed by process, what if you had a tool that was easy to use, actually made your life easier, and resulted in the possibility of more telecommuting? What if you had to sacrifice some of the time you spend on "looking at news" and going on Facebook on your mobile device because it's blocked on the network, or whatever else you do? I'm not saying everyone does this, and I'm not even judging this, just speaking to realities. If you had to give up some of this and be more accountable, would that be worth more telecommuting? I think for most people it would. Would you use it?

To summarize, I believe that telecommuting is worth pursuing as a win-win for both employees and managers, and Basecamp would be a great platform for experimentation. The consistent use of a lean project management tool like Basecamp could provide significant productivity gains for just about any company, and that translates into dollars. And the accountability that comes with it, which could also include general time tracking, should alleviate most concerns about people napping at home.

I think it's a win-win, and I hope more companies think about it. No matter who you are, you could help work toward it, and be a hero of both management and coworkers, by helping people try keeping track of details. Go for it! Then sound off on the Facebook page and let us know how it's going.

CLASSROOM/PERSONAL EXERCISE: ESTIMATE/EVALUATE

In this exercise, you set up a simple project and estimate how long you think it will take. Include Estimated Hours in the to-do item, and then when you complete it, include Actual Hours. Try the project and evaluate how you're doing. This is a valuable exercise for anyone, whether in a class or at work, and it's one of the building blocks that can help with larger project management.

For example, someone might come to a team member and say, "Okay, we need to do x. How long do you think it will take?" Having the ability to answer that question with increased accuracy is a win all around, with every participant.

And with the principle of gamification, the estimated/actual exercise can be fun as you work to get more accurate or faster at the same level of quality.

CLASSROOM/PERSONAL EXERCISE: CHECK IN/TOUCH BASE

So a project manager might be a maestro of many things—brainstorming, the calendar, and keeping track of "dependencies." In some companies, project managers assist others and keep things moving along. In my opinion, everyone could benefit from project management skills. They could be highly relevant to just about any role. It could be that it's awhile down the road before you need to or want to think about dependencies, but I decided that even in a book for beginners, it's worth mentioning, especially if you like the idea of practicing personally or if a class has the opportunity to practice.

In this exercise, I suggest setting up a real or simulated project, with deadlines, and try estimating the hours it might take to do something. Set up a sequence of dependencies, like dependent tasks, and then schedule times for someone, or everyone, to check in on status.

This could mean a regular meeting or people logging in to Basecamp daily and commenting on their assigned to-do items with a status.

A simplified exercise might be a word processing document that combines contributions from each participant. And for the sake of simulation, set it up so person B can't start working on the project until he receives the document from person A. It might not be that the paragraph or project element a person works on is "really" dependent on the prior person, but you set up deadlines and try working on it in that way. Person A is assigned a task, due at a particular point. Then person B works on it, and so on. And then each week or each day, someone checks in. If you want to have some fun with it, introduce delays, and see what happens.

There's no "right" way to do this exercise; it might best be performed with a class. It's not really about what the deliverable or final product is; it's just the process of waiting on someone and collaborating toward a goal. You might try a day-to-day project, maybe with teams, in which a document cycles through three people. (Person A: write the intro. Person B: write a paragraph. Person C: add a graphic.)

Hopefully this book will end up in some interdisciplinary situations. Just about every functional role in business can benefit from project management skills, so it stands to reason that just about any type of class could benefit from exploring this area (and it could provide significant value in helping people launch into careers, no matter the area). So if it's a computer science class, the project might be a set of code. Graphics people might collaborate on a graphic. And so on.

QUESTIONS FOR CONSIDERATION/DISCUSSION

1. What's the difference between estimation and allocation?

2. What's the point of having a milestone?

3. What are two ways to create an event in Basecamp?

4. How might you convince management to allow more telecommuting?

See Appendix A, "Answers to Questions for Consideration/Discussion," for suggested answers.

CONCLUSION

Dear Reader,

Congratulations on making it through the first half of the book!

In this chapter, we reviewed some of the ways you can work with creating events, assigning due dates, and "travelling through time." I also tried to present some perspective on the importance and relevance of these seemingly innocuous tools and how much difference they can make in the real world.

In the next part of the book, we'll look at branching out a bit, starting with text documents and working with files, and continuing on with some tasks associated with working with multiple projects and other fun items.

The goal is to make this as enjoyable and motivating as possible, especially for beginners, because I really do think this stuff is important.

I also want to comment that if you're going through this book and have no plans to use it in the "business" world, it applies equally to the nonprofit world. The more someone can help a nonprofit run more efficiently, or more like a business, the better. Basecamp can help nonprofits, too!

And if you're just using Basecamp to keep track of personal projects, I wish you the best. There are plenty of people who do just that.

Regards,

Todd

P.S. So how'd I do with this chapter? Feel free to sound off at www.facebook.com/basecampbook.

CHAPTER 9

WORKING WITH TEXT DOCUMENTS

In 140 Characters or Less

- Ch 9—Discusses the creation and editing of collaborative text documents in Basecamp.

In This Chapter

- Creating and Editing Text Documents
- Working Around Export
- Discussing Documents
- Deleting Text
- Moving Text
- Comparing Text Documents in Basecamp to Google Docs
- Classroom/Personal Exercise: Google/Basecamp Challenge

Why This Chapter Is Important

In this chapter, we'll look at creating and editing text documents in Basecamp, and some of their features. Then in the next chapter we'll look at how to work with files.

It's important to be familiar with text documents, because they can provide a way to invite people to collaborate and discuss longer sets of content. You can upload a word processing document and attach it to comments for a to-do item, as we've already seen, but putting text right into an editable format makes it easier for people to make changes. It can also be a way to get a document started as part of a project.

CREATING AND EDITING TEXT DOCUMENTS

To create a document, access a project in Basecamp, and click the Text Document link.

Source: 37signals, LLC.

This opens a blank text document.

If you already have a text document in the project, the link is on the left.

Source: 37signals, LLC.

Clicking the link brings up a list of any text documents that are already in the project. You can click the Create a Text Document link.

Source: 37signals, LLC.

When you have a text document, you can click in the upper area and start typing to give it a title, or you can click in the lower area to type the body of the document. There's no Save button; the document just automatically, constantly saves, and Basecamp confirms that it has saved the document with a message "Saved a second ago."

Source: 37signals, LLC.

When you start a document, you might like to put a message at the top of it as a note for people collaborating on it.

There are basic formatting options that might be familiar to you; for example, Ctrl+Z, the undo function, applies here. Still, it's a good idea to try each one, just to be familiar with it. You can either click (a single or double-click will work) on the format buttons and then type text, or you can select text and then click the formatting buttons.

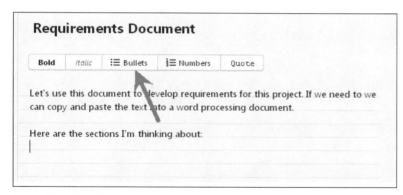

Source: 37signals, LLC.

The bullet formatting indents the text and inserts square bullets.

Source: 37signals, LLC.

Or you can select the text in separate lines and then click the Bullets or Numbers button at the top for the same results.

The Quote feature is a simple formatting option that changes the style of the text and indents it a little less than the bullet points.

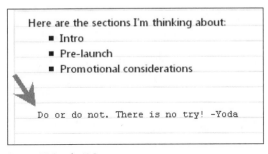

Source: 37signals, LLC.

Working Around Export

There isn't a straightforward export feature in the current version of text documents in Basecamp. If you collaborate on a document in Basecamp, and you want to incorporate that text elsewhere, you just have to select it, copy it, and paste it into an email or word processing document.

Step by step, you can select the text, press Ctrl+C, open your destination—an OpenOffice document (free word processing; go to www.openoffice.org), a Microsoft Word document, or even an email—and paste the text (Ctrl+V).

Source: 37signals, LLC.

Tip

When you're using this technique, first you might want to copy the title at the top of the page and paste it down into the body, because you can't easily select both the title and body text at the same time.

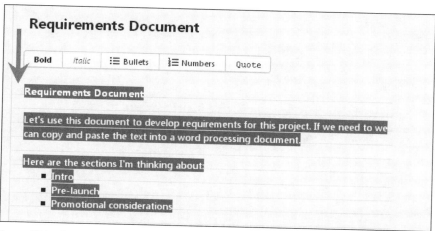

Source: 37signals, LLC.

DISCUSSING DOCUMENTS

The main benefit that text documents provide to a Basecamp project is the ability to collaboratively work on text and then to discuss it.

But a text document can also be a place to simply post guidelines. You can attach entire documents to comments in Basecamp, but it might be easier to just post guidelines or other kinds of text in a text document. Text documents are easy to create and easy to paste.

The comment/discussion feature allows you to easily post some text and notify others to read or add to it.

You just scroll down to the bottom of a text document and click in the Add a Comment area.

Source: 37signals, LLC.

Then you can type/format text as desired, attach documents or files if you want, and choose who you want to notify. When you're ready, click Add This Comment.

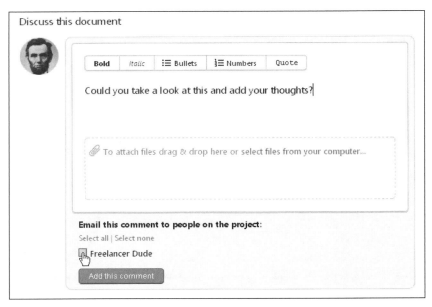

Source: 37signals, LLC.

DELETING TEXT

To delete a text document, access it and click the Delete link on the right.

Source: 37signals, LLC.

You can edit or delete comments to text documents, although there are limits. You can only edit or delete your own comment within several minutes of typing it.

MOVING TEXT

The move feature allows you to move a collaborative text document into another project. For example, one Basecamp project might be R+D or Planning, and you might use collaborative text documents to make plans for several products, events, or projects. Then you can move the text documents into new projects as a way to get things moving.

To move a text document, access it, and on the right, click the Move link.

Then click the Move To drop-down menu. If you want to spawn a new project, choose the Start a New Project option, or choose an existing project to move the document into.

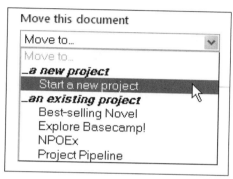

Source: 37signals, LLC.

If you move the document to a new project, choose a name for it, and click Move and Create Project.

Source: 37signals, LLC.

If you chose an existing project to move the document into, click the Move This Document button.

Source: 37signals, LLC.

And remember, you can always use the Nevermind option!

COMPARING TEXT DOCUMENTS IN BASECAMP TO GOOGLE DOCS

It's worth comparing the features of text documents in Basecamp with Google Docs. As a personal exercise, you might like to try collaborating on a document using both tools, so you can be familiar with the pros and cons of each.

The general value of using Basecamp is that it keeps everything in one place. If you create a Google Doc, you have to go through the steps of inviting people, and they either need to have a Gmail account or create a Google account with their email address. It would probably be helpful for everyone to have Gmail tools because they're powerful and free, but using Google might involve another step, so it might be easier just to keep a text document in one place if you need basic collaboration and everyone is already on Basecamp.

You can try using text documents in Basecamp first. Then if you need the more advanced features in Google Docs, try those.

Google Docs offers more advanced formatting, the ability to insert images, and the ability to easily download and export into several formats, including PDF and Microsoft Word. Google Docs also allows you to easily publish a Google Doc as a live web page. Even though it's separate from Basecamp, you can include a link to a Google Doc from within Basecamp.

Both tools have a provision to let you know that someone else is working on a document. You can use either on a conference call. Basecamp adds a little note in the upper-right corner as an alert.

Source: 37signals, LLC.

Google Docs includes an icon showing where a person is typing. Neither Basecamp nor Google Docs is immediately real time, but Google seems to have more indicators.

Both Basecamp and Google tools are great. I recommend trying them both and seeing how they might complement each other.

Classroom/Personal Exercise: Google/Basecamp Challenge

As a personal learning or classroom exercise, I invite you to create a project in Basecamp. Part of the project could involve collaboratively developing a presentation using Google Presentations. Then you can export the Google Presentation into PowerPoint format and attach it to the Basecamp project.

To take it one step further, make a group website using http://sites.google.com, and try inserting the Google Presentation into a live web page. Pretend you need to update it; change some things in the presentation, and the presentation is automatically updated in the website.

Going through some of these steps can help you learn how to use various tools together to work on a project and make a related presentation and private or public website. Marketing groups/classes might like to think along the lines especially of collaboratively developing a microsite—using Basecamp for the discussion, planning, and timelines, and using Google tools for some of the execution. Best wishes!

Questions for Consideration/Discussion

1. What are some scenarios in which you can use a text document to collaborate on something?

2. How might the comment feature come in handy?

3. In what situation would you want to use Basecamp instead of Google Docs, or vice versa?

4. How do you invite someone to participate in a text document?

See Appendix A, "Answers to Questions for Consideration/Discussion," for suggested answers.

Conclusion

Dear Reader,

Congratulations on making it through your ninth chapter!

The text document feature is one you might not use as much as to-dos or the calendar, but it's helpful to be aware of, and in some situations you might rely on it more than to-do lists. Sooner or later you'll want to have text developed in a central place (as opposed to circulating a word processing document, for example). As with other features in Basecamp, a text document provides a common point of reference.

Best wishes with collaborative editing!

Regards,

Todd

P.S. So how'd I do with this chapter? Feel free to sound off at www.facebook.com/basecampbook.

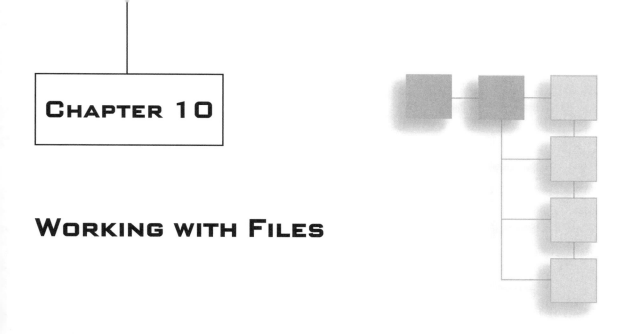

CHAPTER 10

WORKING WITH FILES

In 140 Characters or Less

- Ch 10—A review of how to upload and manage files in Basecamp projects.

In This Chapter

- Uploading Files
- Accessing and Managing Files
- Moving and Deleting Files
- Discussing Files

Why This Chapter Is Important

It's important to know how to add files to Basecamp projects. Some project management can occur without external files, but you can attach files in comments and view them in the Files section.

UPLOADING FILES

You can upload just about any kind of file to your project, up to 2 gigabytes in size. You can attach a file to a Basecamp project in several ways. You can upload it using the main File area to make it available generally, or you can attach it to specific comments, under either to-do items or text documents.

To upload a file using the main File function, access a project, and click on the File link.

The Next iPhone ☆

| 12 To-dos | 1 Text document | Dates | Add the first: | Discussion | File |

Source: 37signals, LLC.

If there are already files in the project, the File link appears on the left.

The Next iPhone ☆

| 12 To-dos | 1 File | 1 Text document | Dates | Add the first: | Discussion |

Source: 37signals, LLC.

In that case, you are led to a screen showing existing files, and you can click the Upload Files button.

The general process is to either drag files into the window or click the Select Files from Your Computer link.

> ✎ To attach files drag & drop here or select files from your computer...
>
> **Email this upload to people on the project:**
> Select all | Select none
> ☐ Freelancer Dude
>
> Loop-in someone who isn't on the project to share this by email only
>
> [Upload] or Cancel

Source: 37signals, LLC.

Then you can select people in the system to notify by clicking on the appropriate check box, or you can click the Loop-in Someone Who Isn't on the Project link and enter an email address.

Before you click Upload, you get a visual confirmation of your attachment. If you have attached a standard image file, an image preview appears. Otherwise, an icon appears, like those shown here.

If you decide that you don't want to upload a file after all, you can click the little X icon.

When you're ready, click the Upload button.

After you upload files, they appear on the Files function in the project.

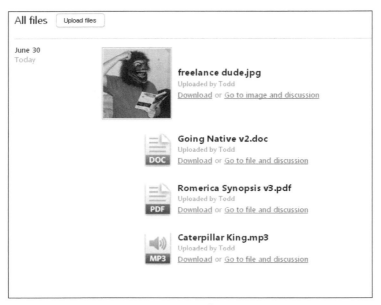

All files   Upload files

June 30
Today

freelance dude.jpg
Uploaded by Todd
Download or Go to image and discussion

Going Native v2.doc
Uploaded by Todd
DOC   Download or Go to file and discussion

Romerica Synopsis v3.pdf
Uploaded by Todd
PDF   Download or Go to file and discussion

Caterpillar King.mp3
Uploaded by Todd
MP3   Download or Go to file and discussion

ACCESSING AND MANAGING FILES

To access files that have been uploaded to a project, access the project, and click on the Files link at the top.

Then you can access each file in different ways, depending on the file type.

For an image file, such as JPG or PNG, you can click directly on the preview. A larger preview window opens, but its only function is to display the image. If there's a larger version available, you can also click the View Full Size button. To leave the window, click the X.

freelance dude.jpg   View full size

For other types of files, there is a Download link, which allows you to download a copy of the file, or a Go to File and Discussion link, where you can perform other functions, including commenting on the file.

Source: 37signals, LLC.

Tip

Depending on which operating system you have and what your browser settings are, clicking the Download link may present you with the option of opening or saving the file. You could also have a setting that makes your computer try to open the file rather than save it. This might be the case with PDF files. If the computer tries to open the file in the browser window, it can be a little tricky to save it. One alternative to clicking the Download link directly is right-clicking it and choosing Save Target As, Save File, Download to Disk, or some function like that. In certain situations, that might be the best option.

MOVING AND DELETING FILES

To move or delete a file, access the project and then choose the File link. On the list of All Files, go to the desired file and click the link that says Go to Image [or File] and Discussion.

Source: 37signals, LLC. © 2013 Cengage Learning®, All Rights Reserved.

Then click the Delete or Move links on the right side of the screen.

The Move link allows you to either start a new project around the file or move the file to another project.

DISCUSSING FILES

To discuss a file, access it by going to a Project > File > (find the files you want) > Go To _____ link (image and discussion/file and discussion), just as you would if you were going to delete or move the file.

Instead of deleting or moving the file, you can decide to Discuss This Upload by clicking in the Add a Comment field.

As with other comment functions throughout Basecamp, in addition to typing in comment text, you can add files.

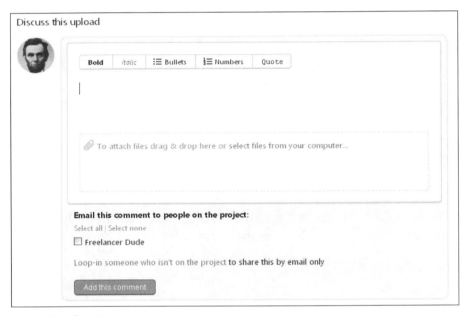

Source: 37signals, LLC.

In this case, the File function might be helpful for uploading a prototype, or an image from the web, and asking a designer to come up with some ideas. The designer could upload them as separate files, or comment on the first file and attach the files in the comment.

After you've made a comment, attached any files you like, and chosen to notify people, click the Add This Comment button.

Any file that has been uploaded to a Basecamp project shows under All Files. For example, you can upload files directly as we've shown, or you can attach comments on to-do items or text documents. Regardless of how the file got into the project, you can always access it in the All Files area (in your Project > File link). When a file has been attached to a discussion around a particular item, there will be a note about it, so you don't have to worry about any files being lost because of their attachment location.

In this situation, Basecamp allows the user to easily access the item's discussion. Here, the user could click on Re: Design Screen to access the comment (and be able to participate in the original discussion).

Note that every uploaded file can have its own discussion, too. For example, in this scenario, there was a to-do item and then a discussion started around it. Then a file was uploaded.

But because each image can also have its own discussion, the Go to Image and Discussion link allows someone to comment on the image itself.

Knowing these options might help you trace a discussion, if someone gets confused, sees a file in the All Files list, and is expecting to participate in a preexisting discussion but clicks Go to Image and Discussion and finds nothing there. In that case, he might need to click on the comment link.

The best way to understand this is just to play around with it.

Basically, Basecamp allows you to upload, access, and discuss files any way you'd like. It gives you as many simple options as possible for getting around and for developing discussions around files, which in the case of images might mean providing feedback to a designer or giving an opinion on various ideas.

It's also worth noting that if there is a discussion around a file, someone coming into the project can see what's going on by going right to the discussions area, which shows any active discussions. (And then he could click on the filename to join the discussion.)

Source: 37signals, LLC.

Questions for Consideration/Discussion

1. What kind of files can you upload to Basecamp?

2. What's the file size limit in Basecamp for an individual file?

3. What kinds of files have previews?

4. Why would you want to generate a discussion around a file?

5. If you upload a design for a logo, and a designer has a new version, how could he upload the new version?

6. How would uploading a word processing file to Basecamp be any better than just emailing it to people?

7. How would you upload a file like a graphic or word processing document and assign it to someone?

See Appendix A, "Answers to Questions for Consideration/Discussion," for suggested answers.

Conclusion

Dear Reader,

Congratulations on making it through your tenth chapter!

In this chapter, we covered the various ways to work with files on Basecamp. With this chapter, we've pretty much wrapped up all the main functions in Basecamp.

In the next two chapters, we'll look at more advanced features and functions, such as working with multiple projects, and some extra fun you can have. (I'll keep it a surprise.) Then, in the final four chapters, we'll go further and look at using Basecamp on a mobile device, connecting Basecamp to other calendars, and using two other products from 37signals, Highrise and Campfire, because of their natural connection to Basecamp.

Best wishes on your adventures in keeping track of files!

Regards,

Todd

P.S. So how'd I do with this chapter? Feel free to sound off at www.facebook.com/basecampbook.

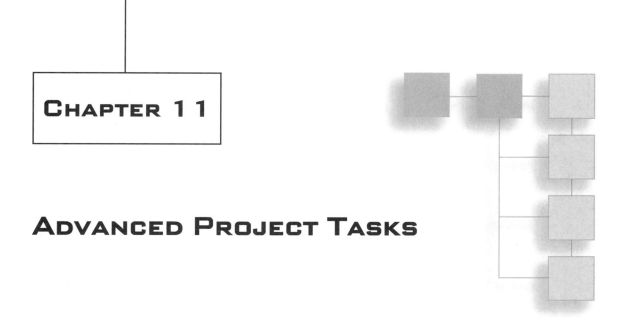

CHAPTER 11

ADVANCED PROJECT TASKS

In 140 Characters or Less

- Ch 11—The soul of the book: a brainstorming exercise. Plus: task completion/notification, deleted items, misc. project tasks.

In This Chapter

- Check Boxes and Completed Items
- Pros/Cons of Check Boxes
- Classroom/Personal Exercise: Brainstorming and Setting Ideas in Motion
- Recovering Deleted Items from the Trash
- Using Multiple Projects Views

Why This Chapter Is Important

As I was writing, I came to feel that the heart and soul of the book is in this chapter—in a brainstorming exercise and in the Conclusion. All the features and options in Basecamp are worthwhile, but brainstorming's importance makes this discussion one to consider.

Also, you need to know how to apply some of the additional features of Basecamp to individual and multiple projects.

Task completion is pretty simple, but it represents a system and philosophy that some people might like to try from the beginning, and others might wait until they're more familiar with it; some groups might find it helpful, and others may just want to use the basic features without completion. Basecamp is written to make working on multiple projects pretty easy, but classes or individuals might like to learn the basics first and then approach advanced tasks later. We'll take a look at the options.

CHECK BOXES AND COMPLETED ITEMS

You can click on a checkbox next to a to-do item, to mark it as being complete.

To try this, go to your project, and click the To-Dos link.

Source: 37signals, LLC.

Then choose/create a to-do list with several items, and try clicking a check box next to an individual item.

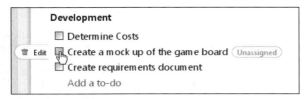

Source: 37signals, LLC.

Checking an item temporarily moves it to the bottom of a list and then moves it to a separate list of "completed" items, which we'll cover in this section.

Source: 37signals, LLC.

When an item is complete, you see a little link on the right of the To-Do Lists page in your project, called See Completed To-Dos. If all the to-do items in a list are completed, a similar link shows up later on the page, called See Completed To-Do Lists.

The to-do lists themselves go away when all the items on them are completed. This might affect the way you organize to-do items. You might want to have stages of the project represented by each item; as one stage is completed, it disappears, and the remaining stages still show.

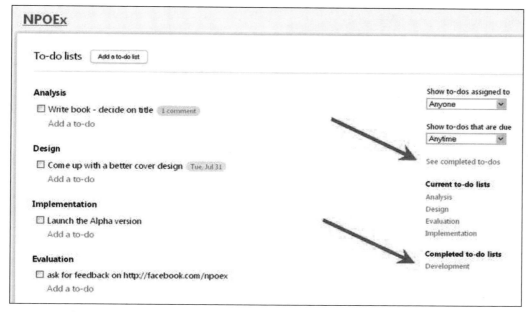

Source: 37signals, LLC.

So even though completed tasks/to-dos "disappear," they are always accessible. If you click on the See Completed To-Dos link, they show up like this.

Source: 37signals, LLC.

Similarly, if you use the link to access a completed to-do list, it shows up like this.

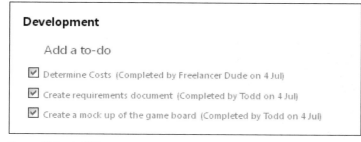

Source: 37signals, LLC.

Tip

If you ever find that a task is not really complete, you can uncheck the item in the Completed To-Do list (Development in this example).

Pros/Cons of Check Boxes

There's no right or wrong about using check boxes.

Pros of the check box method include notifying people who create the to-dos, and clearing items and lists off the table when they're taken care of. Cons include not having all the to-do items in a list easily accessible in the main view.

The simplest approach is to not use check boxes until you need them; understanding their features will help to determine when to use them. For brainstorming lists, you might not need to use them at all.

Classroom/Personal Exercise: Brainstorming and Setting Ideas in Motion

As a classroom or personal learning exercise, try setting up a project in which you have one to-do list called Brainstorming and another called Put into Action. Brainstorm some ideas, and then move one or more of them into the Put into Action list. Then, using the moving techniques discussed later in this chapter, you could move the list into a new project and then expand the initial idea into a series of tasks that need to be completed. This would be a way to represent a full life cycle of brainstorming, all the way to task completion.

There's also a case to be made for having not only separate lists like "Analyze, Design, Develop," but separate projects that serve as project hubs, such as an R + D project, which you might use primarily to capture and discuss ideas. Then at some point you might use the techniques suggested in this section to move the idea from the brainstorm list into a project. And that's exciting, because you begin to realize how powerful Basecamp is as a way to bring things from the idea stage into action. If you haven't been in a corporate or nonprofit work setting yet as an employee, you might end up learning software like Basecamp without realizing how challenging it can be to make ideas come about. But ask someone you know who works at a company or organization how ideas are handled. Perhaps you'll get a variety of answers, but it wouldn't surprise me if you didn't often get the answer "yes" when you ask whether ideas are handled well. And this might represent another personal/classroom exercise to interview people about how they manage projects and handle ideas.

I've seen time and again how easy it is for precious ideas to fall through the cracks and not even reach the discussion stage. But I believe that companies that do actively listen to employees and cultivate a way of capturing ideas are more successful than those that don't. And it's not just asking for ideas (very common), or capturing ideas (also common), but *setting something in motion* to review ideas that makes a difference.

The thing is, you get so busy that you feel like you barely have time to think, much less deal with the emails in your Inbox. (Corporate veterans are nodding their heads.) But don't be alarmed. The beautiful thing is that a tool like Basecamp makes it possible to have a simple way of not just capturing ideas, but reviewing them.

Note

Remember, in a brainstorming meeting, you should capture everyone's ideas without critiquing yet, so every voice can be heard. Then you can schedule a separate critique meeting with the appropriate people.

Once you know how to move an idea from one list to another, you can try moving that brainstorming list of ideas into a new project. This might help you to see how you can provide significant value to a company or organization, by letting people experience what it's like to bring ideas to life.

I'm going to put in a little request here. I'd love it if someone could try this brainstorm sequence I'm describing at a company or organization you work for and then post your attempt and the results at http://facebook.com/basecampbook.

Then I'll put it on the Basecamp book page at www.toddkelsey.com/books/basecamp. (Feel free to check whether anyone else has posted anything.) If we can get a few instances of brainstorming posted, it will encourage people to try brainstorming for themselves.

What I'm saying is that, based on my years of experience, brainstorming is a really valuable thing that people from the CEO down would appreciate. Ideas do matter, and innovation = being competitive.

To conclude this section, what we're talking about here folks is bringing ideas to life—not just capturing them, but setting them in motion. The possibilities are unlimited.

As Pedro said in *Napoleon Dynamite*, "All your wildest dreams will come true!"

(Don't forget that you can use Basecamp for your personal projects, too!)

RECOVERING DELETED ITEMS FROM THE TRASH

Did you know that when you delete items, you can still retrieve them?

To access the trash, click on the Projects link in Basecamp to see all your projects.

Source: 37signals, LLC.

The trash can appears somewhere on the screen depending on what view you are using. You might need to scroll to see it. Go ahead and click on the Trash Can link.

The trash can shows items that were deleted as a chronological list. Trash is removed (deleted items are permanently deleted) after 30 days.

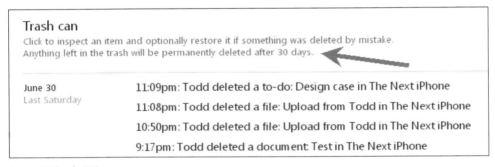

Source: 37signals, LLC.

To access a deleted item, just click on it.

The trash can view has links for Bring It Back and manually Permanently Delete It.

Source: 37signals, LLC.

USING MULTIPLE PROJECTS VIEWS

Basecamp is designed to make it easy to manage not just one project, but multiple projects at the same time. People start using this software for one project, and then that blossoms into using it for multiple projects because it's so easy to use. So you can quickly end up with several projects.

When working with multiple projects, it's helpful to be familiar with certain functions. We'll cover those next.

Choosing a View

I like the default view in Basecamp, which shows big icons for each project. When you click the Projects link at the top, beneath the New Project icon, three little icons affect the project view. The leftmost icon represents the Standard view.

Click the middle icon to see the List with Icons view.

Source: 37signals, LLC.

This is a nice way to be able to easily see more projects but still have some show at the top when they're starred, which we'll cover later.

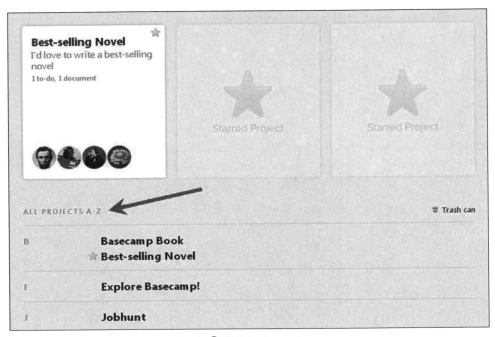

Source: 37signals, LLC. © 2013 Cengage Learning®, All Rights Reserved.

To see the List view, click the third icon.

This is a Straight List view, which might be the easiest way to list things when you have several projects.

Source: 37signals, LLC.

Searching

You can use the search feature to find anything in Basecamp. This is especially useful when you have a lot of projects. In the search box, just type in whatever you want in the upper-right corner of the Basecamp screen.

Source: 37signals, LLC.

Moving

Moving project elements has been mentioned in a few different places in the book. It's a feature found in parts of projects that enables you to move the item/element to a different project and generate a new project from it. This "spawning" capability is marvelous, especially for brainstorming.

Generally, the move feature is found at the item level, in to-do lists, text documents, and so on. For example, to move a to-do list, just click on it, as shown next. (To move an individual to-do item, you might have to create a separate to-do list first, move the item to that list, and then move the list.)

🗑 Edit   **Analysis**
        ☐ Write book - decide on title   1 comment
        Add a to-do

Source: 37signals, LLC.

Then, on the right side of the screen, click Move.

Click the Move To drop-down, and either start a new project or select an existing project.

If you create a new project, you need to give it a name. Try it!

Move this to a new project

Name the project

Move and create project   Nevermind

Source: 37signals, LLC.

Archiving/Unarchiving

Archiving is a way to set aside a Basecamp project. It's helpful, especially if you begin to outgrow your current Basecamp project level. The archiving feature allows you to archive projects that you aren't using anymore so they don't count against the "total project account" of your Basecamp plan. This is another case for having projects like R + D that you keep around, and then more time-based Get It Done projects that you can clear out and archive.

To archive a project, access it so you see the standard project view.

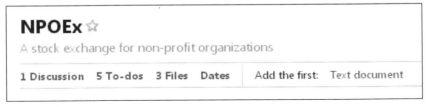

NPOEx ☆

A stock exchange for non-profit organizations

1 Discussion   5 To-dos   3 Files   Dates | Add the first: Text document

Source: 37signals, LLC.

And then scroll down to Project Settings and click on it.

⚙ Project settings...

Source: 37signals, LLC.

Note

The Project Settings link may only appear to the project creator.

Click the Archived radio button, and then click the Save Changes button.

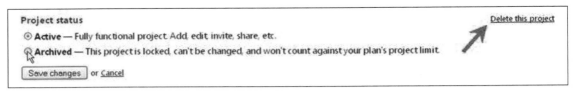

Project status   Delete this project

⊙ **Active** — Fully functional project. Add, edit, invite, share, etc.

○ **Archived** — This project is locked, can't be changed, and won't count against your plan's project limit.

[Save changes] or Cancel

Source: 37signals, LLC.

This is also where you can delete a project.

Then you see a view of the project with the following notice.

Source: 37signals, LLC.

When a project is archived, a link appears somewhere on the projects screen, indicating the existence of archived projects. You can then click on the archive link.

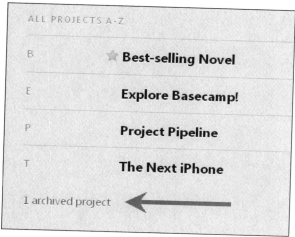

Source: 37signals, LLC.

Then select the project.

You see the banner indicating that the project is archived, and you can click the Project Settings link.

Source: 37signals, LLC.

Then you can click the Active radio button and Save Changes button to unarchive the project.

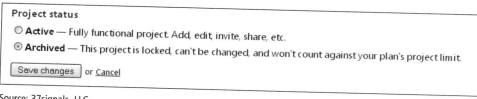

Source: 37signals, LLC.

Starring

Starring allows you to highlight particular projects so they appear at the top of particular views. To star a project, click on the small star in the upper-right corner, in the Icon view of a project.

Source: 37signals, LLC. © 2013 Cengage Learning®, All Rights Reserved.

Then you can see how a project you star appears at the top of a multiple project view, such as the Icon view.

Source: 37signals, LLC. © 2013 Cengage Learning®, All Rights Reserved.

QUESTIONS FOR CONSIDERATION/DISCUSSION

1. When might it be helpful to use the completion/notification method for working with tasks in Basecamp?

2. How do you delete a project?

3. How do you archive a project?

4. How do you restore a file that's been deleted?

5. What kind of value can brainstorming provide to a company or nonprofit organization?

6. Why is brainstorming important?

7. How can software like Basecamp make it easier for a company or organization to bring ideas to life?

8. Would you consider becoming a hero and helping someone or some company or organization to brainstorm? Calling all heroes!

See Appendix A, "Answers to Questions for Consideration/Discussion," for suggested answers.

CONCLUSION

Dear Reader,

Congratulations on making it through Chapter 11!

Wow! It feels like we're making real progress here.

In this chapter, we reviewed some additional features in Basecamp, and I've tried to introduce, and re-introduce, some excitement around the idea of brainstorming. You could spend endless amounts of time brainstorming but never end up setting things in motion. This might be an especially acute danger for creative people (like me). It's easy and fun to brainstorm, but it can be intimidating to know what to do next. Don't just be "an idea person" and give up on the idea of accomplishing your dreams because managing projects and taking concrete action seems out of reach or inaccessible. Brainstorming in Basecamp is cool because it offers a perfect setting to actually do something about those ideas. The move feature and the brainstorming exercise represent one of the most exciting opportunities for using Basecamp.

And, make no mistake, brainstorming isn't only for new ideas. You can use it for everyday projects, too. But brainstorming with to-dos in Basecamp is one of the easiest ways to jot things down and set things in motion, whether everyone's in the same room or people log in and add individual thoughts. May the brainstorm be ever in your favor!

And yes, I really do believe the bit about the opportunity to be a hero in the list of questions for discussion/consideration. I'm hoping that I may have captured a corner of your imagination with excitement, starting with keeping track of details, and turning project management into the stuff of superheroes. But if you consider and experience the difference that project management and brainstorming can make, "hero" isn't an understatement. You might find it really satisfying to master Basecamp and then help people in your organization or company do better. Heck, you might even discover that you can benefit other companies or organizations. It's not just a valuable role you can play in whatever your current situation is, but a value you can bring to others.

Part of the magic is how easy Basecamp is to use. I need to remind you, especially if you've never engaged in project management, especially if you haven't had experience in corporate or nonprofit realms, that it's common to find that project management is about the last thing people want to do. And it can be frustrating when there's not a good way to do it. But pure and simple, Basecamp is an *excellent* way to manage projects. Millions use it, and millions don't, and therein is the opportunity. Want to be part of something revolutionary? Learn Basecamp, use it, and help others use it.

Calling all superheroes!

Thanks for giving this book a chance and for playing along. I really hope it's useful and maybe even inspiring.

Regards,

Todd

P.S. So how'd I do with this chapter? Feel free to sound off at www.facebook.com/basecampbook.

CHAPTER 12

EXTRA FUN

In 140 Characters or Less

- Ch 12—A few additional fun things you can do, such as emailing content into a Basecamp project and using RSS to subscribe to a project.

In This Chapter

- Commenting on To-Do Lists
- Emailing Content to Basecamp Projects
- RSS: Subscribing to a Project
- Nourish: Getting an Email of RSS Activity
- Accessing Support
- Signing Up for the Email Newsletter
- Checking Out New Features

Why This Chapter Is Important

These are a few "extras" that are worth knowing about, in case you or someone you work with might end up wondering if it's possible to do *x, y,* or *z.* A couple of items in this chapter also relate to "learning how to learn." 37signals regularly improves its software, and it's likely that by the time you read this, there will be some new helpful features.

Knowing how to access support can always come in handy. Basecamp is easy enough to use that you may never have a question, but if you do, you have a few options.

COMMENTING ON TO-DO LISTS

A new feature of Basecamp is the ability to comment on to-do lists (in addition to being able to comment on individual to-do items). This might help in a variety of situations, allowing you to group tasks and comment in general on them, or generate discussion around a brainstorming list.

For example, as a personal or classroom exercise, you could invite people to contribute to a brainstorming to-do list by commenting on it and inviting people to either add to-do items or respond by email. When people respond by email, their comments are added to the list, and then someone can go through and add the to-do items. It's a quick way to gather information for a to-do list. You can also use this technique in other situations to gather information quickly and easily.

To comment on a to-do list, just click on the to-do's title.

Source: 37signals, LLC.

Then a standard discussion field appears below the list. You can click to add comments and use the standard functionality to notify people and companies and to attach files.

Source: 37signals, LLC.

Another scenario or exercise might be to attach a file to a blank to-do list and ask someone to go through and lift out the important information, like the most critical ideas, or whatever information you might want to "extract" from a document, and put it in a to-do list.

EMAILING CONTENT TO BASECAMP PROJECTS

Another nice new feature of Basecamp is the capability to use a simple email to create new project elements and add material to Basecamp. This might be appropriate for experienced users who want a quick way to send an email when they think of something or use their mobile device to send an email, without necessarily having to log into Basecamp.

Using this feature, you can do all this:

- Start discussions
- Make a to-do list
- Create a document
- Upload a file
- Forward an email

Here's how it works. Each project has a specially coded email address, and you use a special subject line for the type of content you want to add. There's a helpful set of descriptions for all the steps necessary for each type of content, built right into Basecamp and accessible from a convenient link.

To get started, access the desired project, scroll down to the bottom of the screen, and click the Email Content to This Project link.

Source: 37signals, LLC.

A wizard appears to guide you through the steps required to generate each kind of item.

Note

See the helpful "Questions" section on the wizard screen.

The common element to each approach is the email address, which appears in step 1. Then the wizard describes what steps you need to take to send an email to that address.

Source: 37signals, LLC.

People might want to know particularly about uploading files via email or forwarding emails to Basecamp. These can allow quick, easy connections to projects.

Another nice feature at the bottom of the wizard screen is a link you can click to add the email addresses for each Basecamp project to your address book (for example, to Outlook).

If you really want to rock and roll with this feature, you might want to try setting up templates for each type of email to make it easier to quickly use them.

Personal/Classroom Exercise: Wizard Cheat Sheet

As a personal learning or classroom exercise, I suggest walking through the wizard for each type of item so you can become familiar with it. Then try making some simple notes introducing each feature as a "cheat sheet" that you can share with colleagues.

Suggestion: Lunch and Learn

If you end up collaborating with other people on these new features and other aspects of Basecamp, you might want to introduce them to the program. You're certainly welcome to mention this book if you've found it helpful; you might also want to set up a "lunch and learn" and introduce various features of the program over one or more workshops. It might be a nice way to show people how powerful the program is and help them get more out of Basecamp. Some people might really appreciate knowing how to save time by doing something like forwarding an email into Basecamp. It's one more way for you to be a superhero. Woohoo!

RSS: Subscribing to a Project

RSS is a technology that creates a feed of a blog or other kinds of web content. The most common way people view feeds is through a special reader, such as Google Reader. A reader is an application that allows you to subscribe to a number of blogs and other sites and have their content easily drawn into one convenient place. For example, you can visit your favorite blogs using links and check them regularly, but a feed reader, or RSS reader, allows you to automatically get the content you're interested in as soon as it is available.

The RSS feature in Basecamp is a way of easily monitoring all the activity that happens in a project, without having to log in. A manager who wants to have an easy way to keep track of things would find this feature really helpful.

For more general information on RSS, see http://en.wikipedia.org/wiki/Rss.

To get the RSS link for a Basecamp project, access the project, scroll to the bottom, and click the RSS link.

Source: 37signals, LLC.

You then get a link, ending in .atom, which is considered the feed URL. You might need to log in with the same email address and password you use for Basecamp to access this link.

Google Reader is a popular RSS reader, but it doesn't support secure feeds. Because Basecamp is set up so that you have to have the right credentials to log in, you'd need to use something other than Google Reader. See the following article on the 37signals help site for more information: http://tinyurl.com/bc-rssfeed or http://help. 37signals.com/basecamp/questions/111-why-doesn-t-the-basecamp-rss-feed-work-with-bloglines-or-google-reader-or-firefox-safari-rss.

You can Google each of the products mentioned if you're interested, or you can try accessing the original help article if it is still available at either http://tinyurl. com/bcgreader or http://help.37signals.com/basecamp/questions/111-why-doesn-t-the-basecamp-rss-feed-work-with-bloglines-or-google-reader-or-firefox-safari-rss.

But FeedDemon is one option for PCs, and the preceding article mentions a Mac option as well. To check out FeedDemon, visit www.feeddemon.com.

Then try plugging your project feed (the link ending in .atom) into FeedDemon. It also *might* be possible to synchronize Google Reader with FeedDemon so that you can cobble together a solution by which you end up getting your Basecamp in Google Reader after all.

RSS can get a bit hinky. That is, it might require some tweaking, and it might not work for a variety of reasons. In theory, with FeedDemon and Basecamp, you should be able to try out RSS. Then again, you can contact support for Basecamp (support@37signals.com) if you have any issues, and they might be able to help you.

Nourish: Getting an Email of RSS Activity

Some hardy souls might want to explore whether to use a service called Nourish to take a feed of their Basecamp project and wrap it into an email that is automatically delivered. It's outside the scope of this book, but I thought I'd mention it anyway. Nourish is a cool service for bloggers and people who are into RSS. Not only can it draw together various RSS feeds for you, but it can be a way for a content creator to make a nice curated newsletter. It might even be easier than an RSS feed, because it was created to flatten the learning curve of RSS feeds for people who aren't familiar with them.

In the case of Basecamp, it might be possible to get things tweaked to the point where a manager could receive a regular email of all Basecamp activity.

Accessing Support

In the majority of situations, Basecamp is so easy to use and works so smoothly that you probably won't need to contact support. But if you do, you have a variety of options, including emailing support@37signals. I've found customer service to be competent and responsive. Thanks, 37signals!

You can also access support by logging into Basecamp and clicking the Support icon on the left.

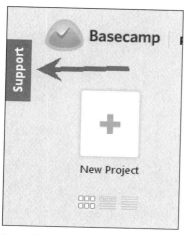

Source: 37signals, LLC.

You'll see various popular articles as well as a few options for contacting the support team.

Note

You might be tempted to Google a question. If you do, you might come up with an article or even a 37signals support article, but be aware that some of those articles are based on the Basecamp Classic version, whereas this book and the current product are focused on the new version.

SIGNING UP FOR THE EMAIL NEWSLETTER

Signing up for the email newsletter is a nice way to keep track of news and announcements. To sign up, log into Basecamp, and click the Support icon.

Then scroll to the bottom and click the Email Newsletter link.

Source: 37signals, LLC.

Type in your email address. (You can always unsubscribe if the emails become overwhelming. As with any other email newsletter you might receive, just look at the bottom for an unsubscribe link.)

Get Basecamp news via email

Email address:

[Subscribe] or Cancel

Source: 37signals, LLC.

CHECKING OUT NEW FEATURES

Another thing you might like to do is check the New Features link at the top of the Basecamp screen. You can review the full articles that 37signals created to discuss some of the new features mentioned in this chapter, such as commenting on to-do lists and emailing content.

Source: 37signals, LLC.

QUESTIONS FOR CONSIDERATION/DISCUSSION

1. How do you contact support?

2. Why would you want to email content to a Basecamp project?

3. Why would you want to comment on a to-do list?

See Appendix A, "Answers to Questions for Consideration/Discussion," for suggested answers.

CONCLUSION

Dear Reader,

Congratulations on making it through your twelfth chapter!

In this chapter, we reviewed some additional things you can do in Basecamp. I do recommend checking out the email newsletter.

In the final four chapters (that sounds nice, doesn't it?), we'll look at "going mobile" with Basecamp by using it on a mobile device; connecting the Basecamp calendar to a separate calendar system, such as Google Calendar; and then exploring two other excellent 37signals products that can enhance your Basecamp experience. Those additional products are Highrise, a CRM package (customer relationship/contact management), and Campfire, which provides secure chat rooms to facilitate remote collaboration.

As always, best wishes on your adventures in keeping track of details and learning how to use Basecamp.

Regards,

Todd

P.S. So how'd I do with this chapter? Feel free to sound off at www.facebook.com/basecampbook.

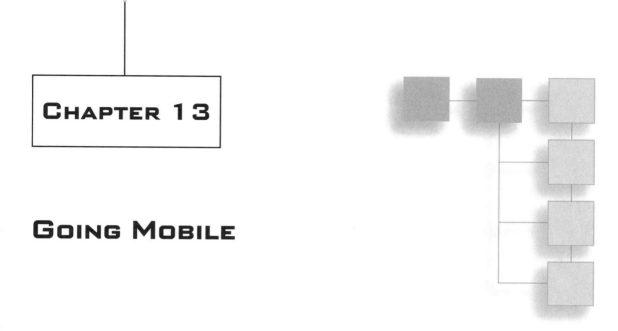

CHAPTER 13

GOING MOBILE

In 140 Characters or Less

- Ch 13—A quick visual tour of how Basecamp works on a sample mobile device (iPhone).

In This Chapter

- Accessing Basecamp
- Connecting Calendars
- Removing the Calendar
- Other Mobile Options, Including Email
- Classroom/Personal Exercise: Mobile Jamboree/Email Test

Why This Chapter Is Important

The new version of Basecamp is particularly mobile friendly, not just for iPhones, but for other devices as well. You might find it helpful to know some of the things you can do to use Basecamp on mobile devices, so this chapter provides a visual tour with some sample tasks. It's not exhaustive, but you'll see some of the things that work.

ACCESSING BASECAMP

You can go to 37signals.com and log in from there, but to get things rolling, you can also just email yourself a link to your Basecamp account/project and then access that link on your mobile device, which is what I did.

I included the link in an email to myself, sent from my laptop.

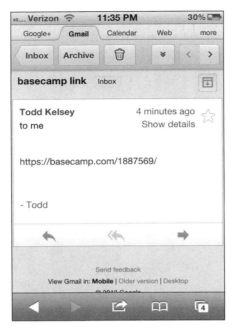

Source: 37signals, LLC.

Then I accessed the email on my iPhone and clicked on the link.

Next, I used the same login that I would on the regular site and clicked the Sign In button.

Source: 37signals, LLC.

The list of projects appears. Depending on how your device works with previewing a website, you might have to zoom in or out. I was able to tap on the Project icon to access it. (And I was holding the iPhone horizontal to get a bigger view.)

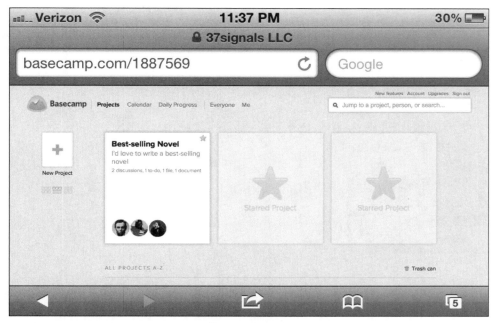

All the same, simple links appear in the Project view, and you can quickly see what's going on.

I tapped the Add This To-Do link. Activating the link may bring up an onscreen keyboard, depending on your device.

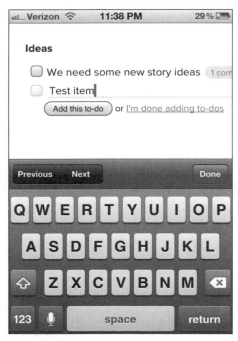

Source: 37signals, LLC.

At the present time, it doesn't seem like you can drag and drop a to-do item, but I think this has more to do with the iPhone's user interface limitations. Most mobile devices are designed to allow keyboard buttons or onscreen tapping for the selection of links, but I haven't seen a touch screen situation allowing tapping, holding, and dragging. (Feel free to correct me if I'm wrong, at http://facebook.com/basecampbook.)

Tapping and holding down a to-do item on an iPhone brings up the standard options for a link, such as just opening it as if you had tapped once without holding your finger down, or opening it in a new page.

Source: 37signals, LLC.

CONNECTING CALENDARS

In this section we discuss an example of connecting a calendar. You may be able to just navigate to the calendar section on the mobile site, or if you're on a device that lets you zoom in and out or hold it at a different angle, you might need to tweak the view to get what you want. Then you can access the Subscribe to iCal link if your device supports iCal. Apple devices support it; if you're on another device, your device might still support it, possibly without additional software, or possibly requiring an app. If you're not sure after Googling something like "(device name)" + "basecamp," you could try emailing support@37signals.com to ask about compatibility.

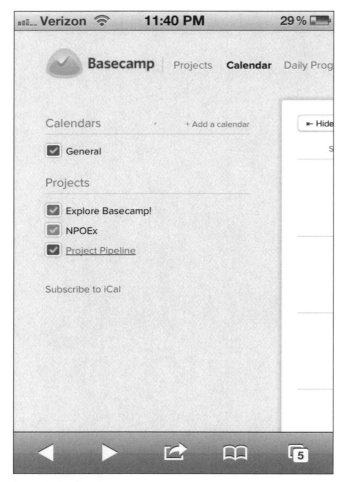

Source: 37signals, LLC.

You can access the Subscription link for either all calendars, or the calendar for the particular project you're interested in. What this does is allow you to access scheduled items (such as to-do items with a deadline) with your personal calendar on your mobile.

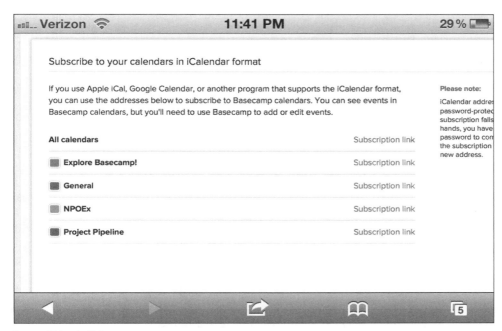

Source: 37signals, LLC.

Then you get a confirmation request like this.

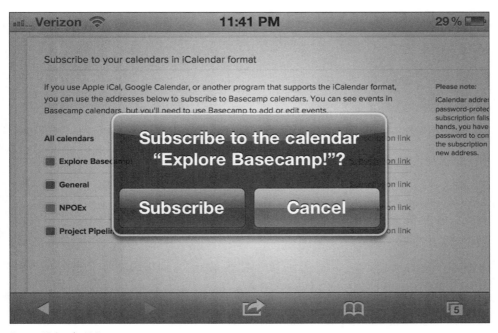

Source: 37signals, LLC.

After you click Subscribe, you can either switch to your calendar (View Events) or access the Done button to remain on that web page.

Source: 37signals, LLC.

If you look at the calendars, you see that an item has been added for a Basecamp calendar to take up residence on your phone.

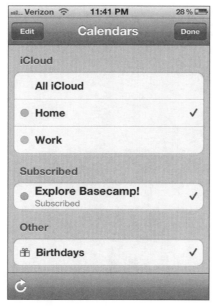

Source: 37signals, LLC.

REMOVING THE CALENDAR

The exact nature of removing an iCal subscription may vary depending on what device/software you are using, but this is how to do it on an iPhone.

The first step is to go to Settings.

Source: 37signals, LLC.

Access Mail, Contacts, Calendars.

Then access Subscribed Calendars.

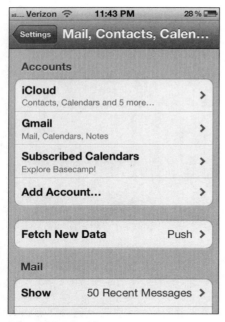

Source: 37signals, LLC.

From there, access the desired calendar.

There are various options, including removing alarms triggered by that specific calendar. You can also access the Delete Account button to get rid of the subscription.

Source: 37signals, LLC.

And that's the tour of a couple mobile features. My experience has been pretty good.

OTHER MOBILE OPTIONS, INCLUDING EMAIL

It's worth trying to access Basecamp from any mobile device that supports the web, just to see what's possible, but another guaranteed option that's universally compatible is to use the email address discussed in Chapter 12, "Extra Fun," to be able to add items easily to a Basecamp project.

In other words, although the mobile functionality is nice, if you're used to emailing on your mobile device, you might want to try the email address technique mentioned in Chapter 12. Maybe you'll find it easier to interact with Basecamp by sending an email. This means that any mobile device capable of sending email can at least "send" items into Basecamp to generate project items. That could make it easy to quickly add things as they occur to you. (And for hardy souls who like a piece of software called Siri, you might take the Siri challenge and try adding a project element entirely through voice. Then you can report on your adventure to http://facebook.com/basecampbook.)

Suggestion: Project as Contact

One way to make the email function easier is to create a contact on your phone, in your email software, or in your web-based email that you access on your phone and make the name of the contact the name of your project. And if you follow the steps in the previous chapter on obtaining the email address for your project, you could type in the email address and add it to your contact on your phone; then it's easier to get an email going. You'd still need to learn what to put in the subject line, but that might be fun and fruitful.

Suggestion: Short URL

This isn't a strictly mobile idea, but one option you do have for sharing URLs for accessing a specific Basecamp project is converting the address into a short URL.

For example, the long link to an example project in this book is https://basecamp.com/1887569/projects/689314-npoex.

But if you want to make it easier for someone to type the URL or remember the address, you can shorten it.

To do this, go to http://tinyurl.com.

Paste in your link, and click Make TinyURL. You're given a few coded letters at the end of the link. But the nice thing about TinyURL is that you can also type in a custom alias before you click the Make TinyURL button to make a more sensible, easier-to-remember link.

You end up with a link like this, which is a little more elegant and easier to type in: http://tinyurl.com/bc-npoex.

Keep in mind that if you go for a custom alias that's already being used, you might have to hunt around a bit for an available alias.

CLASSROOM/PERSONAL EXERCISE: MOBILE JAMBOREE/ EMAIL TEST

A suggestion for a personal or classroom learning exercise is to try accessing Base-camp on as many devices as possible, especially if you can gather a group of people together and then compare and discuss the experience. I invite you to then specifically go through the process of trying to send emails representing each of the possible project item types, discussed in the previous chapter, and have a challenge to add as much as you can from a mobile device. You might even make it a two-part challenge— once at work or in the classroom—and then have people try adding from home, the bus, the train, or wherever. (Don't do it while you're driving, of course. Doing anything on a mobile while you're driving is a bad idea that can result in significant injury and death. Just say no.)

QUESTIONS FOR CONSIDERATION/DISCUSSION

1. What's the value of being able to interact with Basecamp on a mobile device?

2. Why would you want to be able to email Basecamp?

3. How can interacting with Basecamp on a mobile help with remote collaboration?

See Appendix A, "Answers to Questions for Consideration/Discussion," for suggested answers.

CONCLUSION

Dear Reader,

Congratulations on making it through your thirteenth chapter. Woohoo! Thirteen down, three to go!

Thanks for taking a tour of some of the ways you can go mobile with Basecamp. It might not be that you want to use these features until you start using Basecamp more, but believe me, they could come in handy, especially if an idea occurs to you that you want to add to an official or personal brainstorm list. ::ding ding ding::

In the next chapter, we'll look more closely at connecting a calendar to Basecamp, and then we'll move on to Highrise and Campfire, two excellent products from 37signals that you might want to explore.

Best wishes on your adventures in going mobile and learning how to use Basecamp.

Regards,

Todd

P.S. So how'd I do with this chapter? Feel free to sound off at www.facebook.com/basecampbook.

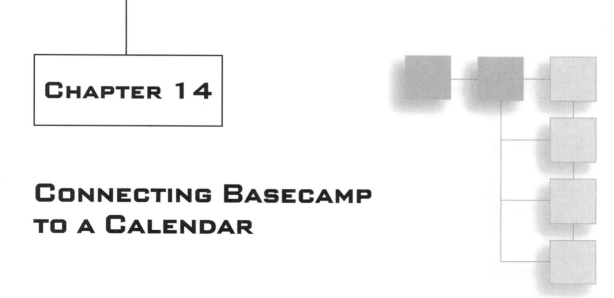

CHAPTER 14

CONNECTING BASECAMP TO A CALENDAR

In 140 Characters or Less

- Ch 14—Connecting Basecamp to a calendar so that you can add events from Basecamp to your calendar system.

In This Chapter

- Accessing the Webcal Link
- Subscribing to the Calendar in Google Calendar
- Removing the Subscription
- Basecamp > Outlook
- Personal/Classroom Exercise: Reminders

Why This Chapter Is Important

Basecamp users might want to subscribe to Basecamp calendars by connecting their calendar system of choice. We saw how this was possible on a mobile device, but it's also possible using other systems. The results will vary with the system, but tying scheduled items and deadlines into the main calendar system people use can provide another way for them to manage their involvement in a project.

In this chapter, Google Calendar is the main example, but we'll also briefly cover Outlook. Whether you use the calendar feature or not, it's probably a good idea to be familiar with it. The main value of going to the effort of learning how to use the Calendar is being able to track deadlines using your own calendar.

In general, even though it might take some effort, I do recommend exploring these options, because it might help you or someone you know be more effective in managing deadlines. Basecamp does generate notifications of a task, and those are helpful, but the real value of figuring out how to connect to your calendar system may be in setting reminders. You might want to try setting reminders on your mobile device, using the techniques discussed in Chapter 13, "Going Mobile," or you might want to try manually setting a reminder yourself when you get notification of a task. But having things *automatically* carried over can be nice.

Accessing the Webcal Link

Basecamp provides a link for each Basecamp project that lets you subscribe to the calendar. In Chapter 13, we saw how clicking on the link directly on a mobile device allowed a connection to Basecamp via the mobile device; in this case, we'll look at how to copy the link and take it into a calendar system.

If you don't use Google Calendar or you use Outlook but can't get this to work, try emailing support@37signals.com to see if you can get the details worked out. Chances are if you're trying a certain combination, someone else has also tried it, and that person might be able to help.

To access the calendar so you can get the Webcal link, log into Basecamp, and click on the Calendar link at the top of the screen; then click the Subscribe to iCal link on the left side.

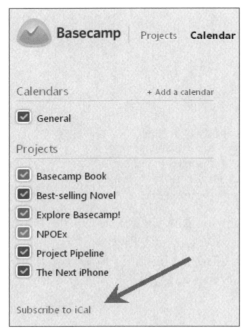

Source: 37signals, LLC.

You will have a list of calendars, including an All Calendars link that gives you everything. We'll be copying the link so that we can paste it into Google Calendar.

Note

Outlook users who want to try something similar may be able to use this technique.

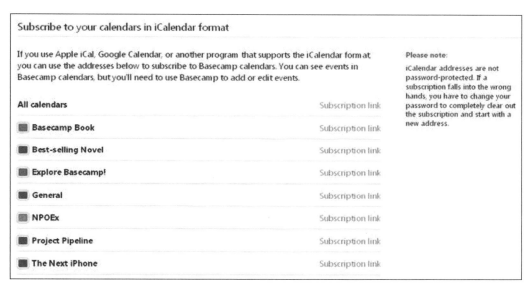

Source: 37signals, LLC.

To get the Webcal link, you need to roll over the desired Subscription link and hover there. Depending on how your browser is configured, you may see a preview of the link in your status bar.

Source: 37signals, LLC.

To copy the link, right-click, and then choose the option to copy the link into memory.

In Firefox, the option will probably be Copy Link Location.

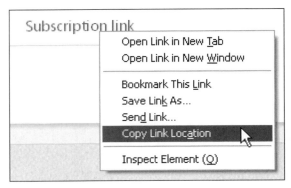

Source: 37signals, LLC.

In Chrome, it will probably be Copy Link Address.

Source: 37signals, LLC.

In Internet Explorer, it will probably be Copy Shortcut.

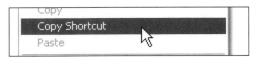

Source: 37signals, LLC.

Then, as I'll show in the next section, with the link now copied into your computer's memory, you will paste it into Google Calendar. Or you might try pasting it into an email that you send to your email address that you access in Outlook. (See the later mention of Outlook in this chapter.)

Note

If you open another program, the link might stay in memory, or you might need to come back and get it in Basecamp. You might want to try opening up Basecamp in one window and Google Calendar in another, or learning how to open up each in different tabs in your browser.

Subscribing to the Calendar in Google Calendar

Google Calendar is a good general-purpose system for keeping track of events. Using Google Calendar, you can schedule reminders that generate emails or even set up text messages to send to your phone. Google Calendar works pretty well on many mobile devices. Using it is as simple as starting a free Gmail account at http://mail.google.com and accessing the Calendar link.

To access Google Calendar, sign into Gmail and click the Calendar link at the top of the screen.

Source: Google.Org™.

Next, on the bottom left, click the little downward-pointing triangle next to Other Calendars, and on the pop-up menu, click Add by URL.

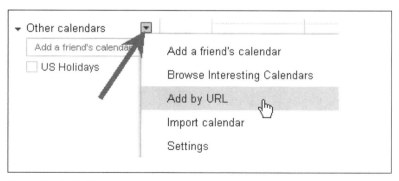

Source: Google.Org™.

Then paste in the Webcal link, and click Add Calendar.

Add by URL   ✕

URL: webcal://basecamp.com/1887569/calendar_feeds/p7(

If you know the address to a calendar (in iCal format), you
can type in the address here.

☐ Make the calendar publicly accessible?

[**Add Calendar**] [Cancel]

Source: Google.Org™.

The project calendar appears in a list of Other Calendars.

▾ Other calendars   ▾

Add a friend's calendar

■ Basecamp Book

☐ US Holidays

Source: Google.Org™.

The way items with due dates from Basecamp appear in Google Calendar depends on the way your calendar is set to be viewed. For example, in some views, they may appear at the top of the column for that day. (See where "2 events" falls in the next graphic.)

	Sun 7/8	Mon 7/9	Tue 7/10	Wed 7/11	Thu 7/12	Fri 7/13	Sat 7/14
GMT-06					2 events	3 events	
12am							
1am							

Source: Google.Org™.

If you click on them, you see a preview of the items.

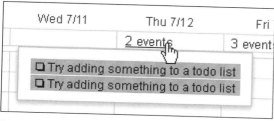

Source: Google.Org™.

Then if you click on the individual items, they open up similarly to Google Calendar items.

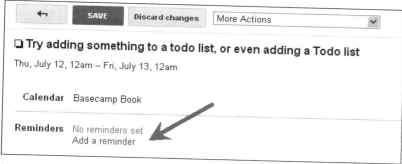

Source: Google.Org™.

Depending on how you like to work with Google Calendar, you could click Add a Reminder to let yourself know of an upcoming item. (In the Month and Agenda views, you might have to click More Details to get there.)

Another thing you might like to do is to click on the More Actions drop-down menu and copy the individual item to your main Google Calendar. (Again, in the Month or Agenda views, click More Details to get to the More Actions option.)

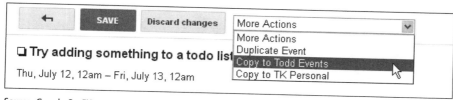

Source: Google.Org™.

For more information and a general introduction on how to use Google Calendar, try http://support.google.com/calendar.

REMOVING THE SUBSCRIPTION

To remove a subscription to a Basecamp calendar, in Google Calendar, click on the Other Calendars pop-up menu, and choose Settings.

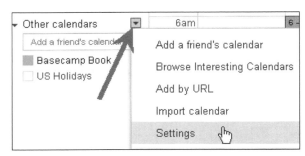

Source: Google.Org™.

Then find the desired calendar, and click Unsubscribe.

Source: Google.Org™.

Special thanks to http://tinyurl.com/johnical for the original hint to some of the steps in this section.

BASECAMP > OUTLOOK

You might be able to subscribe to Basecamp calendars in Outlook using a plug-in (an add-on, like a third-party accessory to the program). Because there are so many variables, I recommend doing a Google search on "Basecamp" + "Outlook _____" (where the underlined space is the version you're using, such as a number or year).

Note

Do use the quotation marks and the plus sign in the search. They tell Google that you want search results with both words.

Another technique is to contact support@37signals.com and ask for help. The support team will want to know what calendar system or version of Outlook you're using. They might know of a plug-in, app, or add-on that might help.

For more recent versions of Outlook, you may be able to take the Webcal link mentioned in the previous section and send it in an email to the address you use with Outlook. When you open the email, click on the link. Ideally, you'll get a request to confirm opening of the link and then an option that says Add This Internet Calendar to Outlook and Subscribe to Updates.

For more information on this technique, try going to either of the following two links (same destination) and looking for the section "Add an Internet Calendar Subscription to Outlook." (They have the same destination; note my use of the TinyURL technique covered previously in this book.)

http://office.microsoft.com/en-us/outlook-help/view-and-subscribe-to-internet-calendars-HA010167325.aspx

http://tinyurl.com/outlook-ical

Even though it might take some doing, I recommend exploring this option, because it might help you be more effective in managing deadlines if you use Outlook as your primary calendar management tool. Basecamp does generate notifications of a task, but the main value of figuring out how to connect to your calendar system may be in setting reminders. You might like to try doing this on your mobile device, using the techniques discussed in Chapter 13. Or maybe you'd like to try manually setting a reminder when you are notified of a task. But having things *automatically* carried over can be nice.

Also, if you have Outlook, depending on the version, it may be possible to take an email you get from Basecamp and simply drag it down to the lower-left corner of the screen, where you will probably have something like this, with or without the Calendar text.

Source: Google.Org™.

Dragging an email in Outlook onto the Calendar icon can automatically open an event so that you can schedule an event or a reminder to perform the task.

PERSONAL/CLASSROOM EXERCISE: REMINDERS

I invite you to consider your method of remembering how and when to do things. Some people manage tasks by keeping open items in their email Inbox; I've done this before and still sometimes do it. Over time I've gravitated toward keeping a list of open items I'm working on in a simple text editor, but I've also found setting reminders to be helpful. Sometimes I manually set them in Google Calendar or on my mobile device. In corporate situations where I've needed to use Outlook, I've done it there.

Many companies are increasingly using Google Apps, including Google Calendar, as a cost-effective alternative to Microsoft Outlook. In a personal or corporate situation in which Google Calendar is used, I would try to subscribe to Basecamp to have a feed of items coming into the calendar and keep my eye on it. I might also contact 37signals or look for a plug-in or add-on that helps to make the process easier. In addition, I might look for a more sophisticated solution using a plug-in or add-on for Outlook, especially if a lot of people were going to be using Basecamp.

In any case, I would probably supplement this by manually setting reminders for myself using Google Calendar, or Outlook, as the case might be, and possibly my mobile device, just as a heads up that something is coming due.

Even with all the bells and whistles, Basecamp, Outlook, and Google Calendar won't do the work for you. One of the best things you can do is make logging into Basecamp one of your daily habits to see what's going on, see how things are going, and see if there's anything you need to do. You could still connect things in the calendar, but you would keep track of things in Basecamp.

For the personal/classroom exercise, think about how you manage things you have to keep track of, things you need to do, and experiment with connecting calendars. This exercise might happen over time. Perhaps you'll discover that logging into Basecamp is the best way for you to keep track of what you need to do.

You can also use Basecamp to make your own to-do lists of things you need to accomplish, even if you're in a shared space.

To-do lists are good for prioritization. Basecamp is effective at managing personal to-dos just as much as project to-dos. Email can work, too, but it's really easy for things to get buried there. (Personal learners or classrooms might like to try having people set up their own "personal" projects, including making to-do lists of what they need to accomplish.)

Also, if you like simplicity, the simplest thing to do might be to set a daily reminder for yourself—"check Basecamp"—and then just make that the way you keep track of items that need doing.

This exercise, in a classroom or personal setting, might be best termed an experiment; try a few things, and see what works best for you. In corporate situations, each person may come to a different conclusion or come up with helpful suggestions that could benefit others.

Best wishes!

Questions for Consideration/Discussion

1. What's the value of being able to import Basecamp calendar items into a calendar system like Outlook or Google Calendar?

2. What are some ways you can remind yourself of things you need to do in Basecamp?

3. How can you get in the habit of checking Basecamp on a regular basis to see what you need to do?

See Appendix A, "Answers to Questions for Consideration/Discussion," for suggested answers.

Conclusion

Dear Reader,

Congratulations on making it through your fourteenth chapter!

In this chapter, we reviewed some calendar techniques and discussed getting in the habit of using Basecamp.

This milestone marks the official end of coverage of Basecamp specifically. Congratulations!

But wait, there's more!

In the next two chapters, we'll look at two related Basecamp products for which you can also start free trials: Highrise, for managing contacts/customer relationships; and Campfire, for group chat sessions. Highrise may be helpful for follow-up with people you interact with, and Campfire can provide a nice alternative to other chat systems for carrying on secure real-time communication. Both are worth looking into.

Best wishes on your adventures in keeping track of details and calendars and learning how to use Basecamp.

Regards,

Todd

P.S. So how'd I do with this chapter? Feel free to sound off at www.facebook.com/basecampbook.

CHAPTER 15

MANAGING CONTACTS AND FOLLOW-UP WITH A FREE HIGHRISE ACCOUNT

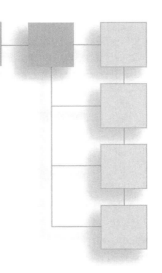

In 140 Characters or Less

- Ch 15—A look at Highrise, a popular tool that integrates with Basecamp, helping you to manage contacts and follow-up. A "Simple CRM" tool.

In This Chapter

- Q: What the Heck Is CRM? A: A Tool for Following Up
- Exploring Highrise
- Taking a Tour
- Why Highrise?
- Plans and Pricing: Starting a Free Account
- Personal/Classroom Exercise: Business Card Party
- Accessing Highrise
- Trying Things Out
- Adding a Contact
- The Art of Following Up
- Cases
- Deals
- Personal/Classroom Exercise: Add a Contact and Follow Up
- Going Mobile

Why This Chapter Is Important

Highrise is a powerful, easy-to-use tool from 37signals that can help even the smallest business or individual keep track of contacts and follow up with people. Similar to the same way that Basecamp ensures that details don't fall through the cracks, Highrise ensures that people and opportunities don't fall through the cracks.

If you're like me, occasionally you meet people who might share an interest, and perhaps they give you a business card. Do you have a pile of business cards from people you haven't followed up with?

In December 2011, I spoke at a TedX conference about the important idea of developing a stock exchange for nonprofit organizations. (If you like, check out the short video of my TedX presentation at http://tinyurl.com/npoexvid.) I've been so busy (sound familiar?) that I haven't gotten around to following up with the people who expressed an interest after the presentation by offering me their business cards.

Highrise is definitely worth looking into because it allows you to capture conventional contact information and provides tools for setting things in motion regarding those contacts, just like Basecamp does for details. Highrise doesn't do the work for you, but it provides the next best thing: an easy-to-use environment for capturing information and then acting on it. Highrise is integrated with Basecamp, as you'll see. When you're logged into Basecamp, Highrise appears at the top of the screen, and vice versa. For example, you might enter a new contact in Highrise, set yourself a reminder to follow up with that person, and then click over to a related project in Basecamp. Or you might work on a Basecamp project that includes a high-level item—such as following up with interested parties, or brainstorming a list of people you could contact—and then flip over to Highrise and use it as a tool for capturing the contact information and acting on it.

In addition to being immediately useful to anyone with a need for managing contacts and follow-up, Highrise happens to be a powerful customer relationship management (CRM) tool. Like Basecamp, it's simple and powerful. If you're in sales, you might already have a CRM tool in place. But if you don't, consider Highrise, especially if you are a small or medium-sized company trying to figure out new strategies for following up with people.

Q: What the Heck Is CRM?
A: A Tool for Following Up

Regardless of your position within a company or organization, it's highly likely you'll need to follow up with people at some point. CRM has evolved so that, instead of just keeping contact information of potential or existing customers, you have ways of taking notes about them so you can be sensitive to their interests and their history with the company. A sales rep might gather business cards at a conference and then follow up with a brochure or sales material. The Highrise CRM tool enhances this experience by allowing the rep to take notes on existing customers, such as when they call in for support.

If you work in a nonprofit organization, you can use CRM for information on volunteers, donors, and potential donors.

Even if you're in a corporate or nonprofit organizations where other CRM tools are used, it won't hurt to look at Highrise. This is especially true if you're not part of the sales force, because it might be helpful for you to follow up on opportunities for collaboration.

Speaking of collaboration, if you have more than one person to work with, multiple people can access the tool and use it for keeping track of opportunities, clients, and customers, and they can share the list of contacts. Having a central tool can be helpful for developing a history of conversations, notes, and files.

A number of tools, integrations, and apps have evolved around Highrise, allowing you to use information from Highrise in another tool, import it, or share it.

Highrise is people centered. And any individual project, group project, organization, or company could benefit from a tool that makes it easier to be people centered.

Exploring Highrise

This section introduces several of the excellent intros and tours that 37signals provides to help you get a sense of what you can accomplish with Highrise. Review this section, and then go on the site and check out some of the materials at http://37signals.com/.

Source: 37signals, LLC.

Then click on the Highrise icon. You can also go to http://highrisehq.com.

This page offers general information on the software and has a link in the upper-right corner for logging in once you have an account.

Source: 37signals, LLC.

Of course, 37signals isn't perfect, but it makes great products. I appreciate the kind of data that's shown here. Seven million happy customers can't be wrong!

Source: 37signals, LLC.

You can click on the add-on link from the earlier page, or you can visit http://highrisehq.com/extras directly for some of the additional options.

Some companies use tools to help them leverage Highrise by tying it into customer support systems.

Source: 37signals, LLC.

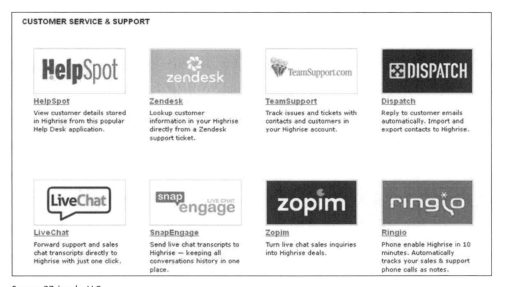

Source: 37signals, LLC.

Then, of course, there are opportunities for integrating with sales and marketing.

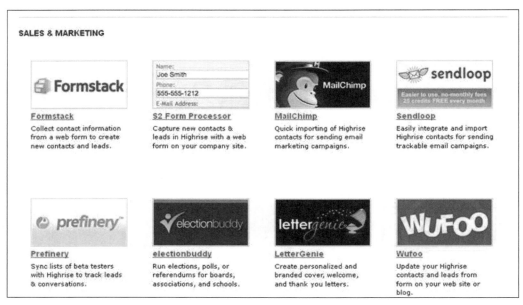

Source: 37signals, LLC.

There are further opportunities for integrating with business productivity and reporting.

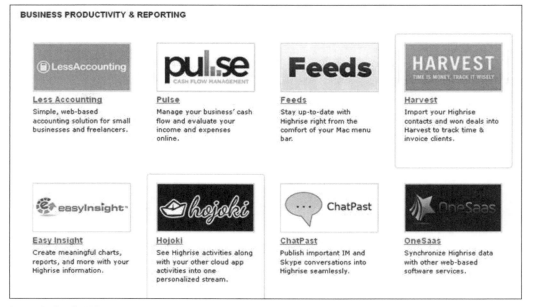

Source: 37signals, LLC.

TAKING A TOUR

You might have more fun going directly on a tour of Highrise. To do so, visit http://highrisehq.com/extras and click the Tour link at the top, or just visit http://highrisehq.com/tour directly.

Source: 37signals, LLC.

Highrise has brief, concise visuals that enable you to just scroll down the page to get a sense of what you can do with the tool. As you're scrolling down, try clicking the Audio/Video Tour link.

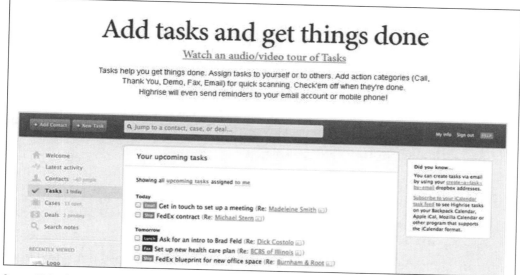

Source: 37signals, LLC.

In addition to the straightforward contact management features of Highrise, more sophisticated tools are oriented toward sales of services or products, which salespeople will particularly appreciate.

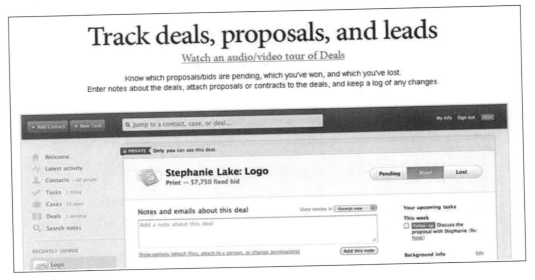

Source: 37signals, LLC.

The Tour page includes more of these visual intros, where you can also take the video tour. Frankly, I think it might be a helpful set of information for anyone to review, just to become more familiar with the kinds of things that are done in business. You can learn from it by looking at how the need for a tool has given rise to products like Highrise. It's a good personal learning exercise to broaden your horizons, and it should make professors proud as well.

Why Highrise?

When you have a chance, I recommend looking at the "Why Highrise" section of the site, at http://highrisehq.com/why.

This section can help you understand some of the traditional uses of Highrise. Highrise is relevant even if you're not in a corporate setting, because it can help you manage contacts. Don't be overwhelmed by all the options. This includes beginners who are starting to venture out with their own business and working through the challenge of doing a little bit of everything themselves. If you fall into this category, focus on what you do best, and hire others to do the rest. Said another way, if you're a visionary, focus on the vision and wear multiple hats when you don't have the option, but whenever you can, work toward collaborating or hiring people to focus on areas you don't have time for. One of those areas might be CRM, but you can still use Highrise to capture some of your early opportunities.

I'd also like to suggest for beginners, as well as students, that you explore things in a tool like Highrise incrementally. That is, don't feel like you have to know everything about CRM to use it. Just think of it as a way to manage contacts, and try some of the features shown in this chapter. You might think of Basecamp and Highrise as career-long tools that you can become familiar with and put in your toolbox.

PLANS AND PRICING: STARTING A FREE ACCOUNT

Convinced that Highrise is worth looking at? Cool. Look for the plans and pricing link on http://highrisehq.com, or if you're on one of the other interior pages on the site, look for the Plans and Pricing link at the top.

Or just go to http://highrisehq.com/signup.

Here are the prices for Highrise at the time of writing, but note that these may change by the time you read this. In the fine print, where I've placed the arrow, note that there's also a free plan.

Source: 37signals, LLC.

It's my hope that 37signals will continue to offer an entirely free plan. If you don't see that link, I recommend starting a free trial. You might set a goal of getting 250 contacts in the free version, which is the limit. I bet that a fair percentage of you have at least 100 business cards sitting around in various drawers.

Click on the Free Plan link, or start a free trial if there's no longer a fully free version. Then click the Sign In Here link on the next screen. That allows you to sign in with your Basecamp account to get started with Highrise.

You're just 60 seconds away from your new Highrise account.

Already have a Basecamp, Highrise, Backpack or Campfire account?
Sign in here to skip this form and use the username you already have.

A few details and you're on your way

First name [   ]

Last name [   ]

Email [   ]

Company [   ]
(Or non-profit, organization, group, school, etc.)

Source: 37signals, LLC.

Go ahead and enter your login/password that you use with Basecamp to get your Highrise account started and integrated with your Basecamp account.

Already use a 37signals product?

Basecamp

Highrise

Backpack

Campfire

Sign in below with the username and password you already have from your existing Basecamp, Highrise, Backpack or Campfire account.

Username [   ]

Password [   ]
I forgot my username or password

[Sign in] or Cancel

Source: 37signals, LLC.

You get a message like this. You can continue filling out information.

You're just 60 seconds away from your new Highrise account.

Hi Todd, (I'm not Todd)

You already have a 37signals ID because you use Basecamp.

After your account is created, you can sign in with the same **username and password** that you use with your Basecamp account.

Source: 37signals, LLC.

The company name you enter will become part of the address of your account. If you don't have a company, just make up a name. You could also try leaving it blank and seeing what happens.

A few details and you're on your way

Company CFTW
(Or non-profit, organization, group, school, etc.)

Got a referrer?

You have selected the Free plan. There is no time limit on the free plan — you can use it for free as long as you'd like. You can always upgrade to a paying plan later if you need file uploading, more cases, more contacts, etc.

By clicking **Create my account** you agree to the Terms of Service, Privacy, and Refund policies.

Create my account

Source: 37signals, LLC.

Then click the Create My Account button. After reading the confirmation message, click the OK, Let's Go button.

You're all set, Todd. Thanks!
You may want to bookmark this page so you can come back to it later. We've also sent you an email with a link to get back here.

OK, let's go!

Source: 37signals, LLC.

Personal/Classroom Exercise: Business Card Party

Have a business card party! Make it a two-step party, and go through your business cards and then throw them in recycling. First, find the people and invite them to connect on LinkedIn. Are you on LinkedIn? Start a LinkedIn account at www.linkedin.com if you don't have one already—especially if you're a student. It's never too early to start building your career network. LinkedIn is becoming the de facto way to network, and it's an increasingly common way to find job opportunities.

Once you're up and running on LinkedIn, you can have a business card party with all your contacts from various business cards. First, find the people and invite them to connect on LinkedIn. Second, enter their information into Highrise. (Or enter the information into Highrise first.) Now it's business card party time! (P.S. It would be amusing if someone had a business card party at work over lunch, took a picture of the pile of business cards that everyone went through, and posted it on http://facebook.com/basecampbook.)

If you hit the ceiling of the free Highrise version, consider the paid one. Or input your contact information and start trying to follow up with people. Individuals may want to get the contact info in the system and then have a spouse, partner, or friend work on following up on people. Tag team! Classrooms might like to simulate something like this by having one student enter in some contacts, whether those contacts are other students or professors. And then the other student in the two-person team could try following up.

Accessing Highrise

After you sign up, you get an email from 37signals with a helpful link and some other information. Your link will have a format like this in your browser:

> https://cftw2.highrisehq.com/welcome

You can shorten it as shown here and make it your login link:

> https://cftw2.highrisehq.com

Or you can just visit the main Highrise site at http://highrisehq.com/ and click the Sign In button.

Trying Things Out

So let's take a look! Looking at Highrise has a familiar, simple, friendly look and vibe. Upon sign-in, you'll notice the general areas of Highrise on the left. That's where you'll find the two common functions of adding a contact and adding a new task. Then there's a central area with a Get Started link and some introductory information.

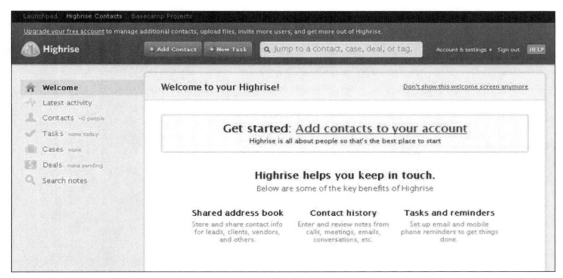

Source: 37signals, LLC.

When you start a Highrise account, your menu options expand at the top, so you can easily flip back and forth between Basecamp and Highrise. Cool! Click Basecamp Projects.

And boom! You're back in Kansas—I mean Basecamp.

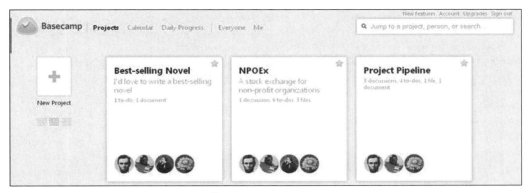

Source: 37signals, LLC. © 2013 Cengage Learning®, All Rights Reserved.

ADDING A CONTACT

To get started with going through that pile of business cards, click the Add Contacts to Your Account link in the Get Started area.

Source: 37signals, LLC.

Or if you don't have it, click the Add Contact button.

Source: 37signals, LLC.

Then just start entering information. You can always come back and add more later, but there are spaces for the most common kinds of high-level contact information for people to get the file rolling.

🏠 Welcome	**Add a new person** or <u>add a new company</u>
〰 Latest activity	
👤 **Contacts** ~0 people	**First name** Freelancer
✓ Tasks none today	**Last name** Dude
🖼 Cases none	**Title** Add a title
💲 Deals none pending	**Company** Add a company
🔍 Search notes	**Phone** Add a phone number
	Email Add an email address
	IM Add an instant message account
	Websites Add a website address
	Address Add an address

Source: 37signals, LLC.

Notice on the right side of the screen some other ways to bring information into Highrise. It's helpful to know about these options. In certain cases, you might be able to export information from another tool, in a format like CSV or Excel, even if that tool isn't in this list.

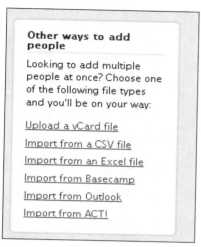

Source: 37signals, LLC.

Other information you can enter includes custom fields that you can set up, such as whom a potential customer may have been referred by, or a customer ID field, as well as social media URLs and high-level background information.

Source: 37signals, LLC.

When you're ready, click Add This Person.

Then you might like to try adding a note about the person by clicking in the Add a Note field, typing in some information, and clicking the Add This Note button.

Source: 37signals, LLC.

You start to see how easy it is to capture background information that could be help-ful for following up with this person in the future, either for you or for someone else who is following up on your behalf.

Next, you might want to click the Add a Followup Task link to see how you can actually keep yourself accountable to follow up.

Source: 37signals, LLC.

For example, you might tell yourself to follow up, look at the contact's LinkedIn pro-file, or invite the contact on LinkedIn. You can click the When's It Due drop-down menu to set a reminder timeline, and then click the Add This Task button.

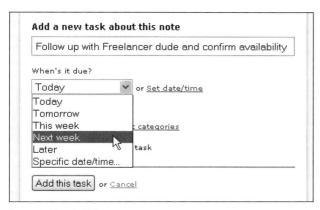

Source: 37signals, LLC.

Being able to add a task when you're creating a contact is nice, because it allows you to take action on the contact or at least set a reminder to do so. This immediacy is what prevents people from falling through the cracks.

The task shows up on the main screen on the right. It appears as something you have to do, and then you get an email reminder.

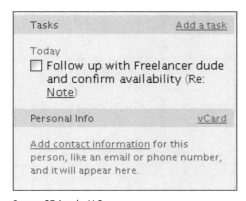

Source: 37signals, LLC.

When you're making contacts, you might also like to try the LinkedIn tab.

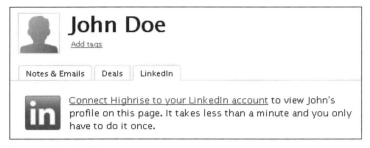

Source: 37signals, LLC.

It's a good idea to connect your LinkedIn account to Highrise so it's easier to work between the two programs. By the way, regardless of whether you already have a LinkedIn account, you're welcome to invite me as a LinkedIn contact. In fact, as a personal learning or classroom exercise, if you don't have a LinkedIn account yet, it's now homework! To invite me, look for "Todd Kelsey" on LinkedIn, or just search under my email address, which is tekelsey@gmail.com. In a nutshell, LinkedIn is important because the network of people you meet and are acquainted with can help you find work and opportunities. LinkedIn can connect the dots between you and someone at a company you want to contact. It can also be a way for recruiters to find *you*. As an example, I just had a phone interview today for a position that came about because a recruiter was on LinkedIn, came across my profile, and said, "Hey, would you be interested in this position?" And I said, "Heck yeah!"

Source: 37signals, LLC. © 2013 Cengage Learning®, All Rights Reserved.

So when you make the initial connection, enter your LinkedIn login and password, and click the OK, I'll Allow It button.

The nice thing about this LinkedIn connection is that, depending on how much information you include as you're entering in a contact, Highrise can suggest the profile of the person you want to link into Highrise.

Source: 37signals, LLC.

Then Highrise pulls in a bit more information.

Source: 37signals, LLC.

If you click the Visit link, you can see more information about the person. You don't have to connect to the person on LinkedIn to see background information. In general, the way LinkedIn works is that you meet someone, and say, "Hey, let's connect on LinkedIn," and they generally frown on contacting someone out of the blue and asking them to connect (though some people are totally fine with this out of the blue). But depending on how you're using Highrise, you might identify people you want to contact, even if you haven't met them, and make their profile easily accessible so you can see more background information.

Especially for people you meet—and for the business card party that I invited you to have earlier—this little technique of linking Highrise and LinkedIn can be great. Highrise can help you follow up with people, and you can use the LinkedIn steps just discussed to find the right profile.

Clicking the little Visit link brings you right into LinkedIn, where you can then click the Connect button.

This is the kind of thing you might want to do if you met someone and exchanged business cards. The more you follow up on connecting with people on LinkedIn, the stronger your LinkedIn network will be. Keep in mind that what goes around comes around. I certainly urge you to consider how you might be able to help other people connect to someone you know.

Note

> When you send an invitation to connect on LinkedIn, you can add a little message and indicate how you are acquainted with the person (such as "we've done business together") and then choose a company you worked with. But there's also an Other option, if connecting with the person doesn't fall neatly into one of the prescribed categories. When you choose that option, you generally need to plug in the person's email address to demonstrate that you know them. So having that email address in your Highrise contact can help you connect.

If you end up visiting a LinkedIn profile that turns out to be the wrong person, in Highrise, you can click Edit This Person on the contact page.

And then in the Social Networks area, you can just select and delete the link to the specific LinkedIn profile.

Source: 37signals, LLC.

Then you can click the Save This Person button.

Sweet! Okay, now we'll try thinking about the art of following up, and then we'll try adding a general task in Highrise.

THE ART OF FOLLOWING UP

At a high level, many businesses have extensive strategies and entire departments devoted to follow-up. For example, sales organizations might define potential custo-mers as prospects, or leads, and sales people might then follow up and send more information about a product.

For a small business or a nonprofit organization, following up can be just as important. In a way, you could think of Highrise as "Basecamp for customers/clients." Highrise allows you to be people centered by keeping notes and contact information. And, like Basecamp, it allows you to set things in motion.

Highrise is scalable, just as Basecamp is.

Collaborating: Pooled Resources

Another thing worth considering is the idea that Highrise, like Basecamp, is collaborative. So one feature is a shared address book, where different users can contribute toward the information about a particular contact or client. When that customer/client contacts you, there's a ready supply of information, or you could have multiple people accessing this shared information for follow-up.

Adding a Task

Okay, so let's add a general task in Highrise. It could be just about anything. Frankly, I think there should be an entire book on Highrise (feel free to chime in on this at http://facebook.com/basecampbook), but in the space we have here, I'll just say that when you start establishing a routine for following up with people, there can be any number of tasks you might like to schedule as part of it.

To do this in Highrise, just click on the New Task button.

Source: 37signals, LLC.

Then try adding a new task, such as "send more information" or "invite to lunch."

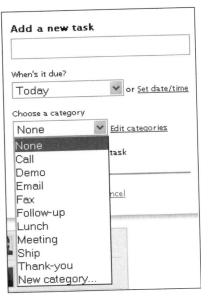

Source: 37signals, LLC.

The Choose a Category drop-down menu is helpful, because it might allow you to sort your tasks easily and work through a number of tasks at the same time—or pass them along to someone else.

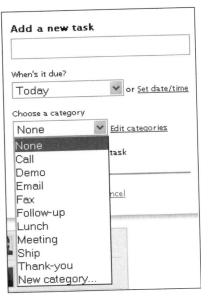

Source: 37signals, LLC.

The Category drop-down menu can also help beginners consider the kinds of follow-up that might occur:

- **Call**—You might want to call the person to inquire how he's doing, see if he'd like to talk further, confirm interest, or invite him to something.

- **Demo**—If you have a product or service, sometimes follow-up includes scheduling a demonstration.

- **Email**—Send the person an email to convey information, a document, or an opportunity.

- **Fax**—Yes, some people still use fax machines. I'd love to hear the response from a professor asking his class, "Who knows what a fax is?" or, "Has anyone ever sent a fax?" I'm curious whether we've reached the point of certain generations never encountering the term before or never sending one. Feel free to relate the results on http://facebook.com/basecampbook.

- **Follow-Up**—This is a general "bucket" for follow-up, as you define it.

- **Lunch**—"Let's have lunch" is a common way to establish business relationships.

- **Meeting**—"Let's meet" is another common way to establish and maintain relationships.

- **Ship**—Someone might have requested a product, sample, or some other material. Yes, people still use conventional mail services to send physical products. Not *everything* is emailed.

- **Thank-You**—This is one of the most important as far as I'm concerned. Follow-up on job interviews and meetings might be as simple as, "Thanks for taking the time to talk," or "Thanks for your thoughts."

- **New Category**—You might want to make your own categories of tasks.

Categories can help with tasks by allowing you to sort your tasks. As an example, if you had a few emails to send out or calls to make, you could tackle all those at the same time.

CASES

In Highrise, another high-level category is Cases, which appears on the left navigation.

Cases—as in briefcases—allow you to gather anything that might be related to a contact in one relevant place. This feature makes it easy to find things when you or another person might need to come back and have some contact. For example, you might get a PDF about some product or opportunity, and then a month later the person emails and says, "What did you think?" Instead of trying and maybe failing to find the original email with the file in it, you could just look up that contact in Highrise and, because of Cases, access the PDF. Sweet.

Cases keep it together.
Cases help you keep related emails, notes, files, images, and contacts together on one screen. A case is basically like a virtual file folder.

⊕ Add your first case

Source: 37signals, LLC.

DEALS

Deals is a commonly used function of Highrise involving situations that require you to propose something to a potential client or customer. Generally, in such a process, you have as many proposals and bids as possible in a pipeline, and either you or someone else might like to have a central place to be able to look at relevant files.

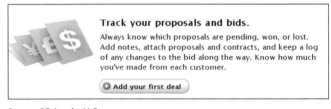

Track your proposals and bids.
Always know which proposals are pending, won, or lost. Add notes, attach proposals and contracts, and keep a log of any changes to the bid along the way. Know how much you've made from each customer.

⊕ Add your first deal

Source: 37signals, LLC.

PERSONAL/CLASSROOM EXERCISE: ADD A CONTACT AND FOLLOW UP

After this whirlwind tour of Highrise, I still think the Business Card Party is probably the most helpful for getting going, to get people to bring in business cards (if you're in a group), or digging them up yourself, but you don't *have* to do that. You might consider just trying to add a contact or two and a follow-up task and see how it works. Then keep it in mind for opportunities that come up.

GOING MOBILE

You can try working on Highrise on the site from your mobile device. There's also a free iPhone app located at http://highrise.comhq/iphone.

QUESTIONS FOR CONSIDERATION/DISCUSSION

1. What does CRM stand for?

2. What does Highrise help with that goes beyond just having people's contact information in your email program?

3. Do you have to be a salesperson to be able to use Highrise?

See Appendix A, "Answers to Questions for Consideration/Discussion," for suggested answers.

CONCLUSION

Dear Reader,

Congratulations on making it through your fifteenth chapter! Wowee! Only one more to go!

In this chapter, we took a brief look at Highrise, and what an interesting building it is! If you don't feel like your feet are quite on the ground with Basecamp, there's no need to get overloaded, but as with Basecamp, you can start simply with Highrise. Start by adding in a contact—a family member and her birthday, even—just to get familiar with it. Chances are at some point you'll find it to be helpful. Many, many others have.

In the final chapter, we'll look at Campfire—an appropriate addition to Basecamp. Boo hoo. It's almost time to part ways. But wait...we can all connect on LinkedIn and Facebook. Woohoo!

Best wishes on your adventures in keeping track of details, as well as people and opportunities.

Regards,

Todd

P.S. So how'd I do with this chapter? Feel free to sound off at www.facebook.com/basecampbook.

CHAPTER 16

EXPLORING GROUP CHAT WITH A FREE CAMPFIRE ACCOUNT

In 140 Characters or Less
- Ch 16—Intro to Campfire, a powerful group chat tool with unique features; and a personal invitation in the Conclusion.

In This Chapter
- Personal/Classroom Exercise: Feedback
- Taking a Look at Campfire
- Trying Campfire
- Comparing Campfire to Skype
- Less Interruption + Remote Collaboration = Telecommuting
- Going Mobile/Campfire Extras
- A Final Invitation

Why This Chapter Is Important

This chapter is important because it discusses another handy tool that many people use to help things run smoothly. Sometimes group chat can help solve issues and maximize the resources of a group. Think of it as a light-years improvement over "reply all" emails. And Campfire approaches group chat in such a way that, like Basecamp, and Highrise, the record of the chat is saved in a central place. That feature alone is worth having, as it can be pretty valuable to go back through ad hoc discussions and look for relevant items that weren't captured elsewhere. Campfire is excellent, in other words. But for skeptics, don't worry; I'll compare it to Skype.

Because it's the last chapter, there's a small treat at the end, in the Conclusion, as a reward for making it through the entire book. So yes, let us gather around the campfire one last time. No we're not going to sing songs. Don't tempt me; we're probably already in enough trouble with the editors, and I fully expect some readers to go on Amazon and write reviews about how there weren't numbered steps or that I shouldn't have mentioned Google so much or that they were turned off by the friendly style even though they were warned by the cover. But if you actually did find this book helpful, please go on Amazon and write a nice review. It will make my editors happy, it will sell more copies, more royalties will be generated for non-profit work, and it will increase my chances of being able to write more books that go out on a limb in a friendly way, like one on Google Apps or maybe one on Highrise. The style is a little different from most technical books, but the intent is to make it as friendly as possible for beginners.

Don't forget to read the Conclusion. There's a personal invitation in it that some of you will appreciate.

Personal/Classroom Exercise: Feedback

I'm going to see if I can get away with issuing a blatant invitation right at the beginning for you, the reader, to go on Amazon.com and write a review. I'm also going to see if I can get away with a blatant invitation to take the book link from the Amazon page, paste it into Facebook, and tell other people about it. If you've come to see how important Basecamp can be, you might actually be doing some of your friends a favor.

Oh wait, this isn't an invitation. This is a homework assignment that you can add to your Basecamp project as a to-do. Woohoo! Thanks in advance to anyone who actually does this and for the dear professors who invite students to do so. Please feel free to make this an exercise in giving feedback to improve the user experience of learning material; feel free to indicate your thoughts in your review or Facebook comments about how the book could be improved.

Taking a Look at Campfire

To take a look at Campfire, visit http://37signals.com and click on the Campfire icon.

Source: 37signals, LLC.

Or you can visit the main Campfire site directly, at http://campfirenow.com.

There's a general high-level intro, a plans and pricing link, and some options at the top of the screen.

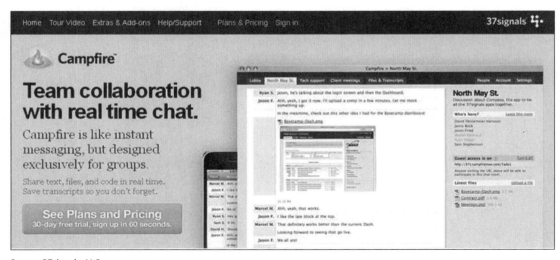

Source: 37signals, LLC.

37signals has created a nice tour of Campfire that is worth watching. To take the tour, just click on the Tour Video link at the top of the main screen.

Starting a Free Account

At the time of writing, there was still a fully free option for trying out Campfire. If that's not available by the time you read this, you can always try a free trial.

Note

Pricing may vary and change from the time of writing, but this section gives a sense of some of the plans.

To start a free account or review plan/pricing info, click the Plans & Pricing link at the top of the screen.

Then cross your fingers and look for a Free Plan link toward the bottom of the plans and pricing info.

Source: 37signals, LLC.

Next, as with Highrise, you can click the Sign In Here link to enter your Basecamp login and password.

You're just 60 seconds away from your new Campfire account.

Already have a Basecamp, Highrise, Backpack or Campfire account?
Sign in here to skip this form and use the username you already have.

A few details and you're on your way

First name	
Last name	
Email	
Company	

(Or non-profit, organization, group, school, etc.)

Source: 37signals, LLC.

Next, you should be led to a screen where you can enter the login/password that you use with Basecamp, to get your Campfire account started and integrated with your Basecamp account.

Already use a 37signals product?

Basecamp

Highrise

Backpack

Campfire

Sign in below with the username and password you already have from your existing Basecamp, Highrise, Backpack or Campfire account.

Username

Password

I forgot my username or password

Sign in   or Cancel

Source: 37signals, LLC.

Then you should get a confirmation message like this. You can continue entering information into the form.

You're just 60 seconds away from your new Campfire account.

Hi Todd, (I'm not Todd)

You already have a 37signals ID because you use Basecamp and Highrise.

After your account is created, you can sign in with the same **username and password** that you use with your other accounts.

Source: 37signals, LLC.

Enter a company name, or try leaving it blank. The name you enter here affects the way the direct address is created to your Campfire account. See how CFTW corresponds to the Access link shown in the "Accessing Campfire" section, next.

A few details and you're on your way

Company CFTW
(Or non-profit, organization, group, school, etc.)

You have selected the Free plan. There is no time limit on the free plan — you can use it for free as long as you'd like. You can always upgrade to a paying plan later if you need more users, more file storage, etc.

By clicking **Create my account** you agree to the Terms of Service, Privacy, and Refund policies.

Create my account

Source: 37signals, LLC.

When you're ready, click the Create My Account button and then the OK, Let's Go button.

You're all set, Todd. Thanks!
You may want to bookmark this page so you can come back to it later. We've also sent you an email with a link to get back here.

OK, let's go!

Source: 37signals, LLC.

Accessing Campfire

You're given a unique link to get into Campfire, something like this: https://cftw3.campfirenow.com/.

You also receive an email with some of the details. And you can always go to www.campfirenow.com and click the Sign In link at the top.

TRYING CAMPFIRE

Campfire is easy to use, but it's also powerful. One of the main values of using a tool like this when working on projects is enabling a forum for ad hoc questions, thoughts, results, and status. Software developers seem to like chat rooms for carrying on this kind of discussion, but it can be helpful for everyone. One thing that it creates is a "network effect," where posting a question could yield an answer from whomever happens to see it next. So it's a hyperspeed improvement over "reply all" emails.

As with other products, 37signals provides some friendly starter messages, and you start off with a single default room. One of the concepts to keep in mind is that you can create different rooms. Various parts of a team might use a room for gathering around particular projects, or a department might like to have a room of its own. A common use of group chat might be to copy just-in-time information into the group chat "stream," such as links, rules, announcements, and so on, in a way that leaves it in a central place where it's easy for people to scan through and catch up on the latest developments. It can be informal, but effective and efficient.

To explore, you can just click on the Room link.

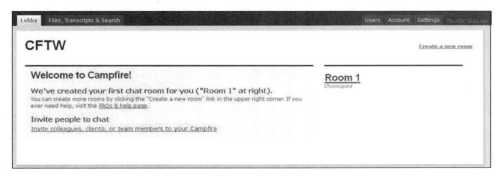

Source: 37signals, LLC.

You might try clicking the link Invite Colleagues, Clients, or Team Members to Your Campfire to see how that feature integrates with people who are already on the system. A classroom or workshop might like to make sure everyone in the workshop is in a test account and then try setting up a group chat window.

One of the scenarios that's especially helpful with group chat is remote collaboration with clients, an agency, a series of freelancers, or whatever. Group chat rooms can facilitate some of the ad hoc communication that goes on as an alternative to "reply all" emails, which can get so easily buried and lost and remain unread.

37signals implements group chat as real time or asynchronous, which is different from a lot of chat. Part of the design of this is intentionally to be less disruptive. For example, instead of having ten different people interrupt you in an instant message storm, or being constantly interrupted by new email queries, you can monitor a chat room at your own convenience. You can scan to catch up with the latest information, and you can keep the window open in real time if you want. But you also have the option of visiting it when you want and having a "gathered stream" of conversation. This feature can be a particularly helpful tool for managers so they have an easy way to catch up on things, jump in, provide guidance, and ask questions.

Chat works pretty easily. When you enter a chat room, Campfire displays the announcement. Then you can type a message and click the Send Message button. Other features include being able to lock the room, include guest access (for someone who is not on Basecamp but you want to loop in), and upload files.

Source: 37signals, LLC.

At this point, you might wonder when to use Basecamp and when to use Campfire. Basecamp is more of a planning tool, a "keeping track" tool, with its facilitation of deadline tracking and accountability and discussions about specific items. Group chat in Campfire is a good ad hoc "execution" tool; it allows work to be done, and the network effect of posting queries and your status can happen on an informal basis. Campfire is also a nice way to have a sense of community in the midst of remote collaboration. So the answer of when to use which tool is best found by exploring both tools in your particular situation.

I experimented with resizing the Campfire window, because I like to have chat and instant messaging easily accessible on my screen. Given the way Campfire is coded, it does pretty well, "collapsing down" as you resize a window into something that you might easily position alongside other windows.

Source: 37signals, LLC.

Notice in this visual the nice way that Campfire, Highrise, and Basecamp are integrated in links at the top of the screen. For example, someone in the group chat window might think of a question that could be answered by consulting Highrise, or an ad hoc discussion might lead to entering a to-do item into Basecamp. The tight integration can expedite and keep things running smoothly and efficiently, all at your fingertips.

Here's the smallest I could resize the chat window down to, in Firefox on Windows. It might be different on various browsers and operating systems, but it seems to work pretty nicely.

Source: 37signals, LLC.

Also, be aware that some apps and integrations can connect Campfire to mobile apps. For example, iPad users might like to try the Pyre app and have their iPads set up on a stand to monitor and interact in the group chat window, while focusing on other work on their laptop or PC. See the "Using Campfire Extras" section later in this chapter.

COMPARING CAMPFIRE TO SKYPE

Campfire is not the only group chat tool out there. Skype is pretty common, is free, and has some advantages of its own. I found Skype pretty helpful for posting into the group chat window while I was interacting with some colleagues on a volunteer project. When people's email Inboxes were filled to the brim and people were not likely to respond to each other, the group chat room provided an easier way to post something. I also experienced the "network effect," which meant you could pose questions, and the next person who was on, or whoever was available, could answer. But the loading of "history" in Skype group chat felt a little clunky, and I remember having some issues when wanting to preserve the contents. I think it had to do with the question of the chat room availability; whoever created the chat room might have control, but it was unclear where the history went when that person closed down the chat window. Experimenting with the very latest version may resolve some issues.

Skype group chat has history capability, but it is up to the individual to set it up, manually find it, archive it, and so on. It's more distributed, peer to peer. In Campfire, the history of chat rooms is more managed, in a central place, so it's easier to keep track of. I prefer Campfire to Skype, because I do think it's valuable for anyone on a project to be able to search through some of those conversations.

If you compare "history" in group chat to email, in a series of "reply all" emails and conversations, yes it might be searchable, but it is distributed over different computers and is a lot "looser." (That is, you might wonder if everything was captured.) It's debatable how important it is to have such an archive, but I think it's a good business practice, especially when you want to have continuity or allow a new employee, volunteer, or participant to catch up on what's going on. Ad hoc discussions can be disorganized in some ways, but a centrally captured history might help.

While it is good to create individual items and track things in Basecamp, the reality is that not all discussion around a project is going to occur there. The ability to notify people or start discussions in Basecamp is great, in the sense that people can respond by email, but Basecamp is still capturing the discussions (so you have history). Basecamp is not going to capture informal discussion, but sometimes little details will come up, and being able to search back in a history might be helpful. All things considered, Campfire is probably better than Basecamp.

I found an interesting article that compares Campfire to Skype. It's compelling because it's written by Jaanus Kase, the person who developed group chat functionality in Skype. He uses both Skype and Campfire and thinks both are excellent. Go to www.quora.com/Should-a-small-team-of-developers-use-Campfire-or-Skype-for-text-chatting, or take a shortcut by using http://tinyurl.com/chatvschat.

One of the themes of the article is the advantage of having the web archive in a central place.

Kase's review wasn't even speaking to the integration benefit that Campfire provides, which, again, is the ability to have Highrise, Campfire, and Basecamp all easily accessible from the top-screen menu.

Launchpad   Highrise Contacts   Campfire Chat   Basecamp Projects

Source: 37signals, LLC.

The advantage of integration is easily being able to transition back and forth between the three programs. There's also the feature of inviting colleagues and guests who are not in the system, with a minimum of hassle to install new software. Campfire is nice in that it is web based; it doesn't require installation.

So while Skype is certainly an option for chat, there are compelling reasons to try Campfire. For me, the most compelling reason is the centrally available "history" of ad hoc conversations.

LESS INTERRUPTION + REMOTE COLLABORATION = TELECOMMUTING

Campfire can structure workflow so that people are less interrupted. If you think how interruptive email and instant messaging can be, you might be interested to know that one of the underlying design philosophies of 37signal's products is to provide an alternative that allows efficient, clear communication, but without the interruption. Interruptions can waste a lot of time—not only the time it takes to interact with the interruption, but also the time that's lost when your concentration is broken. It's pretty common for people to come in early or stay late at work because they feel like they get more done when other people aren't around. (::raise hands::)

This might be a good opportunity to raise the question about workflow philosophy regarding meetings, telecommuting, and cross-pollination. I certainly respect all viewpoints, but I gravitate toward the idea that enabling remote collaboration with accountability can make telecommuting a truly viable option. It makes sense from an efficiency standpoint, using fewer resources. Less commuting also means less pollution. A lot of time is wasted in commuting that could be spent doing other things. Some companies have taken advantage of telecommuting and have saved a significant amount of money toward office space. Setting the goal of more remote collaboration gives any company, individual, or organization more flexibility for collaboration with other people, including working effectively with freelancers and others.

There is, of course, the management philosophy and common preference to have in-person contact, and I think to a certain extent, yes, in-person contact is a good thing. In an increasingly socially connected online world, people report an ironic sense of disconnectedness and less meaningful relationships. I've also known people who really disliked "total" telecommuting because they missed having human contact. In my opinion, the solution is local, shared offices, where people work together, not even necessarily from the same company, but just not necessarily having to commute.

I did encounter one person who claimed that Google, despite being a tech leader, specifically discouraged telecommuting because of the value of in-person cross-pollination—that is, the casual conversations that happen when one person walks over to another's cubicle or a few people are gathered at the water cooler and strike up a discussion. These same conversations might not happen over email.

But the tools from 37signals offer an excellent way to capture ideas—a way that doesn't leave as much to chance as in-person cross-pollination does. I think a mixture of in-person collaboration and remote collaboration is the best balance. In-person collaboration is effective for a period of time to establish relationships, where text might convey 20% of meaning, tone of voice 40%, and body language 40%. Also, to counter the "Google philosophy," if it's still there, I'd contend that the negative impact of interruptive technology might drag overall efficiency, and even eclipse innovation, more than spontaneous in-person cross-pollination might help.

But the basis for resistance to telecommuting is the fear of accountability—or the lack of it. That's where tools that make it easy to do project management could advance a company so far, in terms of efficiency and accountability, that the telecommuting would be worth it.

That's my 1.5 cents' worth. If you're interested in the philosophy of developing less interrupted workflow or even workspace, see the little gem at the beginning of Appendix B, "More Cool Stuff."

GOING MOBILE/CAMPFIRE EXTRAS

You can try working on Campfire from your mobile device. There's also a free iOS (iPhone) app and other mobile apps for using Campfire at http://campfirenow.com/extras.

Note

Prices/availability may have changed by the time you read this.

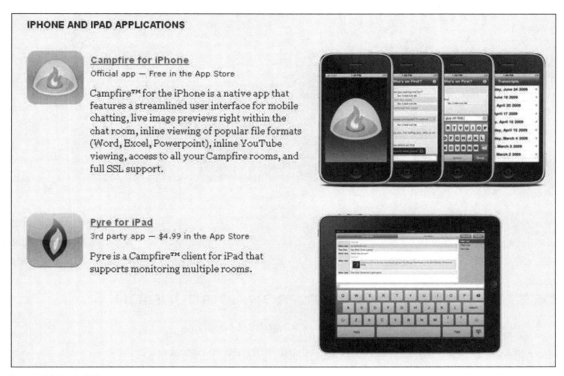

Source: 37signals, LLC.

It's worth visiting the extras site. Because so many millions of people are using 37signals products, apps and additional tools have evolved that can cover some of the situations that come up. These are just a few.

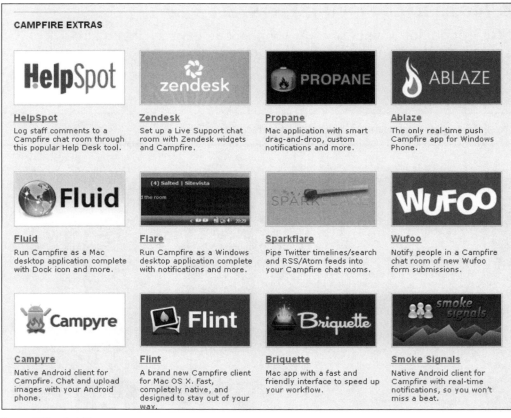

Source: 37signals, LLC.

QUESTIONS FOR CONSIDERATION/DISCUSSION

1. How can group chat add value to managing projects?
2. What's the difference between real-time and asynchronous chat?
3. What's the "network effect" of posing a question in group chat?

See Appendix A, "Answers to Questions for Consideration/Discussion," for suggested answers.

CONCLUSION

Dear Reader,

Congratulations on making it through your final chapter on Basecamp! It's been very nice to have you along for all these chapters. Be sure to visit the appendixes before you head home.

I'd like to take this opportunity to share one last image, a picture that captures a couple of the fundamental opportunities that come with tools from 37signals. I also hope that it might help connect the audience of this book a bit, by showing something that might be universal to many members of the reading audience. In that sense, I like to think that people who are using Basecamp, even at separate companies, are participating in popularizing a tool that can be quite revolutionary for a company or organization. So we're all in this together!

What struck me as I was finishing this final chapter of the book is the thought that many of us have magnets on our refrigerators. And maybe those magnets say something about us and about what tools like Basecamp can help us accomplish.

So here are my fridge magnets of things I appreciate, care about, dream about. There are magnets from the Woodstock Museum, because my goal is to play at the 100th anniversary; see http://2069.us. There's a picture of kids who are helped by an organization called Warm Blankets. I keep it as a "this is what I work for" reminder to myself because of the idea that something like a stock exchange for nonprofit organizations could provide resources to meet the world's needs.

In a very real sense, our magnet collections can remind us of something powerful: *this* is what Basecamp can free up time to pursue. In the case of the nonprofit stock exchange,

Basecamp can help *me* pursue that dream and find collaborators to work with to help change the world.

So I'm curious about what's on your fridge. Feel free to share at http://facebook.com/basecampbook.

So all I really wanted to say is that adopting a tool like Basecamp can help free up time for doing the things we care about. Stress can kill, and work/life balance can be hard to achieve. Basecamp isn't a magic solution for everything, but I look to the millions of people who've found it helpful, and I bet that many could step back and confirm that adopting the tool has led to a relative peace of mind and a feeling that they are more on top of things than overwhelmed. And, if my sense is right, it can also lead to leaving work where it belongs: at work.

One idea I'm fond of is quoted in an article I saw awhile back on the CEO of the successful company Curves. The CEO was busy, but he had a pretty audacious and strict rule: he *never* stayed at work past 6 p.m. His reasoning was that, "It never ends anyway." In other words, there might be a psychological desire to "complete" and "get things out of the way," but at some point, if you have the freedom, you have to set limits. And a tool like Basecamp can help you keep to your limits.

The easier it is to use a system, the more likely it is to be used, and the more effective it is, the more confidence you can place in it. A tool like this can also mean maintaining more detachment, knowing that things are fine and that you can "jump back in." A smoothly running system for managing contacts, people, and ad hoc conversations can make a real difference.

A Final Invitation

Part I of this invitation is pretty simple. Take a look at a photo album I made on Facebook at http://tinyurl.com/heropics, which includes people who have been heroes to me, including Craig Muller, creator of Warm Blankets and one of my personal heroes. Visit at your own risk—there are personal thoughts—but I want you to feel welcome.

Part II of my invitation is to consider the idea I mentioned about the stock exchange for nonprofits. If you would like to give back to the world somehow and aren't sure how you might be able to participate, consider this idea. If there was ever a need for remote collaboration, this is it. If you're interested, check out the TEDx video at http://tinyurl.com/npoexvid, and then visit the Facebook page for that project and post some feedback. Then if you'd like to connect, maybe I can put you in Highrise, or vice versa, or I can connect you to the NPOEx Basecamp project. Individuals, students, professors, project managers, technical people, nontechnical people—anyone is welcome, and anyone can provide valuable feedback. I don't think of it as "my" project; I think of it as a critical need and an alternative to some of the present systems. It's like the way that 37signals looked at project management and tried to engineer a good alternative. NPOEx might be taking a look at the for-profit stock market, learning from it, and considering the way that nonprofits currently are funded and unable to meet the needs of the world. It's trying to engineer an alternative that builds opportunity and invites people to "invest" in nonprofits from a portfolio standpoint. End of pitch.

Part III of my personal invitation is a welcome to "friend" me on Facebook or invite me to connect on LinkedIn. In the same way that I truly appreciate the spirit of collaboration in 37signals products, I love the idea of building community, making friends with people, and developing open communication.

And with that, this book, is a wrap! Remember to visit the appendixes on your way out, and I hope to see you on Facebook or LinkedIn. I hope this book will provide real value for you in a way that you will want to share it with others. I also recognize there is room for improvement, and I'm glad to hear whatever feedback you'd like to give. Feel free to sound off at www.facebook.com/basecampbook.

Thanks again for reading this book. Best wishes on your adventures in keeping track of details, managing projects, and helping your company or organization. Happy graduation! You've earned it.

Regards,

Todd

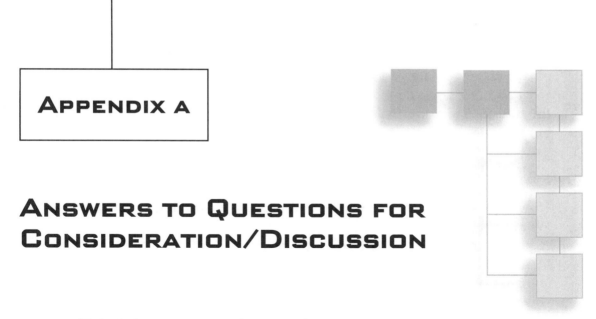

APPENDIX A

ANSWERS TO QUESTIONS FOR CONSIDERATION/DISCUSSION

Here you'll find the questions and *suggested* answers from each chapter's "Questions for Consideration/Discussion." Bon appétit!

CHAPTER 1

1. **What does this mean: no tool will do the work for you?**

   Keeping track of details with a tool requires a time commitment. A tool is worthless unless you keep using it, even when you're working against a deadline. The temptation is to drop it when things get busier, but that makes it harder to keep track of details and to provide a common point of reference for everyone on the project. That's why it's important to be as lean as possible, so that no one feels like the overhead is pointless; the tool has to be relevant, but lean. Basecamp is great for that.

2. **How is a "lean" tool with less overhead helpful?**

   A lean tool allows you to adequately keep track of details, carry on discussions, and keep things organized without taking time from actually working on the project. The less overhead you have, the more you can get done. And the less overhead you have, the easier it is to "keep the commitment" even when things get crazy.

3. **What's the point of trying different tools?**

   It helps you understand the strengths and limitations of each tool. Learning how to do something in one tool can help you appreciate and understand when another tool might be more useful. Trying different tools gives you options. And even if you have a basic commitment to a specific tool, there's no "one size fits all" for every situation, so it's helpful to have a toolbox. Mechanics don't use just one tool; they keep a variety available for different situations. Trying different tools also helps you develop the skill of exploring new things and focusing on the transferable skill—that is, how to accomplish something similar with different tools, in different situations.

CHAPTER 2

1. **How does a project management tool provide a common point of reference? What's the purpose?**

   A project management tool can keep track of things centrally—that is, you log in and update information, and anyone involved in the project can see what's going on. It allows you to pick up where you left off, with all the information you need, instead of having to dig for it or email someone to ask about it— especially if you are on different schedules, in different time zones, or in different countries. The point of having a common point of reference is also to keep things consistent so that you have an "authoritative reference" if a number of options are discussed but one is decided on, or people need to use the latest version of a file or consult the latest version of a set of guidelines.

2. **How can you use a to-do list to reprioritize ideas?**

   You can enter in ideas, capture them all in a brainstorming meeting, and then think about which are the most important or which ones you want to consider first by dragging the most important items to the top of the list.

3. **In what situation would it be helpful to be able to carry on a discussion based on an uploaded item? Why would people want to be notified?**

   A designer might create a mock-up of a graphic and ask people to weigh in on it. Instead of waiting in someone's Inbox, the file is right there in the project site. The notification allows the person who uploaded the file to know about subsequent comments and tell others that the item has been uploaded.

4. **What's the point of having a log of discussion and activity kept in a central place? Why not just use email?**

   Email is quick and familiar. Email Inboxes also quickly get full, and it's easy to lose track of emails. Some email systems even delete emails after a certain period of time. It's good to have a log of a discussion so anyone can find out the latest about what's going on. Instead of filling up everyone's email Inbox with "reply alls" every day, you can keep the discussion focused, on an as-needed basis, and then when necessary, anyone can consult the latest comments in a central place.

5. **What kinds of things could you do with all the time you free up from managing a project effectively?**
You could read a book, spend time with friends, try learning something new, ask someone to join you on a date or an adventure, dye your hair a new color, get a Basecamp tattoo, or try planting sunflowers. The possibilities are endless—hours of fun for the whole family!

CHAPTER 3

1. **What are the strengths of Notepad and TextEdit?**
   - Extremely simple.
   - Easy to create, save a file, take notes.
   - No setup or login required in a time crunch.

2. **What are Notepad's and TextEdit's limitations? What can't you do with these tools?**
   - No calendar.
   - Easier to lose data (for example, if you forget to click Save).
   - Harder to share with other people.
   - Can't collaborate on the document.
   - No sophisticated features.

3. **What are some advantages of NoteTab Light?**
   You can have it set to autosave, and you can open multiple documents under tabs.

4. **What are the strengths of Google Docs?**
   - Entirely free.
   - Documents are embeddable in blogs (for example, blogger.com) or sites (any conventional website, or a free site such as you can make through sites.google.com).
   - Powerful formatting and collaborative features.
   - More or less a full and free online equivalent to Microsoft Office, including some things you can't do in Office.
   - Reorderable tasks.
   - Can schedule deadlines for tasks.

5. **What are the limitations of Google Docs? What can't you do with it?**

   ■ Documents are not situated within a "project" environment.

   ■ In Gmail tasks, even though you can email a task list, in the present version, you can't collaboratively edit a task list.

   ■ The Google Doc formatting capability in the word processing features is powerful and improving all the time, but the formatting might not be as "tight" as in the standalone Microsoft Word or OpenOffice.org application. This limitation may go away, but I've experienced changes in the formatting when I've created a Google Doc online and then downloaded it into Word format.

   ■ The "track changes" feature in Google Docs is powerful, allowing you to see what changes are made, but it might not work like what you're used to in Microsoft Word.

   ■ Google Docs is a set of tools, and it's fairly integrated, but it's not integrated around project management as Basecamp is.

6. **What are the strengths of Excel and Google Spreadsheets as project management tools?**

   ■ Excel is really helpful for anything involving numbers. It's built to make it easy to do calculations (such as when you learn how to use formulas to perform math for you), or report on hours or money spent. It's a portable, common format. Free alternatives include openoffice.org's spreadsheet program and Google Spreadsheets.

   ■ Google Spreadsheets is awesome for tracking details collaboratively, inviting people in.

   ■ Both Excel and Google Spreadsheets have charting capability. This can be part of project management, showing how things are doing, with a simple visual. Bottom line—learn how to use charts.

7. **What are the limitations of Excel and Google Spreadsheets? What can't they do?**

   ■ Excel can exist as a shared document on a network, but it has limited collaboration capability. Microsoft is gradually moving online, but Google Spreadsheets is more mature. Neither Excel nor Google Spreadsheets is *focused* on project management. They're separate tools that might come in handy.

- Google Spreadsheets is great, but there's no integrated calendar, and it does take some effort to learn. It's not meant to be a project management tool.

- Excel and Google Spreadsheets don't have discussion capability, per se, not to the extent that Basecamp does, where you can discuss individual items.

8. **How can you make sure to revisit whatever tool it is that you're using?**

- Keep the window open in Notepad and TextEdit.

- Put a shortcut in Notepad's or TextEdit's Start folder.

- If you try using Google Docs to collaboratively manage a project, you could use Google Calendar to set event reminders, such as a daily reoccurring reminder to "go and check your task list." This could be a Google Doc that has the latest details people are using or your personal task list.

- You can also enable the reminder feature in Google Calendar to send a reminder to your cell phone.

- In this case, if you're using an Excel spreadsheet to track details, or you have it on a network, the best defense is habit—check it.

- If you need to, set a reminder using your phone, Microsoft Outlook, or Google Calendar of "Check project sheet," or however you'd like to phrase it. Remember that no tool does the work for you, and it's only as good as your ability to actively use the tool for updating and consulting information.

CHAPTER 4

1. **What does the Me link do?**
   In Basecamp, the Me link allows people to access their personal settings, including their name, email, and profile icon.

2. **How do you delete a project?**
   Go to Project Settings > Delete Project.

3. **Why would you want to archive a project instead of delete it?**
   The Archive setting allows you to store a project you don't need anymore but might want to access sometime in the future. It gets it out of the way so you can concentrate on current projects, and it frees up "slots" for new projects if, for example, your account allows for 10 projects and you've used up 10; then you can archive one of them and create a new one.

4. **Where can you turn off the Daily Recap email?**
   Go to Me > My Basecamp Settings > Daily Recap.

5. **What are some techniques you can use to keep your eyes from glazing over while learning about project management?**

Truckers sometimes have a container with ice cubes. In theory, you can't fall asleep when you're sucking on an ice cube. Or you might try to think of a project you could develop and manage that is exciting to you, such as ideas for wooing someone you'd like to develop a relationship with, what steps you'd need to take to become president, how you'd spend a million dollars, or what your dream job would look like. Another thing you can do is consider the value you bring to an organization or company by learning these things. It's really valuable, it's crucial, and it can help you maintain your job security or even be promoted. It's quite possible that these skills can help you or your organization or company achieve goals, and it can translate into free time or even money. So you could think of how meaningful it would be to have made a significant contribution to your group or organization, or you could think of what it would be like to have some extra money.

CHAPTER 5

1. **What does ADDIE stand for? What's the point of that concept?**

ADDIE stands for analysis, design/planning, development, implementation, and evaluation. It's an example of a model for project management that views projects in stages. The point is to start off by analyzing the situation and then design the project, develop it, implement it, and follow up by evaluating how things went to see if there are any lessons you learned. Sometimes breaking a project into stages can get some momentum going and help you think of what resources you need. And if you have general stages, you can make time tables within them. What are the milestones that you'd want to achieve when designing the product/project? Maybe the milestones would be mockup, alpha, beta, and approved.

2. **What's the difference between editing and accessing a to-do item? What can you do when you select/access a to-do item?**

Editing a to-do item involves changing its text. Accessing a to-do item involves making comments and posting files.

3. **How do you assign a to-do item?**

Roll over the to-do and click the Unassigned link at the right, and then choose a name from the drop-down menu. The person has to have been previously invited into the project for you to be able to assign it.

4. **How do you make a due date for a to-do item?**
Roll over it and click the Unassigned or No Due Date link at the right, and choose a date in the pop-up calendar.

5. **How do you get a to-do item to show up on the calendar?**
Assign a due date.

6. **What's the point of assigning due dates for to-do items?**
Establishing deadlines for individual pieces of the project allows you to start setting a project in motion.

7. **What's the airspeed velocity of an unladen swallow?**
African or European? See http://www.youtube.com/watch?v=tFylQ6_1bgQ.

CHAPTER 6

1. **How do you add people to Basecamp?**
When you're creating a new project, you can invite them there, or you can click the Invite More People link on a Project page.

2. **What kinds of permissions and access can you grant?**
You can grant access to individual projects and calendars, and you can grant people the ability to create new projects. A Billing Liaison can upgrade the account and adjust billing details, and an Admin can do everything, including creating and deleting people.

3. **What are companies in Basecamp?**
Companies allow you to organize people into groups to make it easier to invite them into projects.

CHAPTER 7

1. **In what kinds of scenarios could you start a discussion as part of a project?**
Requirements—Sometimes projects start with defining requirements—that is, what needs to happen, who is involved. Sometimes requirements can be a document. So you could start a discussion to get some momentum going and talk about the element required for the project, and then you could create a text document (Chapter 9, "Working with Text Documents") as a way to bring it to life.

Strategy—You might start a discussion around strategy. For example, everyone's talking about a new social network called Pinterest, and you want to have a strategic discussion about it, posing some questions. Should we be on it? How do we do it? Can an agency help us? Who's going to be responsible?

Roles and responsibilities—A discussion could be started, asking a pool of people who'd like to be involved in a project and who might want to do A, B, C. This discussion might end up as a to-do list or a text document where you start building a list of who's going to do what.

Brainstorming—A discussion could be a way to start brainstorming, and someone could be assigned to review the discussion and put it into a to-do list for prioritization. (Remember that you can rearrange items in a to-do list.)

2. **What's the value of having a web-based project management tool like Basecamp gather information in a central place? How does it compare to email?**
The value is in helping to keep things from falling through the cracks, to keep things clear, and to keep them organized. It reduces stress and makes your life better. It inspires confidence with your clients and internal partners because your department can be relied on to keep things organized and keep things moving.

3. **What is cross-pollination?**
Cross-pollination is when people collaborate to exchange ideas and people "rub off on each other." It's also known as synergy.

4. **How would you invite discussion by commenting on something in Basecamp?**
Go to a to-do item or text document, post a comment, choose specific people to notify, and invite reaction within your comment.

5. **How would inviting someone to brainstorm in Basecamp keep ideas from "falling through the cracks"?**
Getting ideas into a central place provides you with a way to come back to them. No tool does the work for you, and ideas don't spring up on their own. But if you gather ideas in a central place and then review them, they can come to life. There's strength in numbers and strength in collaboration, and having ideas in a central place is better than having them languish in people's minds or be buried in their email Inboxes.

6. **How would the Move feature help you start a new project? What's the point?**
The Move feature allows you to take a discussion and start a new project around it. The point is that sometimes you could be working on a project, and you might want to split something off to make it more manageable. Or you might have an idea that begins to take shape, like R+D (research and development), and the general idea is to brainstorm, start discussions, and spawn other projects, like prototypes, experiments, whatever.

7. **How is it valuable to have tools to "set things in motion," as opposed to just capturing ideas?**

I believe that ideas have some value on their own—as creative expression, poetry, or self-expression. But some argue that ideas have no value unless they're used for something. Creativity, brainstorming, and innovation are a crucial part of being competitive and making the world better. So doing the work of actually setting things in motion is wonderful; it's like bringing things to life. Maybe that makes project management sound more exciting?

8. **What are some ideas for projects you could do or brainstorming lists you could make that you could discuss with others and might motivate you to use Basecamp?**

This is meant to be a personal question. If you're learning Basecamp as part of a personal learning exercise, at work, or in a class, if you don't have something specific to work on yet, I invite you to think of ideas that would be exciting. Think of dreams—no limits. Just start brainstorming ideas and trying out the features.

Examples might be starting your own business, finding a mate, writing a novel, starting a band, learning an instrument, finding a new career, catching up on loose ends, becoming a millionaire, or getting a degree in _____.

CHAPTER 8

1. **What's the difference between estimation and allocation?**

It means different things to different people, but in terms of deadlines, allocation can mean being handed an arbitrary deadline and having to allocate time. Estimation would involve participating in the planning process and providing an estimate of when you could complete an element of a project. Estimation would be part of a more mature approach to project management in my opinion; it's not necessarily more conservative or cautious, but it's arguably more sustainable and consistent in changing conditions.

2. **What's the point of having a milestone?**

Setting milestones can be a helpful starting point for breaking down a project into doable chunks. You might set general milestones and then go about the business of establishing due dates for tasks.

3. **What are two ways to create an event in Basecamp?**

There might be more than two, but one way is to click on the Calendar link at the top of the screen and click on the calendar itself. Another way is to access a project, click on the Dates link within the project, and then add an event there.

4. **How might you convince management to allow more telecommuting?**

One way to allow more telecommuting might be through demonstrating a commitment to project management, which could mean taking steps toward it without any kind of agreement in place. You might be able to bring a tool like Basecamp into a situation where it hasn't been used before (or use another tool, if your IT department kills it over security issues) and ask management if they'd consider allowing more telecommuting if the use of project management tools were broadened and led to more accountability. You might emphasize the way that lean project management could help with productivity by reducing wasted time and helping to improve estimation.

Or, depending on the political climate, you might be able to take the first step and share internally that the goal is to convince management to allow more telecommuting and work hard on adopting it. Of course, project management has a world of benefits outside of the possibility of telecommuting, but this could help motivate people. Then if you can show a significant change in the transparency, accountability, and clarity of the organization, it might be good evidence for taking a step up the food chain and addressing the traditional concerns about telecommuting. You might also aim to fully exploit the cross-pollination capabilities of Basecamp, in terms of capturing ideas, brainstorming, and working to actually bring things into being, and compare them internally to efforts that never really got off the ground before because they got lost in the cracks. Make sure you're not making anyone look bad. Just approach things positively, and involve everyone you can.

On the note of security, you could point to all the companies that are using Basecamp, some of which are very large. (See the logos of these companies on the 37signals.com site.)

A final note might be to explore some of the complementary tools, such as Highrise and Campfire, mentioned in the latter chapters, to see if they might help to strengthen remote collaboration. In some cases, if you have no telecommuting presently, you might experiment by working in the evening and show how helpful Basecamp can be. And if you do work with agencies, people from offices in other locations, or freelancers, experimenting with Basecamp can demonstrate the accountability and value of the remote collaboration, which can provide a precedent for telecommuting.

Best wishes! Feel free to share success stories, pleas for advice, or valiant yet failed attempts at http://facebook.com/basecampbook. It would especially be fun to hear from people who may have bought this book for a manager, or a manager who is reading this and trying things the other way around—offering telecommuting as an incentive for working with project management. And if anyone wants to buy a bunch of copies of this book, as I've said, royalties are going to nonprofit research. Feel free to get in touch with me or with the publisher directly to discuss large volume orders for print or electronic editions.

Also, if anyone gets this far wading in the appendix, I'm open to setting up a LinkedIn group, which could make it a bit easier to commiserate and share ideas. You might look for existing Basecamp-related LinkedIn groups or project management groups to join. But there's nothing wrong with starting simple and setting up one ourselves. Email me at tekelsey@gmail.com.

CHAPTER 9

1. **What are some scenarios in which you can use a text document to collaborate on something?**
   It might be helpful to develop promotional messages, requirements documents, guidelines, instructional material, proposals—anything where you need to develop text as part of a project. The text document might also be a place to develop guidelines for the project so that it contains messages or instructions for those participating in a project. An example could be welcome guidelines for freelancers.

2. **How might the comment feature come in handy?**
   The comment feature allows you to easily generate discussion and commentary on an item.

3. **In what situation would you want to use Basecamp instead of Google Docs, or vice versa?**
   If you want to keep everything directly in the Basecamp project or you don't want to require a Gmail address or Google account, Basecamp works. If you'd like to be able to easily export text directly into PDF or Microsoft Word format, Google Docs is nice.

4. **How do you invite someone to participate in a text document?**
   Just generate a comment and choose the person you want to notify.

CHAPTER 10

1. **What kind of files can you upload to Basecamp?**
   You can upload just about anything but manila paper files.

2. **What's the file size limit in Basecamp for an individual file?**
The limit is 2 gigabytes. Keep in mind that Basecamp plans have total file storage limits. (Another option is to include links to files uploaded using systems like www.dropbox.com.)

3. **What kinds of files have previews?**
Standard web image files such as JPG and PNG have previews.

4. **Why would you want to generate a discussion around a file?**
A Basecamp discussion allows you to post a file and get comments. You might post a file and ask for feedback, for further ideas, or for instructions on how to proceed. Or you might post a file and allow the comments section to be a forum for asking questions.

5. **If you upload a design for a logo and a designer has a new version, how could he upload the new version?**
You can add a designer to the project, comment on the original file, notify the designer, and invite him to join the discussion and upload the file. Or you could show him how to access the project, click on the File link, and upload the new version (and delete the old one).

Classes might want to simulate working with a designer on a project like a logo. You'd invite the designer, the designer would post the file, and there would be discussion around it and a new version. Or you might like to try it live by working with a site like www.99designs.com.

6. **How would uploading a word processing file to Basecamp be any better than just emailing it to people?**
If you upload a word processing file to Basecamp, you can comment on it and notify desired people, who can then participate in discussion. They don't even have to log on; they can just click Reply in their email to post a comment. The advantage over email is that Basecamp comments occur in a central place, and all files, discussions, and so on, are easy to find, regardless of who gets involved. For example, projects might start with a planning phase. Then you'd invite software developers, designers, freelancers, or volunteers to participate, and the Basecamp project would be a good way to pass off a project to the next stage. You can also use several projects—maybe a planning project—with the most sensitive information and then have a separate design project that you invite more people into.

7. **How would you upload a file like a graphic or word processing document and assign it to someone?**
You could upload a file using the techniques in this chapter. You'd directly upload it, comment on it, and notify the desired person. But to keep track of

who the file is assigned to, it's probably better to create a to-do item, assign it to a particular person, and attach a file to the comment. Then both you and the assignee have an easy way to track what's going on. It allows you to go back to a list of tasks and see which tasks are assigned to whom. This system is also better for assignees because they can log into Basecamp and have a list of all the things that are assigned to them (on the Me screen).

CHAPTER 11

1. **When might it be helpful to use the completion/notification method for working with tasks in Basecamp?**

   If you'd like to-do items cleared off the list when they're completed, or if the person who assigns the to-dos would like to be notified when they're completed, the completion/notification method might be a good fit. When someone completes a to-do item, he can always comment on it and indicate that it's done, but clicking a check box might be easier. Also, the completion/notification method might be good for straightforward items with a clear completion, like "website configuration." If there's a task that might go through several versions, you might want to use discussion/comments around a to-do item to post/notify when a version is done, and then only check the item when it's all done.

2. **How do you delete a project?**

   You can't. Just kidding. When accessing a project, you just need to scroll down to Project Settings, click on it, and click Delete on the right. (To permanently delete a project, you need to go to the trash, select the item, and permanently delete it.)

3. **How do you archive a project?**

   Access the project, scroll down to Project Settings, click it, select the radio button, and save changes.

4. **How do you restore a file that's been deleted?**

   Access the general Projects link at the top of the screen, scroll down to find the Trash Can icon/link, click it, select the desired item, and click Bring It Back.

5. **What kind of value can brainstorming provide to a company or nonprofit organization?**

   Well, thanks for asking! Brainstorming can provide a significant value by using all available resources and employee potential to think of ideas or potential solutions to problems. It's called maximizing resources, or pooling resources. Brainstorm in a way that lets everyone be heard, and then use a tool like

Basecamp to set things in motion. It can help a company or nonprofit organization function better, gain a competitive edge, and work more efficiently. Brainstorming is really, really helpful.

6. **Why is brainstorming important?**

Brainstorming is important because you can cover a lot of ground by bringing people together to add ideas to a "brainstorming" to-do list and then review it later.

7. **How can software like Basecamp make it easier for a company or organization to bring ideas to life?**

Basecamp allows you to not only capture ideas, but use tools in close proximity to set projects in motion, form tasks, assign them to people, and make deadlines.

8. **Would you consider becoming a hero and helping someone or some company or organization to brainstorm? Calling all heroes!**

Why yes, I would be glad to consider this. I just watched *Avengers*, and I, too, would like to be a superhero.

CHAPTER 12

1. **How do you contact support?**

You can contact Basecamp support by emailing support@37signals.com, or you can log into Basecamp and click the Support icon.

2. **Why would you want to email content to a Basecamp project?**

Emailing content to a Basecamp project might provide a convenient way to forward an email, add a file, or start other project elements without having to actually log in.

3. **Why would you want to comment on a to-do list?**

Commenting on a to-do list might be an easy way to discuss an entire set of to-do items, or a way to invite people to add items to a list. Commenting on a list might also be a way to attach a file and ask someone to go through it and "lift out" items to add to a to-do list. These items might include important information from a white paper or taking a "traditional" requirements document and translating it into Basecamp.

CHAPTER 13

1. **What's the value of being able to interact with Basecamp on a mobile device?**

Being able to interact with Basecamp on a mobile device gives you a lot of flexibility. It could be that you are away from your computer and are notified of something you can respond to, or it might allow you to be productive, away from your desk, cubicle, home, wherever. It can be healthy to get up from wherever you're sitting or working once in a while, so think of it as an exercise in health.

2. **Why would you want to be able to email Basecamp?**
Emailing Basecamp is a really easy way of adding new items to Basecamp projects. See Chapter 12, "Extra Fun." Being able to email items provides options for people whose phones might not be able to access Basecamp per se.

3. **How could interacting with Basecamp on a mobile help with remote collaboration?**
When people on your project are spread out in different time zones or you're working with vendors or freelancers, it's nice to have options for people you are inviting into a project. Let them work on it in their preferred way, on their preferred device. Also, it's handy if someone is away from his computer but can pull up Basecamp on his mobile device and talk to you at the same time on a headset. Fancy that.

CHAPTER 14

1. **What's the value of being able to import Basecamp calendar items into a calendar system like Outlook or Google Calendar?**
It allows you to use your favorite tool to keep track of deadlines and to set reminders.

2. **What are some ways you can remind yourself of things you need to do in Basecamp?**
You could set a reminder on your mobile device manually, or you could create an event/appointment in a tool like Google Calendar or Outlook and set a reminder along with that event/appointment. You might even set up a to-do list of items you need to do, as a "personal space" in Basecamp. To-do lists are good for prioritization, and Basecamp can be just as effective at managing personal to-dos as project to-dos. Then you could just check Basecamp regularly and make it your tool for managing what you need to do personally. Email can work, too, but it's really easy for things to get buried that way.

3. **How can you get in the habit of checking Basecamp on a regular basis to see what you need to do?**
Learn how to set a reoccurring/repeated reminder, maybe going off each work day at a certain time.

CHAPTER 15

1. **What does CRM stand for?**

   CRM stands for customer relationship management.

2. **What does Highrise help with that goes beyond just having people's contact information in your email program?**

   Highrise provides a way for you not just to have contact information, but to gather other kinds of relevant information, including background notes, so that you can have context when you're following up with someone. Highrise also allows you to create specific tasks so that you can follow up. Basecamp keeps *tasks* from falling through the cracks, and Highrise keeps *people* and *opportunities* from falling through the cracks or being buried in your email Inbox.

3. **Do you have to be a salesperson to be able to use Highrise?**

   Nope, you don't. Highrise can be a valuable tool for helping anyone follow up with people. You don't need to be in sales or even at a company. Nonprofits, educators, researchers, volunteers, and individuals can all make use of it. What Highrise does is help "with the avalanche" by giving you an easy way to keep track of things.

CHAPTER 16

1. **How can group chat add value to managing projects?**

   It can provide an "ad hoc forum" for posing questions and carrying on conversations that are less likely to be buried in an email Inbox. It also helps you jump into the stream of conversation and catch up on what's going on.

2. **What's the difference between real-time and asynchronous chat?**

   Real-time chat is instant chat, which can be done in Campfire. Campfire also offers asynchronous chat, where you may post a question that someone answers later. Asynchronous = different times.

3. **What's the "network effect" of posing a question in group chat?**

   The network effect would be posing a question and having any of the participants in the group chat being able to respond to it. It's a maximization and pooling of resources, in a way that's much less chaotic than "reply all" emails.

   Feel free to discuss this appendix on the Facebook page http://facebook.com/basecampbook.

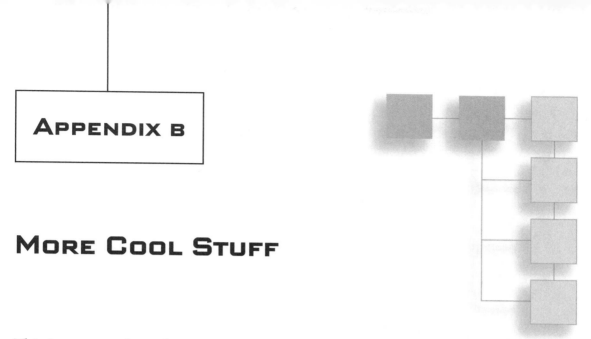

APPENDIX B

More Cool Stuff

This is meant to be a short appendix to introduce, or reintroduce, you to a few items that are important to mention.

"Why Modern Workplaces Don't Work"

I came across an article with an interesting mention of a video and discussion based on thoughts from Jason Fried, one of the founders of 37signals. I like its discussion of constant interruption in workplace activity. I highly recommend taking a look.

You can find it at www.liventerprise.com/news/3580/.

Rework

I want to invite you to consider reading a book called *Rework*, written by the founders of 37signals. It's a useful book for any businessperson.

Here are a few quotes to give you a sense of the book:

> "If given a choice between investing in someone who has read *Rework* or has an MBA, I'm investing in *Rework* every time. A must-read for every entrepreneur."
>
> —Mark Cuban, co-founder of HDNet, owner of the Dallas Mavericks

> "The wisdom in these pages is edgy yet simple, straightforward, and proven. Read this book multiple times to help give you the courage you need to get out there and make something great."
>
> —Tony Hsieh, CEO of Zappos.com

You can buy *Rework* at http://tinyurl.com/rework-bk.

OTHER INTERESTING BITS

Invest some time checking out the bottom of the page at the 37signals site (http://37signals.com) for several nuggets that are easy to overlook.

Our services	Our books
The Job Board Find (or post) a programming or design job.	**REWORK** Our take on building a great business.
37signals Speaks Videos of our keynotes and interviews.	**Getting Real** Learn how to build software the easy way.
Feature stories	Our open-source contributions
Bootstrapped & Proud We profile successful small businesses.	**Ruby on Rails** A powerful & simple web app framework.
Exit Interviews Interviews with companies post-aquisition.	**Open Source** A list of projects we've released & contributed to.

Source: 37signals, LLC.

The folks at 37signals are wise, and they have some interesting material on their site that's worth your time investment to read.

Feel free to discuss the content of this appendix on the Facebook page at http://facebook.com/basecampbook.

INDEX

37signals
  Backpack, 33
  Basecamp. *See* Basecamp
  Campfire
    accessing, 266
    accounts, signing up, 264–266
    apps, 273–274
    extras, 273–274
    logging in, 266
    mobile devices, 273–274
    overview, 33–34, 263–264
    Skype comparison, 270–271
    telecommuting, 271–272
    using, 266–270
  Highrise (CRM), 236
    accessing, 246–247
    accounts, signing up, 243–245
    benefits, 242–243
    business cards, 246
    cases, 257–258
    collaborating, 255, 258
    compatibility with other programs, 239–240
    contacts, adding, 248–254
    deals, 258
    following up, 254–258
    LinkedIn, 246, 251–254
    logging in, 246–247
    mobile devices, 258
    overview, 33–34, 236–242
    tasks, adding, 255–258
    tour, 241–242
    website, 237–242
  resources, 296–297
  Rework, 12, 295–296
  website, 11, 19, 33
45-day trial accounts, 76–77

accessing
  Basecamp (mobile devices), 209–213
  calendars, granting, 112–113
  Campfire, 266
  Highrise, 246–247
  projects, granting, 112–113
  to-dos, 97–100
accounts
  Campfire, 264–266
  Google, 45–48
  Highrise, 243–245
  multiple, 126
  overview, 75
  prices, 76–77
  projects, 83–84
  signing up, 77–79
  trial accounts, 76–77
ADDIE model, 93
adding/creating
  administrators, 113, 117
  comments
    text documents, 138
    to-dos, 97–100
  companies, 121–126
  events (calendars), 147–148
  Google accounts, 45–48
  Highrise
    contacts, 248–254
    Tasks, 255–258
  people, 111–112
  projects, 80–81
  Tasks
    Highrise, 255–258
    lists, 56
  text documents, 138, 166–168
  to-dos, 94–96, 106–107
    comments, 97–100
    due dates, 101–102
    files, 97–100
  web pages (Google Docs), 49
administrators (projects), 113, 117
allocation (project management), 142–145
Amazon, feedback, 262
applications. *See* **programs**
archiving projects, 82–83, 193–195

article, "Why Modern Workplaces Don't Work," 295
asynchronous collaboration (online), 49
attaching files (discussions), 128
author (Kelsey, Todd)
  personal invitation to readers, 276–277
  Twitter, 72
  website, 45, 63, 76
avatars, 86–87

Backpack, 33
Basecamp
  accounts. *See* accounts
  calendars. *See* calendars
  collaborating, 202
  discussions. *See* discussions
  email relationship, 16–17, 33, 134–135
  files. *See* files
  Google Docs comparison, 50
  homescreen, 78–80
  logging in, 20
  mobile devices. *See* mobile devices
  New Features, 206
  permissions, 31–32, 112–113, 117
  point of reference, 19
  programs. *See* programs
  reasons to use, 11–13
  security. *See* security
  text documents. *See* text documents
  to-dos. *See* to-dos
  website, 76–77, 79
Battleship website, 62
benefits
  discussions, collaborating, 139
  Highrise, 242–243
bit.ly website, 47, 49, 219–220
Blogger, 47
blogs (Google Docs), 47
book, feedback, 262
brainstorming, 188–189
business cards (Highrise), 246

calendars

events

comments, 148

creating, 147–148

deleting, 148

discussions, 148

email, 146

general calendar, 147

milestones, 149–159

project-specific calendars, 147

to-dos, 152–159

Google Calendar, 50–51, 147

ICal/Webcal, 224–227

items, 228–229

reminders, 229, 232–233

subscribing, 227–230

unsubscribing, 230

mobile devices

deleting, 217–219

iCal/Webcal, 213–219

subscribing, 213–216

Outlook, 19, 147

email, 231

reminders, 231–233

subscribing, 230–231

overview, 21–24, 29–30

people, granting access, 112–113

Tasks, 57

to-dos, 104–106

due dates, 102

events, 152–159

Campfire

accessing, 266

accounts, signing up, 264–266

apps, 273–274

extras, 273–274

logging in, 266

mobile devices, 273–274

overview, 33–34, 263–264

Skype comparison, 270–271

telecommuting, 271–272

using, 266–270

cancelling comments, 135

cases (Highrise), 257–258

categories (to-dos), 92

chapter answers to questions for consideration/discussion

Chapter 1, 279–280

Chapter 2, 280–281

Chapter 3, 281–283

Chapter 4, 283–284

Chapter 5, 284–285

Chapter 6, 285

Chapter 7, 285–287

Chapter 8, 287–289

Chapter 9, 289

Chapter 10, 289–291

Chapter 11, 291–292

Chapter 12, 292

Chapter 13, 292–293

Chapter 14, 293

Chapter 15, 294

Chapter 16, 294

charts (Excel), 69–72

chat (Campfire)

accessing, 266

accounts, signing up, 264–266

apps, 273–274

extras, 273–274

logging in, 266

mobile devices, 273–274

overview, 33–34, 263–264

Skype comparison, 270–271

telecommuting, 271–272

using, 266–270

cheat sheets, managing expectations, 117–119

check boxes (to-do items), 186–188

checking in (project management), 161–162

choosing views (projects), 191–192

collaborating. *See also* **people**

asynchronously, 49

Basecamp, 202

Campfire

accessing, 266

accounts, signing up, 264–266

apps, 273–274

extras, 273–274

logging in, 266

mobile devices, 273–274

overview, 33–34, 263–264

Skype comparison, 270–271

telecommuting, 271–272

using, 266–270

discussions, 134–135, 139

Excel, 66–69

Google Docs, 46–50, 66–69

Google Spreadsheets, 68–69

Highrise (CRM), 236

accessing, 246–247

accounts, signing up, 243–245

benefits, 242–243

business cards, 246

cases, 257–258

collaborating, 255, 258

compatibility with other programs, 239–240

contacts, adding, 248–254

deals, 258

following up, 254–258

LinkedIn, 246, 251–254

logging in, 246–247

mobile devices, 258

overview, 33–34, 236–242

Tasks, adding, 255–258

tour, 241–242

website, 237–242

mobile devices, 220

Tasks, 57–58

comments. *See also* **discussions**

deleting, 133

editing, 133

events (calendars), 148

files, 180–182

Nevermind, 135

overview, 32–33

text documents, 138, 169–170

to-dos

adding, 97–100

discussions, 136–138, 200

common point of reference (Basecamp), 19

companies, creating, 121–126

compatibility of Highrise, other programs, 239–240

completed to-do items, 186–188

completion, tracking details, 9–10

conferences (discussions), 134–135

configuring people

avatars, 86–87

Daily Recap, 88

icons, 86–87

notifications, 88

overview, 84

settings, 87–88

updating personal information, 85–86

consideration/discussion answers

Chapter 1, 279–280

Chapter 2, 280–281

Chapter 3, 281–283

Chapter 4, 283–284

Chapter 5, 284–285

Chapter 6, 285

Chapter 7, 285–287

Chapter 8, 287–289

Chapter 9, 289

Chapter 10, 289–291

Chapter 11, 291–292

Chapter 12, 292

Chapter 13, 292–293

Chapter 14, 293

Chapter 15, 294

Chapter 16, 294

contacts (Highrise), 248–254

conversations. *See* **collaborating; discussions**

creating/adding

administrators, 113, 117

comments

text documents, 138

to-dos, 97–100

companies, 121–126

events (calendars), 147–148

Google accounts, 45–48

Highrise

contacts, 248–254

Tasks, 255–258

people, 111–112

projects, 80–81

Tasks
    Highrise, 255–258
    lists, 56
    text documents, 138, 166–168
    to-dos, 94–96, 106–107
        comments, 97–100
        due dates, 101–102
        files, 97–100
    web pages (Google Docs), 49
CRM (customer relationship
      management) and Highrise, 236
    accessing, 246–247
    accounts, signing up, 243–245
    benefits, 242–243
    business cards, 246
    cases, 257–258
    collaborating, 255, 258
    compatibility with other programs, 239–240
    contacts, adding, 248–254
    deals, 258
    following up, 254–258
    LinkedIn, 246, 251–254
    logging in, 246–247
    mobile devices, 258
    overview, 33–34, 236–242
    tasks, adding, 255–258
    tour, 241–242
    website, 237–242
customer service, 204–205
customers, managing. See CRM

Daily Recap, 88
deadlines, rescoping pipelines (Excel), 59–64
deals (Highrise), 258
deleting
    calendars
        events, 148
        mobile devices (iCal/Webcal), 217–219
    comments, 133
    files, 179
    people, 117
    projects, 83, 117, 194
    text documents, 170
    to-do items, 190
    to-dos, 97
dependencies
    project management, 161–162
    taking notes, 40
details, tracking
    completion, 9–10
    importance of, 2–5
    programs, 10–11
    project management, 7–10, 15–16
    unrealized gain, 6
    zombies, 6
devices (mobile devices)
    accessing Basecamp, 209–213
    calendars
        deleting, 217–219
        iCal/Webcal, 213–219
        subscribing, 213–216

Campfire, 273–274
    collaborating, 220
    email, 219–220
    Google Docs, 73
    Highrise, 258
    Siri, 219
disabling/enabling Daily Recap, 88
discussions. See also comments
    answers to questions for consideration/
      discussion
      Chapter 1, 279–280
      Chapter 2, 280–281
      Chapter 3, 281–283
      Chapter 4, 283–284
      Chapter 5, 284–285
      Chapter 6, 285
      Chapter 7, 285–287
      Chapter 8, 287–289
      Chapter 9, 289
      Chapter 10, 289–291
      Chapter 11, 291–292
      Chapter 12, 292
      Chapter 13, 292–293
      Chapter 14, 293
      Chapter 15, 294
      Chapter 16, 294
    collaborating, 134–135, 139
    comments
      adding to text documents, 138
      deleting, 133
      editing, 133
      Nevermind, 135
      to-dos, 136–138, 200
    conferences, 134–135
    email, 130–132, 201–202
    events (calendars), 148
    files, 128, 180–182
    looping in, 130
    moving, 133–134
    notifications, 129–131
    overview, 24–25, 32–33
    participating, 130–133
    posting, 129–130
    social networks, 135
    starting, 128–129, 139
    text documents, 169–170
    to-dos, 32–33, 134–138, 200
documents
    Google Docs
      asynchronous collaboration, 49
      Basecamp comparison, 50
      Blogger, 47
      collaborating online, 46–50,
        66–69
      creating web pages, 49
      embedding, 47
      formats, 49
      Google Apps comparison, 38
      Microsoft Office comparison, 46
      mobile devices, 73

      opening, 47–48
      private/public files, 47
      signing up, 45–47
      taking notes, 49
      text documents comparison, 172
    text documents. See also files
      comments, 138, 169–170
      creating, 166–168
      deleting, 170
      discussions, 169–170
      editing, 166–168
      email, 201–202
      exporting, 168–169
      formatting, 167–168
      Google Docs comparison, 172
      lists, 167–168
      moving, 170–171
      opening, 166
      overview, 30–31
      quotes, 168
      saving, 166
download.com, 45
downloading/uploading
    download.com, 45
    files, 175–179
Dr. Who, 141–142
dragging. See moving
due dates (to-dos), 101–102

editing
    comments, 133
    text documents, 166–168
    to-dos, 97
email
    Basecamp relationship, 16–17, 33,
      134–135
    Daily Recap, 88
    discussions, 130–132
      notifications, 129–131
      projects, 201–202
    Email Newsletter, 205–206
    events (calendars), 146
    files, 201–202
    forwarding, 201–202
    invitations, 114–116
    lists (Tasks), 55
    mobile devices, 219–220
    notifications
      discussions, 129–131
      files, 176
      overview, 32–33
      updating, 88
    Outlook calendars, 231
    RSS, 204
    text documents, 201–202
    to-dos, 201–202
embedding (Google Docs), 47
enabling/disabling Daily
    Recap, 88
estimation (project management),
    142–145, 161

evaluation (project management), 161
events
    calendars
        comments, 148
        creating, 147–148
        deleting, 148
        discussions, 148
        email, 146
        general calendar, 147
        milestones, 149–159
        project-specific calendars, 147
        to-dos, 152–159
    Google Calendar, 50–51
Excel
    formulas, 58–59
    rescoping pipelines, 59–64
    spreadsheets
        charts, 69–72
        collaborating online, 66–69
        overview, 58, 64–65
expectations, managing, 117–119
Explore Basecamp project, 79–80
exporting text documents, 168–169
extras (Campfire), 273–274

Facebook, feedback, 262
features (New Features), 206
feedback
    project management, 142
    this book, 262
files. See also text documents
    comments, 180–182
    deleting, 179
    discussions, 128, 180–182
    downloading, 179
    email, 201–202
    Google Docs. See Google Docs
    managing, 178–179
    moving, 179
    multiple, 44
    notifications, 176
    opening, 178–179
    overview, 28–29
    saving, 44
    to-dos, 97–100
    uploading, 175–178
filtering. See moving
firewalls, 18–19
following up (Highrise), 254–258
formal project management tools, 17–18
formats (Google Docs), 49
formatting text documents, 167–168
formulas (Excel), 58–59
forwarding email, 201–202
Fried, Jason ("Why Modern Workplaces
    Don't Work"), 295

gamification, 141–142
Gmail
    Google Calendar. See Google Calendar
    Google Docs. See Google Docs

Tasks
    Basecamp to-dos comparison,
        53–54
    calendars, 57
    collaborating online, 57–58
    creating lists, 56
    emailing lists, 55
    Highrise, 255–258
    indenting lists (tabs), 55–56
    list order, 54–55
    opening, 51–53
    sharing lists, 55
    taking notes, 53–54
Google
    accounts, 45–48
    Tasks
        Basecamp to-dos comparison, 53–54
        calendars, 57
        collaborating online, 57–58
        creating lists, 56
        emailing lists, 55
        Highrise, 255–258
        indenting lists (tabs), 55–56
        list order, 54–55
        opening, 51–53
        sharing lists, 55
        taking notes, 53–54
    website, 38, 45, 47, 219–220
Google Apps/Google Docs comparison, 38
Google Calendar, 50–51, 147
    iCal/Webcal, 224–227
    items, 228–229
    reminders, 229, 232–233
    subscribing, 227–230
    unsubscribing, 230
Google Docs
    asynchronous collaboration, 49
    Basecamp comparison, 50
    Blogger, 47
    collaborating online, 46–50, 66–69
    creating web pages, 49
    embedding, 47
    formats, 49
    Google Apps comparison, 38
    Microsoft Office comparison, 46
    mobile devices, 73
    opening, 47–48
    private/public files, 47
    signing up, 45–47
    taking notes, 49
    text documents comparison, 172
Google Drive. See Google Docs
Google Presentations, 173
Google Spreadsheets
    collaborating online, 68–69
    websites, 71
groups (Campfire)
    accessing, 266
    accounts, signing up, 264–266
    apps, 273–274

extras, 273–274
logging in, 266
mobile devices, 273–274
overview, 33–34, 263–264
Skype comparison, 270–271
telecommuting, 271–272
using, 266–270

hardware (mobile devices)
    accessing Basecamp, 209–213
    calendars
        deleting, 217–219
        iCal/Webcal, 213–219
        subscribing, 213–216
    Campfire, 273–274
    collaborating, 220
    email, 219–220
    Google Docs, 73
    Highrise, 258
    Siri, 219
Help, 204–205
hiding to-do items, 186–187
Highrise (CRM), 236
    accessing, 246–247
    accounts, signing up, 243–245
    benefits, 242–243
    business cards, 246
    cases, 257–258
    collaborating, 255, 258
    compatibility with other programs,
        239–240
    contacts, adding, 248–254
    deals, 258
    following up, 254–258
    LinkedIn, 246, 251–254
    logging in, 246–247
    mobile devices, 258
    overview, 33–34, 236–242
    tasks, adding, 255–258
    tour, 241–242
    website, 237–242
homescreen, 78–80

iCal/Webcal
    Google Calendar, 224–227
    mobile devices
        deleting, 217–219
        subscribing, 213–216
icons
    people
        PicResize.com, 119–121
        projects, 114–115, 119–121
    updating, 86–87
    views (projects), 191–192
importance of tracking details, 2–5
indenting lists (Tasks), 55–56
Internet. See collaborating; websites
inviting people
    email, 114–116
    multiple accounts, 126
    overview, 109–110

projects, 81, 85
readers, 276–277
sending, 110–114
iPhones (mobile devices)
  accessing Basecamp, 209–213
  calendars
    deleting, 217–219
    iCal/Webcal, 213–219
    subscribing, 213–216
  Campfire, 273–274
  collaborating, 220
  email, 219–220
  Google Docs, 73
  Highrise, 258
  Siri, 219
items
  Google Calendar, 228–229
  to-dos
    check boxes, 186–188
    completed, 186–188
    deleting, 190
    organizing, 186, 188–189
    recovering, 190
    viewing/hiding, 186–187

Jira, 19

Kelsey, Todd
  personal invitation to readers,
    276–277
  Twitter, 72
  website, 45, 63, 76

LinkedIn (Highrise), 246, 251–254
links (ICal/Webcal), 224–227
lists
  brainstorming, 188–189
  Tasks
    creating, 56
    email, 55
    indenting, 55–56
    order, 54–55
    sharing, 55
  text documents, 167–168
  to-dos. *See* to-dos
  views (projects), 192
Live Enterprise, 19
logging/signing in
  Basecamp, 20
  Campfire, 266
  Highrise, 246–247
  people (projects), 116
looping in (discussions), 130

magnets (refrigerators), 275–276
managing
  customers (CRM) and Highrise, 236
    accessing, 246–247
    accounts, signing up, 243–245
    benefits, 242–243
    business cards, 246

cases, 257–258
collaborating, 255, 258
compatibility with other programs,
  239–240
contacts, adding, 248–254
deals, 258
following up, 254–258
LinkedIn, 246, 251–254
logging in, 246–247
mobile devices, 258
overview, 33–34, 236–242
tasks, adding, 255–258
tour, 241–242
website, 237–242
files, 178–179
people's expectations, 117–119
projects
  ADDIE model, 93
  allocation, 142–145
  checking in, 161–162
  dependencies, 161–162
  Dr. Who, 141–142
  estimation, 142–145, 161
  evaluation, 161
  feedback, 142
  formal tools, 17–18
  gamification, 141–142
  SurveyMonkey, 142
  telecommuting, 159–161
  time travel, 141–142
  to-dos, 92
  tracking details, 7–10, 15–16
  websites, 92
Microsoft
  Excel
    charts, 69–72
    collaborating online, 66–69
    formulas, 58–59
    overview, 58, 64–65
    rescoping pipelines, 59–64
  Outlook, 19, 147
    email, 231
    reminders, 231–233
    subscribing, 230–231
  Project, 17–18, 73
  Google Docs comparison, 46
milestones (calendar events), 149–159
mobile devices
  accessing Basecamp, 209–213
  calendars
    deleting, 217–219
    iCal/Webcal, 213–219
    subscribing, 213–216
  Campfire, 273–274
  collaborating, 220
  email, 219–220
  Google Docs, 73
  Highrise, 258
  Siri, 219

moving
  discussions, 133–134
  files, 179
  projects, 193
  text documents, 170–171
  to-dos, 96–97, 103–104
multiple accounts (invitations), 126
multiple files (taking notes), 44

naming to-dos, 95
Nevermind, 135
New Features, 206
newsletters (Email Newsletter), 205–206
Notepad/TextEdit, 39–43
notes
  dependencies, 40
  Google Docs, 49
  Notepad/TextEdit, 39–43
  NoteTab Light, 43–45
  opening multiple files, 44
  reprioritizing, 42
  saving files, 44
  Tasks, 53–54
NoteTab Light, 43–45
notifications
  discussions, 129–131
  files, 176
  overview, 32–33
  updating, 88

Office
  Microsoft Office. *See* Microsoft
  Open Office, 59
One Laptop Per Child website, 66
online collaborating. *See* collaborating
Open Office, 59
opening
  files, 44, 178–179
  Google Docs, 47–48
  Tasks, 51–53
  text documents, 166
order (lists), 54–55
organizing. *See also* prioritizing
  to-do items, 186, 188–189
  to-dos, 96–97, 103–104, 107
Outlook, 19, 147
  email, 231
  reminders, 231–233
  subscribing, 230–231

participating in discussions,
  130–133
people
  adding, 111–112
  author's personal invitation to readers,
    276–277
  calendars, granting access, 112–113
  Campfire
    accessing, 266
    accounts, signing up, 264–266
    apps, 273–274

people (*Continued*)
    extras, 273–274
    logging in, 266
    mobile devices, 273–274
    overview, 33–34, 263–264
    Skype comparison, 270–271
    telecommuting, 271–272
    using, 266–270
cheat sheets, managing expectations,
    117–119
collaborating. *See* collaborating
comments. *See* comments
companies, creating, 121–126
configuring
    avatars, 86–87
    Daily Recap, 88
    icons, 86–87
    notifications, 88
    overview, 84
    settings, 87–88
    updating personal information, 85–86
CRM. *See* Highrise
discussions. *See* discussions
Highrise (CRM), 236
    accessing, 246–247
    accounts, signing up, 243–245
    benefits, 242–243
    business cards, 246
    cases, 257–258
    collaborating, 255, 258
    compatibility with other programs,
        239–240
    contacts, adding, 248–254
    deals, 258
    following up, 254–258
    LinkedIn, 246, 251–254
    logging in, 246–247
    mobile devices, 258
    overview, 33–34, 236–242
    tasks, adding, 255–258
    tour, 241–242
    website, 237–242
inviting
    email, 114–116
    multiple accounts, 126
    overview, 109–110
    projects, 81, 85
    sending, 110–114
permissions, 31–32, 112–113, 117
projects
    creating administrators, 113, 117
    deleting, 117
    granting access, 112–113
    granting superpowers, 113, 117, 126
    icons, 114–115, 119–121
    permissions, 31–32, 112–113, 117
    PicResize.com, 119–121
    profiles, 114–115
    signing in, 116

permissions, 31–32, 112–113, 117
personal information, updating, 85–86
personal invitation to readers, 276–277
phones (mobile devices)
    accessing Basecamp, 209–213
    calendars
        deleting, 217–219
        iCal/Webcal, 213–219
        subscribing, 213–216
    Campfire, 273–274
    collaborating, 220
    email, 219–220
    Google Docs, 73
    Highrise, 258
    Siri, 219
photos (icons)
    people
        PicResize.com, 119–121
        projects, 114–115, 119–121
    updating, 86–87
    views (projects), 191–192
PicResize.com, 119–121
pictures (icons)
    people
        PicResize.com, 119–121
        projects, 114–115, 119–121
    updating, 86–87
    views (projects), 191–192
pipelines, rescoping (Excel), 59–64
plug-ins. *See* programs
point of reference, 19
posting discussions, 129–130
powers, granting to people, 113, 117, 126
Presentations (Google), 173
prices (accounts), 76–77
prioritizing. *See also* organizing
    reprioritizing (taking notes), 42
    to-dos, 107
private files (Google Docs), 47
profiles (people), 114–115
programs
    Campfire
        accessing, 266
        accounts, signing up, 264–266
        apps, 273–274
        extras, 273–274
        logging in, 266
        mobile devices, 273–274
        overview, 33–34, 263–264
        Skype comparison, 270–271
        telecommuting, 271–272
        using, 266–270
    compatibility with Highrise, 239–240
    formal project management tools, 17–18
    Gmail Tasks
        Basecamp to-dos comparison, 53–54
        calendars, 57
        collaborating online, 57–58
        creating lists, 56

    emailing lists, 55
    Highrise, 255–258
    indenting lists (tabs), 55–56
    list order, 54–55
    opening, 51–53
    sharing lists, 55
    taking notes, 53–54
Google
    accounts, 45–48
    website, 38, 45, 47, 219–220
Google Apps/Google Docs comparison, 38
Google Calendar, 50–51, 147
    iCal/Webcal, 224–227
    items, 228–229
    reminders, 229, 232–233
    subscribing, 227–230
    unsubscribing, 230
Google Docs
    asynchronous collaboration, 49
    Basecamp comparison, 50
    Blogger, 47
    collaborating online, 46–50, 66–69
    creating web pages, 49
    embedding, 47
    formats, 49
    Google Apps comparison, 38
    Microsoft Office comparison, 46
    mobile devices, 73
    opening, 47–48
    private/public files, 47
    signing up, 45–47
    taking notes, 49
    text documents comparison, 172
Google Drive. *See* Google Docs
Google Presentations, 173
Google Spreadsheets
    collaborating online, 68–69
    websites, 71
Highrise (CRM), 236
    accessing, 246–247
    accounts, signing up, 243–245
    benefits, 242–243
    business cards, 246
    cases, 257–258
    collaborating, 255, 258
    compatibility with other programs,
        239–240
    contacts, adding, 248–254
    deals, 258
    following up, 254–258
    LinkedIn, 246, 251–254
    logging in, 246–247
    mobile devices, 258
    overview, 33–34, 236–242
    tasks, adding, 255–258
    tour, 241–242
    website, 237–242
importance of, 37
Jira, 19

Microsoft Excel
    charts, 69–72
    collaborating online, 66–69
    formulas, 58–59
    overview, 58, 64–65
    rescoping pipelines, 59–64
Microsoft Office/Google Docs
        comparison, 46
Microsoft Outlook, 19, 147
    email, 231
    reminders, 231–233
    subscribing, 230–231
Microsoft Project, 17–18, 73
mobile devices, 219
Notepad/TextEdit, 39–43
NoteTab Light, 43–45
overview, 38–39
Project Pier, 19
Siri, 219
Skype/Campfire comparison, 270–271
Taskline, 19
tracking details, 10–11
Project (Microsoft), 17–18, 73
project management
    ADDIE model, 93
    allocation, 142–145
    checking in, 161–162
    dependencies, 161–162
    Dr. Who, 141–142
    estimation, 142–145, 161
    evaluation, 161
    feedback, 142
    formal tools, 17–18
    gamification, 141–142
    SurveyMonkey, 142
    telecommuting, 159–161
    time travel, 141–142
    to-dos, 92
    tracking details, 7–10, 15–16
    websites, 92
Project Pier, 19
projects
    accounts, 83–84
    archiving, 82–83, 193–195
    brainstorming, 188–189
    creating, 80–81
    deleting, 83, 194
    discussions. *See* discussions
    email
        discussions, 201–202
        files, 201–202
        forwarding, 201–202
        inviting, 114–116
        text documents, 201–202
        to-dos, 201–202
    Explore Basecamp, 79–80
    Google Presentations, 173
    inviting
        email, 114–116
        multiple accounts, 126

    overview, 109–110
    projects, 81, 85
    readers, 276–277
    sending, 110–114
managing
    ADDIE model, 93
    allocation, 142–145
    checking in, 161–162
    dependencies, 161–162
    Dr. Who, 141–142
    estimation, 142–145, 161
    evaluation, 161
    feedback, 142
    formal tools, 17–18
    gamification, 141–142
    SurveyMonkey, 142
    telecommuting, 159–161
    time travel, 141–142
    to-dos, 92
    tracking details, 7–10, 15–16
    websites, 92
Microsoft Project, 17–18, 73
moving, 193
people. *See* people
Project Pier, 19
project-specific calendars, 147
searching, 192–193
settings, 82–83, 87–88
starring, 196
to-dos. *See* to-dos
unarchiving, 193–195
upgrading, 84
views
    choosing, 191–192
    icons, 191–192
    lists, 192
    overview, 190–191
project-specific calendars, 147
Public Domain Pictures website, 86
public files (Google Docs), 47

questions for consideration/discussion
        answers
    Chapter 1, 279–280
    Chapter 2, 280–281
    Chapter 3, 281–283
    Chapter 4, 283–284
    Chapter 5, 284–285
    Chapter 6, 285
    Chapter 7, 285–287
    Chapter 8, 287–289
    Chapter 9, 289
    Chapter 10, 289–291
    Chapter 11, 291–292
    Chapter 12, 292
    Chapter 13, 292–293
    Chapter 14, 293
    Chapter 15, 294
    Chapter 16, 294
quotes (text documents), 168

readers
    author's personal invitation, 276–277
    RSS, 203–204
reasons to use Basecamp, 11–13
recovering deleted to-do items, 190
refrigerator magnets, 275–276
reminders
    Google Calendar, 50–51, 229, 232–233
    Outlook calendars, 231–233
removing. *See* **deleting**
reprioritizing (taking notes), 42
rescoping pipelines (Excel), 59–64
resources, 296–297
Rework **(37signals), 12, 295–296**
RSS readers, 203–204

saving
    files, 44
    text documents, 166
    to-dos, 96–97
scoping pipelines (Excel), 59–64
searching projects, 192–193
security, 18–19
    calendars, granting access to people,
        112–113
    firewalls, 18–19
    permissions, 31–32, 112–113, 117
    projects
        creating administrators, 113, 117
        granting access to people, 112–113
        granting superpowers to people,
            113, 117, 126
        permissions, 31–32, 112–113, 117
selecting views (projects), 191–192
sending invitations, 110–114
setting things in motion (brainstorming),
        188–189
settings
    projects, 82–83
    updating, 87–88
sharing lists (Tasks), 55
shortening URLs, 47, 49, 219–220
showing/hiding to-do items, 186–187
signing/logging in
    Basecamp, 20
    Campfire, 266
    Highrise, 246–247
    people (projects), 116
signing up
    accounts, 77–79
        Campfire, 264–266
        Highrise, 243–245
    Email Newsletter, 205–206
    Google Docs, 45–47
Siri, 219
size (icons), 119–121
Skype/Campfire comparison,
        270–271
social networks (discussions), 135
software. *See* **programs**

spreadsheets
  Excel
    charts, 69–72
    collaborating online, 66–69
    formulas, 58–59
    overview, 58, 64–65
    rescoping pipelines, 59–64
  Google Spreadsheets
    collaborating online, 68–69
    websites, 71
  Open Office, 59
starring projects, 196
starting discussions, 128–129, 139
subscribing (calendars)
  Google Calendar, 227–230
  mobile devices (iCal/Webcal), 213–216
  Outlook, 230–231
superpowers, granting to people,
  113, 117, 126
support, 204–205
SurveyMonkey (project management), 142

tabs, lists (Tasks), 55–56
taking notes
  dependencies, 40
  Google Docs, 49
  Notepad/TextEdit, 39–43
  NoteTab Light, 43–45
  opening multiple files, 44
  reprioritizing, 42
  saving files, 44
  Tasks, 53–54
Taskline, 19
Tasks
  Basecamp to-dos comparison, 53–54
  calendars, 57
  collaborating online, 57–58
  creating lists, 56
  emailing lists, 55
  Highrise, 255–258
  indenting lists (tabs), 55–56
  list order, 54–55
  opening, 51–53
  sharing lists, 55
  taking notes, 53–54
telecommuting
  Campfire, 271–272
  project management, 159–161
text documents. *See also* **files**
  comments, 138, 169–170
  creating, 166–168
  deleting, 170
  discussions, 169–170
  editing, 166–168
  email, 201–202
  exporting, 168–169
  formatting, 167–168
  Google Docs comparison, 172
  lists, 167–168

  moving, 170–171
  opening, 166
  overview, 30–31
  quotes, 168
  saving, 166
TextEdit/Notepad, 39–43
time travel (project management), 141–142
tinyurl.com, 47, 49, 219–220
to-dos
  accessing, 97–100
  adding comments, 97–100
  adding due dates, 101–102
  adding files, 97–100
  calendars, 104–106, 152–159
  categories, 92
  comments, 136–138, 200
  creating, 94–96, 106–107
  deleting, 97
  discussions, 32–33, 134–138, 200
  dragging, 96–97, 103–104
  editing, 97
  email, 201–202
  events, 152–159
  Gmail Tasks comparison, 53–54
  items
    check boxes, 186–188
    completed, 186–188
    deleting, 190
    organizing, 186, 188–189
    recovering, 190
    viewing/hiding, 186–187
  lists, brainstorming, 188–189
  moving, 96–97, 103–104
  naming, 95
  organizing, 96–97, 103–104, 107
  overview, 21–28, 92
  prioritizing, 107
  project management, 92
  saving, 96–97
  troubleshooting, 102
tools
  formal project management tools, 17–18
  programs. *See* **programs**
tour (Highrise), 241–242
tracking details
  completion, 9–10
  importance of, 2–5
  programs, 10–11
  project management, 7–10, 15–16
  unrealized gain, 6
  zombies, 6
trial accounts, 76–77
troubleshooting
  support, 204–205
  to-dos, 102
Twitter (Kelsey, Todd), 72

unarchiving projects, 193–195
unrealized gain (tracking details), 6

unsubscribing (Google Calendar), 230
updating/upgrading
  avatars, 86–87
  icons, 86–87
  notifications, 88
  personal information, 85–86
  projects, 84
  settings, 87–88
uploading/downloading
  download.com, 45
  files, 175–179
URLs, shortening, 47, 49, 219–220
users. *See* **people**
using Campfire, 266–270

viewing/hiding to-do items, 186–187
views (projects)
  choosing, 191–192
  icons, 191–192
  lists, 192
  overview, 190–191
voice software (Siri), 219

web pages, creating (Google Docs), 49
Webcal/iCal
  Google Calendar, 224–227
  mobile devices
    deleting, 217–219
    subscribing, 213–216
websites
  37signals, 11, 19, 33
  ADDIE model, 93
  Basecamp, 76–77, 79
  Battleship, 62
  bit.ly, 47, 49, 219–220
  Blogger, 47
  download.com, 45
  Google, 38, 45, 47, 219–220
  Google Spreadsheets, 71
  Highrise, 237–242
  Jira, 19
  Kelsey, Todd, 45, 63, 76
  Live Enterprise, 19
  NoteTab Light, 45
  One Laptop Per Child, 66
  Open Office, 59
  PicResize.com, 119–121
  project management, 92
  Project Pier, 19
  Public Domain Pictures, 86
  Siri, 219
  SurveyMonkey, 142
  Taskline, 19
  tinyurl.com, 47, 49, 219–220
"Why Modern Workplaces
  Don't Work," 295

zombies, tracking details, 6